A CABINET
✤ OF ✤
ANCIENT MEDICAL
CURIOSITIES

A CABINET
OF
ANCIENT MEDICAL CURIOSITIES

STRANGE TALES
AND
SURPRISING FACTS
FROM THE
HEALING ARTS OF GREECE AND ROME

J.C. McKEOWN

OXFORD
UNIVERSITY PRESS

OXFORD
UNIVERSITY PRESS

Oxford University Press is a department of the University of Oxford. It furthers
the University's objective of excellence in research, scholarship, and education
by publishing worldwide. Oxford is a registered trade mark of Oxford University
Press in the UK and certain other countries.

Published in the United States of America by Oxford University Press
198 Madison Avenue, New York, NY 10016, United States of America.

Library of Congress Cataloging-in-Publication Data
Names: McKeown, J. C.
Title: A cabinet of ancient medical curiosities : strange tales and
surprising facts from the healing arts of Greece and Rome / J.C. McKeown.
Description: Oxford ; New York, NY : Oxford University Press, [2017] |
Includes bibliographical references.
Identifiers: LCCN 2016010809 (hardback) | LCCN 2016012218 (ebook) |
ISBN 9780190610432 | ISBN 9780190610449 (ebook)
Subjects: LCSH: Medicine, Greek and Roman. | Medicine, Ancient.
Classification: LCC R138 .M394 2017 (print) | LCC R138 (ebook) |
DDC 610.938—dc23
LC record available at https://lccn.loc.gov/2016010809

1 3 5 7 9 8 6 4 2
Printed by Sheridan Books, Inc., United States of America

In gratitude to the doctors and nurses who saved my life one summer's day

CONTENTS

PREFACE

THE HIPPOCRATIC treatise *On the Nature of Man* begins by declaring, "Anyone who is accustomed to listening to discussions of the nature of man in a broader context, and not just in its relation specifically to medicine, will find nothing to interest him in this work of mine." By contrast, the main emphasis in this book is on the wider aspects of life in antiquity as preserved for us in the medical texts, rather than on medicine itself. Here you may expect to find vignettes of doctors wrangling at the sickbed and impressing large audiences with their surgical skills; cures for migraine such as wrapping an electric fish or a woman's brassiere or a bandage containing mouse droppings round the patient's head (headaches, and also baldness, can be prevented by having one's hair cut on the seventeenth or the twenty-ninth day after the new moon); donkeys in the sickroom to ensure a fresh supply of milk; a great profusion of amulets, such as a strangled viper to ward off tonsillitis or a cuckoo in a hareskin pouch to induce sleep; and famous old jokes on the order of "A man went to a doctor and said, 'Doctor, I feel dizzy for half an hour when I wake up, and then I feel fine.' To which the doctor replied, 'Well then, wake up half an hour later!' "

There is no way to mitigate the absurdity of countless assertions about medicine made in antiquity. To take just a few random examples, we can only wonder at such statements as:

Medicines become useless if they happen to be placed on a table before they are administered.

Puberty can be retarded by smearing bat's blood on young girls' breasts and young boys' testicles.

One of Pythagoras's soundest observations was the discovery that a child given a name with an odd number of vowels is likely to suffer lameness, loss of eyesight, and other such defects on the right side of the body, but on the left side if the number of vowels is even.

It may be that there are some medical practitioners nowadays who, if they think about the origins of their profession at all, are glibly dismissive of just about every achievement in the field before the discovery of microorganisms and the technology to study them. Such a complacent attitude, which takes no account of the many brilliant insights into medicine that we owe to antiquity, would be misguided, but this book will do little or nothing to correct it. As will already be obvious from the quotations above, my chief aspiration is to provide glimpses into the world of medicine in the distant past that offer entertainment rather than enlightenment. I do not have the competence to speak with authority on any medical topic, ancient or modern, and my modus operandi unabashedly makes no attempt to give a fair and balanced account of Greek and Roman medicine. The focus is primarily on the odd, the bizarre, and the downright weird, such as prognosis through astrology and the wandering womb (see pp. 17 and 95); few of the texts quoted will even hint at the more rational and scientific aspects of ancient medical thought.

Medicine has developed in such radically different ways since antiquity that the content of this book will often seem rather surprising to a reader more accustomed to the modern medical world. Great prominence is given, for example, to medicine's supposed links with religion and with magic, to quaint procedures such as bloodletting, and to outdated theories such as the extremely tenacious belief in the four humors. On the other hand, voluminous as they are, the ancient sources are conspicuously reticent about aspects of the discipline that are of central significance in modern medicine. Since families were expected to take care of their own infirm and elderly, we hear little about care for the physically disabled and there was no specialization in geriatrics; dentistry involved hardly more than the extraction of teeth (though some people had dentures or gold teeth); addiction, whether to alcohol or to other drugs, is rarely mentioned; sexually transmitted infections seem not to have been as rife or as virulent as nowadays; surgery was widely practiced but, given the ignorance of internal anatomy and the absence of effective anesthetics, it was a dreaded and desperate remedy, and therefore most accounts of such procedures are inevitably brief and superficial.

The advances being made in modern medical science are unprecedented in both their range and their rapidity. Since the turn of the millennium, the human genome has been mapped, minimally invasive and robotic surgery has become commonplace, and the first human kidney and liver have been grown. Expectations are high for decisive breakthroughs in the treatment of cancer, genetic disorders, and cardiac and neurological diseases. These lists could easily be extended. Medical research is looking to the future with the realistic presumption of ever more awesome progress.

It has not always been so. Until relatively recent times, medicine, like most sciences, was firmly focused on the revered past rather than on the unknown future. In antiquity, the physician par excellence was Hippocrates of Cos (fifth/fourth cent. B.C.); because of his great reputation, the seventy or so treatises in the Hippocratic corpus were attributed to him, even though he is not demonstrably the author of any of them and many were probably written after the great man's death. Galen (second/third cent. A.D.) dominated Western medical thought virtually unchallenged till the Renaissance, and some of his teachings were still the accepted dogma well into the nineteenth century. That he remained authoritative for more than one and a half millennia indicates conservatism of a very extreme order. In fact, such commitment to intellectual inertia can be seen to extend over an even longer period, given that Galen's writings were themselves so heavily influenced by the Hippocratic corpus.

More than once in his essay *Recognizing the Best Doctor*, Galen insists that a medical student is not properly educated unless he has acquired a thorough understanding of the teachings of the foremost medical writers of antiquity. Galen is by no means an isolated figure. Respect for and deference to long-established traditional wisdom were pretty well universal features of medical teaching and practice throughout antiquity. For example, when Scribonius Largus published his collection of drug prescriptions in the middle of the first century A.D., he made the following introductory comment:

> *Hardly anyone makes a careful assessment of a doctor's credentials before entrusting himself and his family to his care. By contrast, no one would commission an artist to paint his portrait without first assessing his ability by studying examples of his work. Everyone keeps a set of exact weights and measures, to ensure that mistakes do not occur in aspects of life that are actually quite trivial. This is because people put a lower value on themselves than they do on everything else. As a consequence of this, doctors do not feel the need to work hard at studying medicine. There are even some who are not only ignorant about the writings of doctors in times past, whose works are the bedrock of the medical profession, but actually have the temerity to attribute quite erroneous opinions to those early researchers (Prescriptions Preface).*

Likewise, writing in Alexandria during the death throes of the classical world, just before the city was taken by the Arabs in A.D. 641, Paul of Aegina prefaces his *Medical Compendium* as follows:

> *It is strange that lawyers have legal manuals containing the chief points of all the laws ready at hand whenever they are needed, whereas we doctors have been remiss about this. Lawyers can postpone consideration of any issue for a long time, but we rarely or never have that opportunity. . . . Their business is conducted almost exclusively in the cities, where there is an abundant supply of books, but medical emergencies arise not just in cities, or indeed in the countryside and remote areas, but sometimes even on shipboard out at sea, where delay can have fatal or at least extremely serious consequences. It is very difficult if not utterly impossible to retain in one's memory every medical procedure and all the various medicines. That is why I have collected this digest of material from ancient medical writings, with only a modest contribution of my own, based on what I have seen and tried in my practice as a doctor.*

Paul's "ancient medical writings" are predominantly those of Galen, who flourished nearly five hundred years earlier, and the Hippocratic corpus, written mostly about a millennium earlier. Given this deeply entrenched conservatism, it is hardly surprising that the surviving ancient medical texts preserve very little praise of new discoveries but a great deal of criticism of innovations either as sheer ignorance or else as ephemeral quackery, motivated more often than not by a desire to get rich quick. Such criticism will loom large in the pages that follow; the medical profession has not always been regarded as positively as it is nowadays.

Because of the remarkably static nature of ancient medical practices, it very often does not greatly matter when or by whom something was said. I have presented most quotations without the distraction of a commentary or footnotes. A glossary on pp. 253–263 will, however, provide some basic information about the people, places, and events that feature most prominently in the book.

Ancient medical texts, whether written in Greek or in Latin, can be very challenging to read. Difficulties arise not just from the often highly technical nature of the subject matter but also from the lack of reliable editions of so many texts. Until recently, most of the works of Galen and Hippocrates were still being read in nineteenth-century editions which relied substantially on not always very satisfactory scholarship dating back to the Renaissance. This deficiency is now being made good by the splendid efforts of many scholars in many countries, the quality of whose research is very high. Without their efforts, the ancient medical corpus would present an even more formidable challenge than it does to a nonspecialist like myself, and I would have had no access to those works that have survived only in translations into other languages, most notably Arabic. On a personal level, I owe a considerable debt to friends and colleagues. Debra Hershkowitz read a draft of the whole book, trimming off substantial amounts of excess material unlikely to fascinate anyone but myself. Two busy physicians, Cara Moll and James Nettum, have saved me from numerous errors in modern medical terminology. Julie Laskaris, Susan Mattern, Vivian Nutton, my teacher many years ago, Ralph Rosen, and John Scarborough, my colleague in Madison, have generously shared with me their vast knowledge of ancient medicine and improved the book in very many respects.

MEDICAL ADVICE

Before trying any of the remedies in this *Medicine Cabinet,* consult your physician. If he or she approves more than a tiny percentage of them, change your physician.

May be read a.c., c/c., p.c., h.s., ad lib., s.o.s., *mane, nocte* (before, during, and after meals, at bedtime, as desired, as need be, day or night).

For best results, read not more than two chapters per day. Exceeding this recommended dosage has no long-term ill effects, but may cause drowsiness and, in rare cases, nausea.

I begin to sing of Asclepius, healer of sicknesses,
The son of Apollo, whom shining Coronis, the daughter
Of King Phlegyas, bore on the plain of Dotis,
A great delight to mortals, soother of evil pains

(Homeric Hymn to Asclepius)

A doctor should not quote poetry in support of his opinions,
for such earnest zeal suggests incompetence

(Hippocrates *Precepts* 12)

A CABINET
❦ OF ❦
ANCIENT MEDICAL
CURIOSITIES

· I ·

MEDICINE, RELIGION, AND MAGIC

MEDICAL DEITIES

Asclepius, the son of Apollo, was taught medicine by the Centaur Chiron.
Athena gave him the blood that flowed from the Gorgon's veins, and with
it he healed many people. He used the blood from the veins on the left
side to kill people, and that from the veins on the right to cure them. It is
said that he even restored dead people to life this way. In order to prevent
mortals thinking Asclepius was a god, Zeus killed him with a thunderbolt
(Zenobius *Proverbs* 1.18).

The Greeks have made rather greater medical advances than have other
peoples. Even among the Greeks, however, medicine is just a few gen-
erations old, and does not go back to the origins of the race. Asclepius is
famous as the earliest exponent of the art. Medicine was still rudimentary
and crude in his time, and he came to be reckoned as one of the gods
simply because he developed it in a more sophisticated way (Celsus *On*
Medicine Preface 2).

Fig. 1.1 Apollo, Chiron, and Asclepius.

Asclepius displayed his medical skill only for the benefit of those who were suffering from a specific disease but were otherwise healthy both in their constitution and in their manner of living. Such people he cured with drugs and surgery, instructing them to carry on with their customary lifestyle.... But, when it came to people whose bodies were permeated with disease, he did not attempt to extend their useless lives ... and have them producing children who would probably be just like them. Asclepius did not think that he should treat people whose habits rendered them incapable of living, since treating them did no good either for the patients themselves or for the state (Plato *Republic* 407d).

The unexpected success of Asclepius's cures was the reason why he was thought to have brought numerous dead people back to life. The old stories tell us that Hades accused him of diminishing the importance of his kingdom; he claimed that, because of Asclepius's cures, the number of dead people was steadily decreasing (Diodorus Siculus *The Library* 4.71).

Snakes are sacred to Asclepius.... It is natural that Asclepius should have them as his attendants: since snakes slough off their old skin, they always look young, and likewise the god makes sick people look young when he casts away their illnesses like a snake-skin (Ancient commentator on Aristophanes *Wealth* 773). Since most people nowadays immediately associate snakes with venom and danger, it may seem somewhat paradoxical that such a creature should symbolize healing. The Greeks and Romans, however, did not take such a negative view. Nonpoisonous snakes were sometimes welcomed as rodent-control agents. Even today, a snake appears on the caduceus of Asclepius and on the Bowl of Hygieia as a symbol of various medical associations.

Fig. 1.2 The sacred snake has slithered off Asclepius's staff and is looking up at him like a faithful dog.

Asclepius had two sons, Podalirius and Machaon, who went with Agamemnon to the Trojan War and rendered very considerable assistance to their fellow-soldiers. Even so, Homer makes no mention of them providing any relief from the pestilence [in Iliad 1] or from any of the other diseases that afflicted the Greeks. He says that they used to treat patients with either surgery or drugs. Hence it is clear that these were the only branches of medicine they attempted and that they must be the longest established practices. We can also learn from Homer that diseases were thought to be caused by the anger of the immortal gods, and that it was from the gods that humans sought to obtain relief from sicknesses (Celsus *On Medicine* Preface 3).

The sons of Asclepius helped the Greeks not only with their medical skill but also with their weapons. Machaon laid down his life at Troy when he came out of the Trojan Horse into Priam's city (Pseudo-Hippocrates *The Embassy Speech* 9).

Fig. 1.3 Asclepius with his daughter, Hygieia, and his sons, Podalirius and Machaon, and a human family paying homage. For the difference in scale between the deities and the mortals (esp. the very tiny toddler), see also figs. 3.1 and 3.2.

After Asclepius and his sons, no one of any distinction practiced medicine until literary studies became more widespread. Studying literature may be supremely important for our minds, but it is damaging to our bodies. Medical science was originally regarded as a part of philosophy, and hence the treatment of diseases and the contemplation of the natural world developed from the same sources: for, of course, the people most in need of medical attention were those whose physical strength had been diminished by their restless mental activity through the long watches of the night (Celsus *On Medicine* Preface 5).

HEALING SANCTUARIES

Well over 700 sites have been identified as sanctuaries and shrines in honor of Asclepius.

Neither dancing in the same chorus nor sharing a sea voyage nor having the same teachers establishes such a close camaraderie as does going together on the same pilgrimage to the sanctuary of Asclepius (Aelius Aristides *On Concord between States* 520).

>———●

Customer satisfaction was vital for the reputation and prosperity of a healing temple. The following case histories are found inscribed on large marble slabs set up in the fourth century B.C. at the temple of Asclepius in Epidaurus:

> *A three-year pregnancy. Ithmonica of Pellene came to the temple about having children. She slept in the shrine and had a vision. It seemed that she asked the god to allow her to conceive a daughter, and Asclepius said that she would be pregnant and that he would grant her anything else she asked for. She said that there was nothing more she needed. She became pregnant and carried the child in her belly for three years, and eventually came back to entreat the god about giving birth. She slept in the shrine and had a vision. It seemed that the god asked her whether everything had not happened that she had asked for and whether she was pregnant. He said that she had not asked anything about giving birth, even though he had asked her whether there was anything else she needed and had said that he would grant it. But he said that, since she had come now to supplicate him about giving birth, he would make that also happen for her. She then hurried out of the inner sanctum, and as soon as she was outside the shrine she gave birth to a daughter (Epidaurus Inscriptions Stele A 2).*

> *Epiphanes, a boy from Epidaurus. This boy slept in the temple when he was suffering from kidney stone. The god seemed to stand over him and say to him, "What will you give me if I cure you?" The boy said, "Ten dice." The god laughed and said he would put an end to his suffering. In the morning the boy left the temple cured (Epidaurus Inscriptions Stele A 8).*

> *A cup. As he was walking to the temple a baggage carrier fell down. He stood up, opened his bag, and saw that the cup from which his owner always drank was broken. He was depressed and sat down to try to join the broken pieces together. A passerby saw him and asked, "Why are you wasting your time, you*

idiot, piecing the cup together? Not even Epidaurian Asclepius could make it whole again." After hearing this, the slave put the broken pieces into his bag and went into the temple. When he got there, he opened the bag and took out the cup, and saw that it had been made whole. He told his owner what had happened and what had been said, and when he heard it his owner dedicated the cup to the god (Epidaurus Inscriptions Stele A 10).

A man from Torone, leeches. This man slept in the shrine and had a dream. It seemed to him that the god split open his chest with a knife and took out the leeches, and then put the leeches in his hands and stitched his chest closed. In the morning he left the temple cured, with the creatures in his hands. He had been tricked by his stepmother to drink them down in a potion she had thrown them into (Epidaurus Inscriptions Stele A 13).

Heraieus from Mytilene. This man had no hair on his head, but lots and lots on his chin. He slept here because he was ashamed at being mocked by other people. By smearing his head with a medicine, the god made it have hair (Epidaurus Inscriptions Stele A 19).

Hermon from Thasos. Asclepius cured his blindness. The god later made him blind again because he did not give a thank-offering for the cure, but, when he returned and slept in the temple, the god made him well again (Epidaurus Inscriptions Stele B 2).

A dog cured a boy from Aegina. He had a growth on his neck. When he came to the god, a dog took care of him with its tongue and made him well (Epidaurus Inscriptions Stele B 6).

Hagestratos, headache. This man was afflicted with sleeplessness because of pain in his head. He fell asleep in the inner shrine and had a dream. The god seemed to cure the pain in his head and then to stand him up naked and to teach him the forward thrust used in the pancration [a combination of boxing and wrestling]. *In the morning he left the shrine cured, and not much time later he won the pancration event at the Nemean Games (Epidaurus Inscriptions Stele B 9).*

Gorgias from Heraclea, pus. This man suffered an arrow wound in the lung during a battle, and it suppurated so badly for a year and six months that he filled sixty-seven basins with pus. When he slept here, he saw a vision. The god seemed to remove the arrowhead from his lung. In the morning he left the shrine cured, holding the arrowhead in his hands (Epidaurus Inscriptions Stele B 10).

A woman had a worm inside her, and the best doctors had given up hope of curing her. So she came to Epidaurus and begged Asclepius to free her from the parasite. The god was not present, but the temple attendants laid the woman down where the god was accustomed to heal suppliants. She lay quietly, as she had been instructed. The god's ministers began the procedure necessary for the cure. They took her head off her neck, and then one of them inserted his hand into her body and extracted the worm, a big brute of a thing. But they could not fit her head back on correctly, the way it had been before. The god arrived and was angry with them for trying to do something that was beyond their capability. Then he himself, with his irresistible divine power, fitted her head back on her body, and restored her to health (Aelian *History of Animals* 9.33). A briefer version of this, naming the woman as Aristagora from Troezen, is recorded at *Epidaurus Inscriptions* Stele B 3.

Nearly all the cases recorded on the Epidaurus *stelae* involve treatment of the patient during sleep. Aristophanes makes fun of such cures at *Wealth* 667–83, where a slave reports events in Asclepius's temple when the blind god Wealth is brought there to have his sight restored:

There were many people in the temple, with all sorts of afflictions. The god's attendant extinguished the lamps and told us to go to sleep. He said that, if anyone heard a noise, he was to keep quiet. We all lay down nicely, but I couldn't sleep, for I was being tortured by the thought of a pot of porridge that was lying very close to the little old woman's head. I was awfully keen to creep over and get it. So I looked up, and saw the priest snatching the cookies and dried figs from the holy table. Then he went round all the altars, to check whether any cakes were left, and any he found he sanctified into a sack. I thought this was a fine and holy way to act, so I stood up and headed for the pot of porridge.

Asclepius being a god, cures at his sanctuary could not fail. The inscriptions at Epidaurus and elsewhere attest to his uniform success. Mortal doctors were just as keen to advertise their achievements. Galen declares proudly that, whereas sixteen gladiators died when his predecessor was physician at the amphitheater in Pergamum, he himself lost none. Likewise, of the twenty-two cases described in Rufus of Ephesus's *Case Histories*, only two end with the death of the patient, one through the patient's lack of cooperation, the other through the incompetence of the nursing staff. By contrast, well over half the cases discussed in, for example, the Hippocratic *Epidemics I* and *III* end with the patient's death. Given the pressure on doctors to foster and preserve their reputation, such candor is as surprising as it is commendable.

A doctor, like a savior god, should be on equal terms with slaves, with the poor, with the rich, with kings, and he should help everyone like a brother. For we are all brothers. He should not hate anyone, nor harbor spite in his mind, nor foster self-importance (Supplementum Epigraphicum Graecum 28 [1978] 225). This is part of a damaged inscription from the Sarapion monument in the temple of Asclepius on the Athenian acropolis.

The tragedian Aristarchus of Tegea contracted a disease. Asclepius cured him, and ordered him to make a thank-offering in return for his health. So the poet gave Asclepius the drama that is named after him. But gods would never demand nor accept payment for granting health. How could that be? After all, with a kind and thoughtful love for humans, they provide us free of charge with the greatest blessings [. . . sunlight, water, fire, air . . .] (Aelian *frg.* 101). Aristarchus was a celebrated poet, competing against Sophocles and Euripides, and possibly also Aeschylus, in the great Athenian drama festivals.

To counter a terrible pestilence in the early years of the third century B.C., the Romans sent an embassy to bring the cult-statue of Aesculapius (i.e., Asclepius) from Epidaurus to Rome. The god's sacred snake also boarded the ship, and it swam ashore at the Tiber island. The temple of Aesculapius was therefore built there, and the island was surrounded with stoneworks which gave it the appearance of a ship in commemoration of the god's miraculous arrival. Even today, there is a hospital on the little island, and a pharmacy with an extremely pleasant and knowledgeable staff.

Fig. 1.4 The same patient appears twice in this votive tableau: the doctor treats the boy's shoulder and the snake gives him paramedical assistance.

Where were Rome's ancient deities when the city was forced by a devastating plague to summon Aesculapius from Epidaurus as a god of medicine? Jupiter may be the supreme god who has been sitting enthroned on the Capitol for so long, but his younger days were devoted to sexual escapades, and no doubt they had left him no time for studying medicine (St. Augustine *City of God* 3.17). Attacks on the old pagan religion by the Church Fathers are not always very subtle. Augustine had been a bit of a hedonist himself before he saw the light.

———————

Because it was such a bother to provide their sick and worn out slaves with medical treatment, some people were in the habit of abandoning them on the island of Aesculapius. Claudius decreed that all such slaves were free, and were not to be returned to their owners. Anyone who chose to kill his sick slaves rather than abandon them was liable to a charge of murder (Suetonius *Life of Claudius* 25).

Enter good, leave better (bonus intra, melior exi) (*Corpus of Latin Inscriptions* 8.1.2584). An inscription at the temple of Aesculapius at Lambaesis, in the Roman province of Africa.

VOTIVE OFFERINGS

It was a common practice, when cured of an illness affecting a particular part of the body, to dedicate a picture or carving of that body part to the deity deemed responsible for the cure. Votive body parts could be extremely well crafted, and might occasionally even be gilded. On the other hand, many dedicated body parts were mass-produced.

Fig. 1.5 *Tyche* (dedicates this as a) *thank-offering to Asclepius and Hyg*[i]*eia.* Markedly more dedications to Asclepius were set up by women than by men.

Such was the volume of votive offerings in the temples of the healing gods that they had to be removed periodically to make room for fresh dedications. Often they were buried in pits dug for the purpose. Among many other finds at a sanctuary in the Etruscan town of Tarquinia in northern Latium are over four hundred terracotta models of wombs, measuring on average about eight inches. Nearly all of them have been shown by radiography to contain a model of a fetus, measuring on average about half an inch.

In the sanctuary of Aesculpius near Sicyon, there is a statue of the god's daughter, Hygieia (Health). *It is very hard to see because it has been so thickly covered with strips of Babylonian cloth and with locks of hair cut off by women in the goddess's honor* (Pausanias *Guide to Greece* 2.11.6).

Fig. 1.6 *Thanks, Hyg*[ie]*ia.* An exquisite gold votive offering from about the sixth century A.D. The practice of making such offerings continued long after Christianity became the state religion of the Roman Empire.

MEDICINE AND MAGIC

No one will doubt that magic was born out of medicine, and that under the guise of promoting health it surreptitiously established itself as a higher and holier type of medicine (Pliny *Natural History* 30.1).

The sort of medicine doctors administer at the patient's bedside is practically useless against fever, so I shall propose several remedies advocated by magicians (Pliny *Natural History* 30.98).

Cut the foot off a live hare and remove the fur from its belly, then let the hare go free. Make a strong thread out of the fur, and use it to tie the foot to the sick person's body. This produces a marvelous cure. The cure will be even more efficacious, almost incredibly so, if you should happen to find the actual bone, i.e., the hare's foot, in the feces of a wolf. . . . It also helps a lot if you say to the hare, as you release it, "Flee, flee, little hare, and take the pain away with you" (Marcellus *On Medicines* 39.35).

Motas vaeta daries dardares astataries dissunapiter and *huat hauat huat ista pista sista dannabo dannaustra* and *huat haut haut istasis tarsis ardannabou dannaustra* are incantations approved by the elder Cato for use in treating dislocations and fractures (*On Agriculture* 160). The text of these apparently quite meaningless charms is inevitably in doubt. They may be distortions of phrases in a now unidentifiable language, not Latin at all, or they may have been invented in much their present form, imposing for their sound, not their sense.

Sicy cuma cucuma ucuma cuma uma maa, a charm to staunch bleeding in any part of the body, would seem to be an incantation of the impressive but nonsensical type (Marcellus *On Medicines* 10.35). The spell immediately following, apparently to stop uterine hemorrhaging, is different again, being in good Latin but with little obvious meaning: "a stupid man was going along on a mountain; the stupid man was stupefied; I beg you, womb, do not take this up angrily" (*stupidus in monte ibat; stupidus stupuit; adiuro te, matrix, ne hoc iracunda suscipias*). It should perhaps be noted that, in this same passage, Marcellus also discusses practical measures to stop bleeding.

Contraceptive, the only one in the world. Take some vetch seeds, one for every year that you wish to remain infertile, and soak them in a woman's menstrual blood. She should insert them into her genitalia to soak them. Then take a live frog and throw the vetch seeds into its mouth, so that it swallows them, and then release it alive where you caught it (*Greek Magical Papyri* 36.320). As with so many other practices, whether or not they involved magic, it is hard to see how anyone could have hit on these specific details. Why frogs? Why vetch seeds? Why menstrual blood? Why birth control? We might perhaps also wonder how anyone has ever managed to get a frog to swallow anything.

Menstrual blood was thought to have many dark powers:

> *It turns new wine sour*
> *It makes grain fields sterile*
> *It kills grafted shoots*
> *It dries up seeds*
> *It makes fruit drop from trees*
> *It dulls the bright surface of mirrors*
> *It blunts iron weapons*
> *It dulls ivory*
> *It kills hives of bees*
> *It rusts bronze and iron*
> *It fills the air with a dreadful stench*
> *It makes dogs rabid and gives them an incurably poisonous bite*
> (Pliny *Natural History* 7.64)

On the other hand:

> *If menstruating women walk naked round a field, caterpillars, worms,*
> *beetles, and other pests fall off the crops* (Pliny *Natural History* 28.78).

There are charms to drive away hailstorms and to cure various kinds of
diseases and to soothe burns, but I am very hesitant to mention them, given
that opinions about such measures are so divided. Everyone should suit him-
self in forming his own opinion about them (Pliny *Natural History* 28.29).

Iron has other medical applications apart from its use in making surgical
incisions. Both adults and children are kept safe from harmful drugs if a
circle is traced round them with an iron implement or if an iron spear-
head is carried round them three times. Driving into the threshold nails
that have been pulled out from a tomb wards off nighttime frenzy. Being
pricked lightly with the point of a weapon with which someone has been
wounded helps counter sudden stabbing pains in the side or chest. Cautery
with iron cures some afflictions, most notably the bite of a mad dog; even
if the disease has already taken hold and the victim is afraid to drink,

cauterizing the wound cures him immediately. Drinking water heated up by white-hot iron helps against many diseases, especially dysentery (Pliny *Natural History* 34.151).

Some of the things that drug sellers and root cutters say are, I suppose, rea-sonable enough, but sometimes they make such a song and dance with their exaggerated claims. . . . It seems incredibly far-fetched that, for example, peonies should be dug up only at night, for fear that, if a person is seen by a woodpecker while he is gathering their flowers, he risks going blind, whereas, if he is seen by a woodpecker while he is cutting the root, he may suffer a prolapsed anus (Theophrastus *History of Plants* 9.8).

Especially because of its narcotic properties and the vaguely human shape of its root, mandrake was commonly associated with magic. Josephus describes how mandrake-gatherers avoid the deadly powers of its root:

Fig. 1.7 Harvesting mandrake.

They dig a furrow round it, leaving just a very short part of the root in the earth. Then they tie a dog to the root. When the dog rushes to follow the per-son who tied it there, the root is pulled out of the ground without difficulty, but the dog dies at once, as a substitute for the per-son trying to harvest the plant. (There is no danger in picking it up after the dog dies.) Despite all these risks, it has one property which makes it extremely prized: so-called demons, that is to say the spirits of evil people, enter the bodies of the living and kill them if they receive no help; a simple application of mandrake quickly drives them out (The Jewish War 7.183–5).

Mandrake juice is drunk as an antidote for snakebites and as an anesthetic before surgery or injections, but care must be taken with the dosage: one whiff of it is enough to send some people to sleep (Pliny Natural History 25.150).

AMULETS

πέσσε, πέσσε, πέσσε (*pesse, pesse, pesse* "digest, digest, digest!"): a common inscription on amulets to aid digestion.

Many patients, especially the rich ones, absolutely refuse to take medicines or have enemas used on their stomach, and instead compel us to put a stop to their pain by resorting to magic amulets (Alexander of Tralles Therapeutics 2.375).

Take several threads, preferably dyed with sea purple, put them round the throat of a viper, and choke it. Then tie all the threads round your own neck. This amulet gives amazing relief from tonsillitis and any growths in the region of the neck (Galen The Mixtures and Properties of Simple Medicines 11.860K).

If you catch two lizards copulating and cut off the male's penis and dry it and give the powder to a woman to drink, she will be strongly attracted to you.... Wearing the lizard's tail as an amulet ensures an erection (Cyranides 2.14).

A salamander is a four-footed creature, bigger than a green lizard, that lives in thickets and woodlands.... If a woman wears one attached to her knee, she will not conceive nor have a period (Cyranides 2.36).

Fig. 1.8 Amulets came in many styles, and were worn for many purposes, from warding off evil in general to assuring protection from specific diseases. The other side of this limestone amulet is carved to resemble a walnut shell.

In his Ethics, *Theophrastus tells how Pericles was visited by a friend when he was ill, and showed him an amulet that the women of the household had hung round his neck. He did this to indicate that he must really be ill to be putting up with that sort of nonsense* (Plutarch *Life of Pericles* 38). Theophrastus is talking about the Athenian Plague of 430 B.C. The amulet did Pericles no good, for he died of the plague. Despite dozens of suggestions by modern scholars, the precise nature of the Athenian Plague has not been determined; it has been identified most recently with Ebola.

An amulet of green jasper is good for the stomach and the esophagus. Some people even wear it in a ring with a radiate serpent engraved on it, just as King Nechepsos prescribes in his fourteenth book. I have myself tested this stone carefully: I made a necklace of little pieces of green jasper that I hung round my neck in such a way that they reached down to the opening to my stomach. They were just as efficacious even without Nechepsos's engraving (Galen *The Mixtures and Properties of Simple Medicines* 12.207K).

Some doctors say that amulets are effective. . . . I myself have no time for them. Even so, we should not forbid our patients from wearing them; they may not provide any direct relief, but they do perhaps make sufferers more cheerful through the hope that they inspire (Soranus *Gynecology* 3.42).

MEDICINE AND ASTROLOGY

It was the Egyptians who made the connection between medicine and the prognostic powers of astrology. If they had held the belief that the future could not be moved or altered, they would never have devised ways to ward off, protect against, or treat conditions, whether universal or specific, that assail us or exist among us because of our environment (Ptolemy *Tetrabiblos* 1.3.16).

Ptolemy provides a list of the main parts and functions of the body influenced by the sun, the moon, and such planets as were known in antiquity (*Tetrabiblos* 3.12.147):

Saturn	right ear, spleen, bladder, phlegm, bones
Jupiter	touch, lungs, arteries, semen
Mars	left ear, kidneys, veins, genitals
Venus	smell, liver, flesh
Mercury	speech, reason, tongue, bile, buttocks
Sun	sight, brain, heart, sinews, all the parts on the right side
Moon	taste, swallowing, stomach, womb, all the parts on the left side.

The Egyptian astrologers discovered that the moon foretells whether we should expect good days or bad days, and their predictions apply not just to the sick but to healthy people also. I have kept a record of such forecasts and find them to be perfectly accurate (Galen *Critical Days* 9.911K). Galen was antiquity's most influential doctor, but few doctors nowadays would agree with this view of astrology.

Those who are born when Jupiter is in this particular position will be lawyers or doctors, with such great ability that the affairs of powerful people will be dependent on their intervention. They will be popular, but they will always be engaged in adulterous liaisons, always either on the lookout for ways to satisfy such desires, or actually satisfying them (Firmicus Maternus *Astrology* 5.2.17).

People born when Mars and Saturn are in opposition to each other have a tendency to vomit blood. As for those born when Mars is in opposition to the Moon while he is in Scorpio, Capricorn, Pisces, or Cancer, he will cause them to suffer from impetigo, jaundice, and leprosy. If Saturn is in opposition to the Moon when she is not in her own house nor in the house of Saturn, those born then will have hemorrhoids or be susceptible to boils (Firmicus Maternus *Astrology* 7.20.11). This is a small part of a long catalogue of physical and mental problems that can be predicted by astrologers. In contrast to their modern colleagues, astrologers in antiquity felt no compunction to accentuate the positive.

Crinas of Marseilles combined medicine with another art, astrology, regulating his patients' diet in accordance with the movement of the stars as reckoned in an astrological diary (Pliny *Natural History* 29.9).

There was a rather paradoxical formula used at the end of some Greek horoscopes, meaning "Good luck!," so perhaps medical and other such horoscopes were not meant to be entirely categorical.

· II ·

THE DOCTOR IN
SOCIETY

MEDICAL TRAINING

In medicine, as in all other disciplines, there is a vast difference in skill and knowledge between one practitioner and another (Hippocrates *Ancient Medicine* 1).

There are three kinds of doctor: the ordinary doctor, the high-status doctor, and the doctor who has had a good education. There are the same three types in most professions (Aristotle *Politics* 1282a).

These are the prerequisites for obtaining an accurate knowledge of the medical art:

> *a natural aptitude*
> *good teaching*
> *a sound basic education*
> *a suitable place for study*
> *an appetite for hard work*
> *time.*

A natural aptitude is the first requirement, for if nature does not cooperate, everything else is futile. Learning medicine can be compared to the growing of plants: our natural aptitude is the soil; the instruction our teachers give us is the seeds; our basic education is the planting of the seeds at the right time; our place of study is the nutrients received by the seedlings from the surrounding air; our hard work is the tending of the plants; time ensures strong growth (Hippocrates *The Law* 2).

Medicine has been well organized now for a long time, and has evolved both a set of principles and a method on the basis of which many fine discoveries have been made over a period of many years. What remains to be discovered will be discovered, if the inquirer has the requisite ability and a sound knowledge of what has already been discovered, and uses this knowledge as his starting point. Anyone who undervalues and rejects all this knowledge, and tries to pursue his investigations along some other path, following some other theory, has been, and still is, bound to be disappointed (Hippocrates *Ancient Medicine* 2).

It is not possible to learn the art of medicine quickly. Here is the reason: it is impossible for medicine to have fixed principles, in the way that, for example, anyone who learns a particular method of writing by a particular set of rules has a complete understanding of that method. Everyone has the same understanding of a writing system because the same symbol is used in the same way both now and at all other times, and never becomes its opposite; it is always steadfastly the same, and does not depend on circumstances. Medicine, on the other hand, does different things from one moment to the next, and has quite opposite effects on the same person at different times, these effects actually being contradictory (Hippocrates *Places in Man* 41).

It is difficult to see how a weaver or a carpenter would derive any benefit in his work from knowing the absolute ideal form of weaving or carpentry, or how a doctor or general could be a better doctor or general through having viewed the ideal of their profession. A doctor does not, in fact, seem to regard health in this way: he studies human health, or perhaps indeed the health of a single individual. After all, he treats his patients one at a time. That's enough on this topic (Aristotle *Nicomachean Ethics* 1097a).

From a fragmentary list of anatomical questions and answers, compiled in Greek in Roman Egypt in the third or fourth century A.D., *Lund Papyri* I 7:

> *Why is the rectum so called?*
> *Because it is positioned in a straight* [direct] *line, whereas the other intestines are twisted in a spiral.*
> *Where is the sphincter situated?*
> *At the end of the rectum.*
> *What is it made of?*
> *It is neurocartilaginous.*
> *What is its purpose?*
> *To control* [. . .] *rectum* [. . .] *so that* [. . .] *does not easily* [. . .]

Just as there are some athletes who long to be Olympic victors but undertake none of the training that would help them fulfill their ambition, so there are doctors who say they admire Hippocrates as a doctor beyond comparison, but do nothing that would help them emulate him (Galen *The Best Doctor Is Also a Philosopher* 1.53K).

You should entrust one of your students with the task of administering treatment and ensuring that your instructions are carried out in a timely manner. Pick one who has already been inducted into the mysteries of the medical art, and is capable of administering treatment safely and of modifying the treatment if need arises. He can also make sure that nothing that happens in the intervals between your visits escapes your notice. Never give any such responsibility to a layman, for otherwise, if anything goes wrong, you will be blamed for it (Hippocrates *Decorum* 17).

I was feeling poorly. You came to see me straightaway, Symmachus, accompanied by a hundred student doctors. A hundred fingers chilled by the North Wind took my pulse; I didn't have a fever, Symmachus, but now I do (Martial *Epigrams* 5.9).

Fig. 2.1 Socrates, twinned on a double bust with Seneca (see p. 125).

When Euryphon the doctor was asked with which teacher he had studied, he replied, "With Time" (Stobaeus *Anthology* 1.8).

Men of Athens, I have never learned the art of medicine from anyone, nor have I asked any of the doctors to be my teacher. I have consistently taken care neither to learn anything from the doctors nor even to seem to have learned their art. Nevertheless, I ask you to appoint me as a doctor, for I shall try to pick up the skill by putting your lives at risk (Xenophon *Memoirs of Socrates* 4.2.5). Socrates is making this absurd proposal to point out the illogicality of allowing inexperienced speakers to urge the Athenian democracy to adopt any policy that happens to occur to them.

MEDICINE AND MONEY

If a rich man should fall ill, unscrupulous physicians, aware of their cli-ent's desire for pleasure, would not administer the treatment most condu-cive to good health, but instead they would prescribe the most desirable and pleasant regimen. In any case, they would be unable to administer

*the most appropriate treatment correctly, even if they should wish to do
so. This is because it has never been their intention to apply the art of
medicine properly. Their only aim is to gain money, power, and position*
(Galen *Recognizing the Best Doctor* 1.6). Galen himself had rather a
negative reputation in the Byzantine period and the Middle Ages as a
money-grubber.

*The majority of doctors who are in vogue nowadays have no time for seek-
ing the truth, given that from early dawn they fritter their time away in
paying their respects to their patrons, and spend all evening gorging and
getting drunk* (Galen *The Therapeutic Method* 10.76K).

*I think that even a man with the knowledge and insight of Hippocrates
would have quickly forgotten all his knowledge if he had been distracted by gourmet food, abundant wine, frequent travels, hanging
about on the doorsteps of the rich, and other diversions, all of which
are detrimental to medical treatment* (Galen *Recognizing the Best
Doctor* 9.18).

Money has great power to save those whose bodies fall foul of diseases
(Euripides *Electra* 427).

*It frequently happened to me in my travels that, when either I myself or one
of my attendants fell ill, I had dealings with doctors who were fraudulent
in a variety of ways; some of them sold very ordinary medicines at highly
inflated prices, and others were driven by greed to take on cases that they
had no idea how to cure* (Gargilius Martialis *Appendix to Medicina Plinii*
Preface).

*To the Gods under the ground: The earth hides the best doctor in the
world, Dionysius, who despised gold, but was himself all golden* (*Notizie
degli scavi di antichità* [1941] 193). The inscription has a point only if
most doctors are assumed to be interested in making money.

*To the god Men, and to his power. Prepousa, freedwoman of the priestess, prayed on behalf of her son that, if he were restored to health without her having to pay doctors, she would set up an inscription to show her gratitude. Her prayer was answered, but she did not pay the tribute. Now the god has demanded payment, and has punished her father, Philemon. So she is paying for the answer to her prayer, and will praise the god from now on (*Epigraphica Anatolica *[1989] 42).*

The ideal doctor will despise money and be entirely devoted to his work. Such devotion is impossible for anyone who is addicted to wine or food or sex or—not to mince words—a slave to his penis or his belly (Galen *The Best Doctor Is Also a Philosopher* 1.59K).

No doctor, qua *doctor, considers his own advantage and prescribes accordingly, rather than considering the advantage of the patient* (Plato *Republic* 342d).

If the first thing you did when you met with a new patient was to discuss fees, you would give the wretched sufferer the impression that, unless an agreement could be reached, you would go off and leave him, or that you would neglect him and prescribe no treatment. So do not think about agreeing on payment. The patient has troubles enough, and I think such anxieties do nothing to help, especially if he is suffering from some acute disease. For if the disease's rapid development gives no time to hesitate, that gives the good doctor no incentive to look to his profit margin; no, it focuses him on earning a good reputation through successfully treating the patient. It is better to chivvy patients after you have saved their lives than to extort money from them when they are prostrated by their illness (Hippocrates *Precepts* 4).

I urge you not to be too ruthless, but to take a patient's financial circumstances into account. Sometimes, you should provide your services without charge, bearing in mind either some earlier occasion when you earned grateful thanks or the satisfaction to be derived from the present case. You should give aid especially to impoverished foreigners, if you have an opportunity to treat such people. For where there is love of mankind, there you will also find love of the medical art. Some people, even though they are aware that their condition is perilous, recover their health simply through the reassurance they derive from the doctor's kindness (Hippocrates *Precepts* 6).

What doctor is there now in Athens? None, for there's no art where there's no fee (Aristophanes *Wealth* 407–8).

Heraclitus says that doctors cut, cauterize, and torment the sick in every cruel way, and then, despite inflicting exactly the same pains as do the diseases, they demand from their patients a fee that they do not deserve at all (Heraclitus *frg.* 58).

It is competition between rival doctors that keeps medical bills in check, not a sense of decency (Pliny *Natural History* 29.21).

There is one principle that should be observed in all cases everywhere: the doctor should be in attendance continuously, so as to monitor his patient's strength. . . . Hence it is easy to appreciate that it is not possible for a single doctor to treat a large number of patients. . . . But more money can be made from a throng of patients, and so doctors who are slaves to money-making eagerly embrace those methods of care that do not require them to be so attentive (Celsus *On Medicine* 3.4).

Doctors are in the habit of making up many compounds, but when you come to buy these pricey concoctions, you will pour out vast sums of money for no good purpose and be disappointed. Why not learn how to guarantee your health with inexpensive remedies? (Serenus Sammonicus *The Medical Book* 27.517).

After Hippocrates, there was no limit to the profits to be made from medicine. One of his pupils, Prodicus of Selymbria, invented the ointment cure, thereby discovering a source of income for anointers and medical menials (Pliny *Natural History* 29.4). The elder Pliny may have a low opinion of such people, but his nephew and adopted son, the younger Pliny, thought highly enough of his own ointment-doctor to obtain citizenship of Rome and Alexandria for him by special dispensation from the emperor Trajan (*Letters* 10.5, 6, 7, and 10).

There's not a single doctor, if you really think about it, who'd want even his own friends to be healthy, nor a soldier who'd like to see his city free from strife (Philemon *frg.* 134).

MEDICINE AND THE LAW

In A.D. 74, the emperor Vespasian granted generous privileges to doctors and teachers, but twenty years later his son Domitian had to issue a rescript designed to check abuses of those privileges:

> *I have decided that very strict measures must be taken to curb the greed of physicians and teachers. Their skills should be passed on to selected freeborn young men, but are being sold quite scandalously to many domestic slaves who are trained and then sent out, not for the benefit of mankind, but as a scheme to make money. Therefore, anyone who makes money from training slaves in these professions is to be deprived of the privileges granted by my deified father, just as if he were exercising his art in a foreign community.*
>
> (*Sources of Roman Law before Justinian* 427)

In A.D. 530, the maximum price was fixed for slaves in certain categories (Justinian's *Codex* 6.43.3):

10 solidi:	Slaves under ten years old
20 solidi:	Slaves without a trade
30 solidi:	Slaves with a trade (except doctors and notaries)
50 solidi:	Notaries, eunuchs without a trade
60 solidi:	Doctors and midwives
70 solidi:	Eunuchs with a trade

It would seem that doctors are worth more if they are eunuchs.

We decree that doctors and teachers, along with their property in their own communities, are to be exempt from public obligations. . . . We further rule that they should not be summoned to court or suffer any injustice, and anyone who does them wrong is to pay one hundred thousand sestertii to the Treasury (Theodosian Code 13.3.1).

Even after they had been freed, former slaves still had an obligation to provide services for their former owners. *If a freedman practices the art of dancing, it is proper that he should provide this service free of charge not only for his patron, but also at entertainments put on by his patron's friends. Similarly, a freedman who practices medicine should treat his patron's friends without payment whenever the patron wishes him to do so. For it is not right that, in order to benefit from his freedman's services, a patron should have either to give entertainments constantly or to be ill all the time* (Justinian's *Digest* 38.1.27).

Ideally, a doctor should be outstanding in his medical expertise, and also a person of excellent character. If one of these qualities is missing, it is better that he should be a good man with no learning rather than a thoroughgoing expert, but unscrupulous and immoral. The decency that accompanies good character seems to compensate for lack of knowledge, whereas moral flaws may taint and corrupt medical skill, however great (Erasistratus frg. 31).

Those who are appointed as chief physicians, being aware that their subsistence allowance is paid for out of public taxes, should choose to minister to those who are less well off rather than act like slaves to the rich (*Theodosian Code* 13.3.8).

Some people will perhaps recognize as doctors those who offer cures for just one part of the body or for a particular affliction, for example, those who specialize in ears, ulcers, or teeth. But purveyors of incantations, or invocations, or—to use the vulgar expression used by charlatans— exorcisms, such people are to be excluded from the profession, since those are not branches of medicine, for all that there are some who insist that they have been helped by them (Justinian's *Digest* 50.13.1).

Incompetence counts as culpable, as when, for example, a doctor kills your slave by botching an operation or making a mistake with a medication (Justinian's *Institutes* 4.3).

An old woman with eye trouble called in a doctor. He came and put ointment on her eyes. While she had her eyes closed, he systematically removed every piece of furniture from her house. When it was all gone and he had cured her, he asked her for the agreed fee. She refused to pay it, so he took her to court. She said that she had indeed promised to pay him if he restored her eyesight, but that her vision was worse after the treatment than it had been before it, "for I used to be able to see all the furniture in my house, but now I can't see any of it at all" (Aesop *Fables* 57).

PROFESSIONAL RIVALRY

Galen begins his *On Prognosis* with an uncompromising attack on doctors who prefer the semblance of medical expertise to the reality, pandering to the rich and powerful with their deference and flattery, acting like buffoons to amuse them. Such people wear expensive cloaks and jewelry and have large troupes of attendants and medical instruments made of silver, so as to persuade laymen that they are worth looking up to and envying. *Some of these influential doctors hide their considerable ignorance and there are others who maybe know absolutely nothing.... But these are the people by whom Quintus, the best doctor of his generation, was driven into exile from Rome on a charge of doing away with his patients* (*On Prognosis* 14.601K).

My teacher Eudemus warned me that, if they could not bring me down with their wicked schemes, the clique of jealous doctors would try to poison me. And he told me about a certain young man who had come to Rome about ten years before, and who, just like me, had given practical demonstrations of his medical skill: these doctors poisoned him along with two of his attendants (Galen *On Prognosis* 14.623K).

There is a marvelous medicine for pains in the side, which was known already to doctors long ago, but Paccius Antiochus perfected it and made a lot of money by prescribing it in quite a number of very difficult cases. As long as he lived he never told anyone what the ingredients were. After his death it was written down in a little book dedicated to the emperor Tiberius and deposited in the public libraries. That is how I eventually got my hands on the medicine. Up till then, try as I might, there was no way I could find out about it. He used to make it up with his own hands, behind locked doors, and he did not entrust the recipe to any of his students; in fact, as a way to mislead them, he used to tell his assistants to grind up larger quantities of various ingredients than were actually required (Scribonius Largus *Prescriptions* 97).

All the attendant physicians kept watching my use of these lotions, but none could follow my example in using them because they were unaware of the method of application and the daily required amount of each lotion. . . . The majority of physicians who saw these performances did not know where to find written material on this or on other subjects. Some, after seeing what I did, nicknamed me "wonder-worker", others "wonder-teller" (Galen *Recognizing the Best Doctor* 3.15).

I once attended a public gathering that had met to test the knowledge of physicians. I performed many anatomical demonstrations before the spectators; I made an incision in the abdomen of an ape and exposed its intestines, and then I called on the physicians who were present to put them back in position and make the necessary abdominal sutures— but none of them dared to do this. We ourselves then treated the ape, displaying our skill, manual training, and dexterity. Furthermore, we deliberately severed many large veins, thus allowing the blood to run freely, and called on the senior physicians to provide treatment, but they had nothing to offer. We then provided treatment, making it clear to the intelligensia who were present that physicians who possess skills like mine should be in charge of the wounded (Galen *Recognizing the Best Doctor* 9.6).

QUACKS AND CHARLATANS

Procedures to correct curvature of the spine caused by a fall are rarely successful. I know of no case in which shaking a patient on a ladder has ever yet cured a patient. The doctors who use this method are mostly those who want to attract a large crowd and make them gape, and their audience consists of the sort of people who are amazed by this kind of show, whether they get to see someone suspended or shaken or treated in some other such manner. They always applaud, and the result of the attempted cure does not matter to them at all, whether it does harm or good. Any doctors of my acquaintance who actually use this procedure are incompetent. . . . . I think it is not beyond hope that the curvature can sometimes be corrected, provided one has the proper equipment and the shaking is done properly. But I personally have always been too ashamed to treat patients by any such

Fig. 2.2 Ladder therapy.

methods, given that they are associated particularly with charlatans (Hippocrates *Joints* 42).

Of all arts, medicine is the most splendid. But, because of the ignorance of those who practice it and of those who criticize them so arbitrarily, it is nowadays the least reputable of all arts. The main reason for this error of judgment seems to me to be that medicine is the only profession for which no penalty is laid down for incompetence other than loss of reputation, and that does no harm to those who have no reputation to lose. Doctors of that sort are like the characters that appear on the tragic stage as extras with no speaking role: they look like actors, they dress like actors, they wear the masks of actors, but they are not actors. It is the same with medicine: many people have the title of doctor, but there are very few actual doctors (Hippocrates *The Law* 1).

Medicine consists of three parts: first theory, then diet, and the third one is surgery and drugs. . . . Theory is derived mainly from the schools of Herophilus and Callimachus at Alexandria; it is definitely a significant part of medicine, but the ostentatious and self-promoting manner of those doctors might lead you to think that no one else has any mastery of the discipline. However, when you make them face up to real life by putting an actual patient in their care, it turns out that they are no more use than people who have not read even a single medical text. Sick people have often entrusted themselves to these doctors, won over by their powerful eloquence, and then come close to dying, even if there was nothing seriously wrong with them to begin with. Such doctors are really just like pilots who steer ships according to the instruction manual. And yet, when they parade from city to city, they draw large crowds (Polybius *Histories* 12.25d).

All the ancient writers on the subject made some contribution, whether great or small, to our understanding of medicines, and they did so without resorting to witchcraft and trickery such as Andreas later displayed. . . . You should stay away from Andreas and all other such charlatans, and especially from Pamphilus, for he has never seen, even in his dreams, the plants he attempts to describe. Such people are like heralds who advertise the distinguishing characteristics of a runaway slave whom they themselves have never set eyes on. They learn about him from those who do know him and then they publicize the details as a sort of sing-song, but they would be incapable of recognizing the slave, even if he happened to be standing right beside them (Galen *The Mixtures and Properties of Simple Medicines* 11.795K).

In every aspect of the medical art, absolute priority must be given to curing the sick. If there is more than one way to achieve this goal, you should choose the one that involves least fuss. This is more decent, more professional, the choice made by any doctor who does not aspire to worthless popularity (Hippocrates *Joints* 78).

There are so-called doctors who put on displays in which they sit prominently in front of their audience and explain in detail all about how the joints fit together, the arrangement and relative positioning of the bones, and other such things—the pores, breathing, the filtering of waste products. And the hoi polloi *gawp at them; little children could not be more entranced. But a real doctor does not carry on like that; he does not make long speeches to sick people who really need his help. Out of the question! He tells the patient what he has to do, he prevents him from eating or drinking whatever he wants, and he takes his scalpel and lances any abscesses there may be on his body* (Dio Chrysostom *Orations* 33.6).

What harm would it do if incompetent medical practitioners got what they deserve? As things are, it is their innocent patients who suffer, as if the violence of their illness were not enough for them without the inexperience of their doctor as well (Hippocrates *Precepts* 1).

You imagine that, by owning a large number of books, you will impress people and compensate for your lack of education. What you do not appreciate is that this is just how really ignorant doctors act: they equip themselves with ivory medicine boxes, silver cupping-glasses, and lancets with gold handles, but when they actually have to put them to use, they do not even know how to hold them properly; then along comes a doctor who really knows his stuff and relieves the patient's suffering with a lancet that is covered in rust but has a very well sharpened blade (Lucian *The Ignorant Book Collector* 29).

After spending all their time in libraries and acquiring their vast experience by reading textbooks, "theory doctors" persuade themselves that they are ready for action (Polybius *Histories* 12.25e).

Forty years ago, during the reign of Tiberius, there was a fad for drinking wine on an empty stomach and just before meals. This was one of those foreign customs approved by doctors always straining to make a name for themselves by promoting some novelty (Pliny *Natural History* 14.143).

Fig. 2.3 A Roman surgical knife, with its handle shaped for an easy grip.

Socrates *Suppose someone went up to your friend Eryximachus or his father Acumenus, both of whom are doctors, and said, "I know what medicines to apply, so as to heat or cool a person, and I know how to administer an emetic or a purge, and much else like that. And since I know these things, I claim to be a doctor and to make a doctor of anyone else to whom I pass on this knowledge." How do you think they would respond?*

Phaedrus *They would certainly ask him if he also knew to whom he should give these medicines, and when, and in what dosages.*

Socrates *What if he were to say, "I have no idea at all, for I expect the person who consults me to be able to do these things for himself"?*

Phaedrus *I think they'd say the fellow was insane, to suppose that he had made himself a doctor simply by learning something from some book or because he happened to come across some drugs, when really he had no understanding of the art of medicine* (Plato *Phaedrus* 268a).

WOMEN DOCTORS

In recent years, it has been established that women had a rather more prominent role in the medical profession than had previously been supposed. Even so, ancient society being so male-dominated, prejudice often worked against them.

If you are suffering an affliction we must not talk about, these women are here to help you through it. But if it is an ailment we may mention to men, speak up, so that the doctors may be told about it (Euripides *Hippolytus* 293–6; Phaedra is being addressed by her nurse, and it is taken for granted that the doctors are men).

In the old days, there were no midwives, and women died because their modesty forbade them to consult male doctors. (The Athenians had seen to it that no slave or woman should learn the art of medicine.) But a girl called Hagnodice wanted to learn medicine, so she cut off her long hair, and dressed like a man and apprenticed herself to Herophilus the doctor. She learned medicine and, when she had heard that a woman was having a difficult birth, she tried to visit her. But the woman, under the impression that Hagnodice was a man, was reluctant to entrust herself to her care, so Hagnodice lifted up her clothes and showed her that she was a woman. That was how she started treating women. When the male doctors saw that they were not being allowed to visit women any more, they began making accusations against Hagnodice, alleging that "he" was a smooth seducer of women, and that the women were feigning illness so that "he" would visit them. The court was about to find her guilty when Hagnodice lifted her tunic and showed that she was a woman. The male doctors began to accuse her all the more vehemently [for breaking the law prohibiting women from studying medicine], *but the wives of the leading citizens came to court and protested, "You aren't our husbands, you're our enemies, for you are condemning the woman who has found a way to save our lives". Then the Athenians emended the law, to allow freeborn women to learn medicine* (Hyginus *Fables* 274).

An epitaph found at Pergamum, in which a doctor honors his wife and fellow doctor:

Farewell, my wife, Pantheia, from your husband, whose grief at your devastating death is inconsolable. Hera the goddess of marriage has never before beheld such a wife, excelling in beauty, wisdom, and discretion. All the children you bore resemble me, and you took care of your husband and your children. You kept the tiller of our domestic life on a straight course, and you exalted our shared reputation as doctors. Nor, even though you are a woman, *did you fall short of me in skill. Therefore Glycon your husband built for you this tomb, which also covers the body of our immortal Philadelphus, and in which I myself shall also lie.*

(*Appendix to the Greek Anthology* 190)

Fig. 2.4 The epitaph proudly proclaims: "Mousa, daughter of Agathocles, a woman physician." The dogs are a nice personalizing touch. They do not signify that Mousa worked with pets as well as people. Veterinary medicine was focused on working animals—cows, horses, mules, and donkeys. There were no small-animal vets; most people in antiquity would have thought that a bizarre idea.

An epitaph for a woman doctor, from Rome:

> *To my holy goddess, to Primilla, a physician, daughter of Lucius Vibius Melito. She lived 44 years, of which she spent 30 with Lucius Cocceius Apthorus without a quarrel. Apthorus built this tomb for his excellent, devoted wife and for himself.*
>
> (*Corpus of Latin Inscriptions* 6.7581)

· III ·

ATTITUDES TO DOCTORS

A RANGE OF OPINIONS

The Greeks are a quite worthless and unteachable race. When they bestow their literature on us, they will destroy our whole existence. They will do this all the sooner if they send us their doctors, for they have conspired to murder all non-Greeks with their medicine. They make us pay for treatment, so we will have the more confidence in them and they can ruin us the more easily (The elder Cato, the icon of traditional Roman values, quoted by Pliny at *Natural History* 29.14).

In practically every case, whether it involves a disease or a wound, people blame the doctor for any further suffering that arises as the inevitable consequence of the pain that the patient is already experiencing. They do not understand the constraints that make it inevitable. Suppose a doctor treats someone suffering from a fever or a wound: if there is no immediate improvement in his condition, if indeed by the next day it has deteriorated, people blame the doctor. But if there is an improvement, they do not praise the doctor as much as they blame him for deterioration, for they think the patient was going to improve anyway (Hippocrates *Diseases* 1.8).

The "lazy argument" goes like this: If you are fated to recover from your illness, you will recover, whether you call in a doctor or not. But if you are fated not to recover from your illness, you will not recover, whether you call in a doctor or not. Either you are fated to recover from your illness, or you are fated not to; so calling in a doctor is pointless (Chrysippus *frg.* 957).

If they can see something perfectly well but cannot explain it, many doctors deny that it exists (Galen *The Affected Places* 8.322K).

A doctor who chatters too much is an affliction in addition to the one you are already suffering from (Menander *Sententiae* 379).

In any profession, a lot of fuss, a lot of spectacle, a lot of talk, resulting in no benefit, is a disgrace. This is particularly true when it comes to medicine (Hippocrates *Joints* 44).

So-called "talk-therapy" has nothing at all to do with helping the sick; diseases are cured by medicines, surgery, and diet, not by words (Philo *On Meeting for Education* 53).

Some doctors know how to treat just about every illness, disease, or weakness, but cannot give you a true or reasonable explanation of how they do it, and then there are doctors of the other sort, clever talkers, tip-top at explaining the symptoms, causes, and treatments that make up the science of medicine, but when it comes to the actual treatment of sick patients, they are absolutely useless, incapable of contributing in the slightest way to finding a cure (Philo *The Worse Tends to Plot against the Better* 43).

A sick person does not look for a doctor who is eloquent, but if it so happens that a doctor who is able to cure him can also explain the necessary procedures in an elegant manner, the patient will not take it amiss. That is not to say that he will be congratulating himself on his good fortune in coming across a doctor who is also good with words, for that would be just the same as if a ship's pilot were handsome as well as skillful. Why are you tickling my ears? Why are you trying to amuse me? That's not what you're here to do: I need cautery, I need surgery, I need to be put on a diet (Seneca *Letters* 75.7).

Some of those who take the trouble to put questions to doctors about patients would like to receive answers that are shorter than their questions (Galen *Recognizing the Best Doctor* 8.4). Garrulous and blustering verbosity was regarded as a common occupational trait in the medical profession. Galen frequently complains about other doctors' *glossalgia* ("tongue pain"), by which he means that they talk so much it hurts their tongue. He himself, however, is often criticized for long-winded and tangential meanderings. Such criticism is not always fully justified. For example, at *The Affected Places* 8.442K, he gives an extensive and rather splendid report on his observation of the instinctive behavior of a newborn goat before coming eventually to the point, which is that, just as animals do not need to be taught to act as they do, so the erection of the penis also depends on instinct, not instruction.

If there were no doctors, there would be nothing more stupid than teachers (Athenaeus *Wise Men at Dinner* 15.72). "Galen" is one of the guests attending this fictional dinner, but the man himself was so breathtakingly arrogant that he would hardly have regarded this as a personal attack. His own works are permeated with criticisms, probably more often scurrilous than justified, of his medical colleagues.

Most of those who aspire to be doctors or philosophers nowadays do not even know how to read properly, and yet they attend the lectures of teachers who are to instruct them in the greatest and most beautiful field of human enquiry, the knowledge imparted by philosophy and medicine. This sort of slothful attitude set in many years ago, when I was still a young man, but it was not as rampant then as it is now (Galen *My Own Books* 19.9K).

A medical sect, called the Empiricists because they based their beliefs on experience, was formed in Sicily with the backing of Empedocles of Acragas, the great natural philosopher. But all such schools argued among themselves, and were denounced by Herophilus. The Empirical sect failed, for the ability to read was a requirement for membership (Pliny *Natural History* 29.6).

Galen says of his rivals that "they are so stubborn and contentious that not even Asclepius himself could cure them" (*Critical Days* 9.774K). Later in the same work, he asserts, "I myself am not in the habit of engaging in lengthy disputes with argumentative people" (9.866K). With the possible exception of Socrates, Galen is actually just about the last person with whom anyone would want to get into an argument.

It would be very easy to acquire in a very few years the knowledge that Hippocrates accumulated over an extremely long period, and then devote the rest of one's life to finding out about those aspects of medicine that still remain to be discovered (Galen *The Best Doctor Is Also a Philosopher* 1.57K). He goes on to conclude that it is only their preoccupation with money that prevents modern doctors from bringing medicine to perfection.

The only difference between doctors in Rome and highwaymen is that the doctors do their evil work in the city, not in the mountains (Galen *On Prognosis* 14.622K).

Where there are many doctors there will probably also be many diseases (Strabo *Geography* 6.1.8).

When it comes to acute diseases, laymen are not very good at distinguishing which doctors are outstanding, and they tend to praise or criticize outlandish cures. It is in the treatment of these diseases that ordinary people outdo themselves in their lack of comprehension and those who are not doctors seem most plausibly to be doctors (Hippocrates *Acute Diseases* 2).

If a carpenter is ill, he either expects to obtain from the doctor a medicine that he can drink so as to get rid of the ailment by vomiting, or he expects to be freed from it by purging or cautery or surgery. But if a long course of treatment is proposed, with his head wrapped in bandages and all the fuss that such a cure entails, he hurriedly says that he has no time for being ill and that life is not worth living if it means being preoccupied with his illness and neglecting the work that lies before him. He dismisses doctors who recommend that sort of treatment, returns to his usual way of living, and recovers his health while attending to his own affairs; or, if his body is incapable of bearing the strain put on it, he dies and is freed from all his troubles (Plato *Republic* 406d).

Politicians should not be blamed for political ills, any more than a doctor for physical ones, but they should be thanked for curing them (Pseudo-Demades *On the Twelve Years* 15).

It is utterly disgraceful if a doctor creates work for himself. Many doctors have been known to aggravate their patients' condition, so that they could win all the greater credit for curing them, but then they have proved unable to cure them, or have managed to do so only at the cost of inflicting great suffering on the wretched patients (Seneca *On Benefits* 6.36).

STATUS OF DOCTORS

Mortals never come closer to the gods than when they give good health to other mortals (Cicero *In Defense of Ligarius* 38).

It is not possible to restore every sick person to health. If it were possible, a doctor would be greater than a god (Aretaeus *On the Treatment of Chronic Diseases* 1.5).

A doctor who is also a philosopher is equal to a god. The difference between medicine and philosophy is slight, for all the qualities needed for the pursuit of wisdom are inherent in medicine:

> *a lack of interest in money*
> *respect*
> *modesty*
> *restraint*
> *sound opinions*
> *good judgment*
> *composure*
> *determination*
> *integrity*
> *a pithy manner of speaking*

Both the physician and the philosopher understand what is useful and necessary in life; both purge us of uncleanliness; both are free from superstition; both have god-given superiority; both use their talent against intemperance, against vulgarity, against greed, against lust, against theft, against shamelessness (Hippocrates *Decorum* 5).

Fig. 3.1 Asclepius, with his daughter, Hygieia, being approached with due deference.

Fig. 3.2 A doctor being approached with due deference. As is indicated by the relative size of the figures, he has been heroized, with semidivine status.

Some people are doctors for the financial rewards, some for the exemptions it gives them from public service, some from love of their fellow men, and some for the glory and honor the profession bestows. In as much as they are health workers, they are all called doctors, but in as much as they do such work for different reasons, one is a humanitarian, another is seeking honor, another is seeking reputation, another is out to make money (Galen *The Doctrines of Hippocrates and Plato* 9.5.4).

To have himself recognized as a qualified practitioner, a doctor does not need to give an actual demonstration of his skill, even though medicine is such an eminently practical discipline—all he has to do is claim to have received his training in Alexandria (Ammianus Marcellinus *History of Rome* 22.16).

When patients do not actually require drugs, but merely need to be put on a health regime, even an inferior doctor will suffice. But, when drugs do have to be administered, we know that a more confident doctor is necessary (Plato *Republic* 459c).

Medical treatment varies greatly, depending on the status of the patient:

> *Sick slaves are just about always treated by doctors who are slaves .... Such a doctor never gives or receives a report about an individual slave's particular illness. He merely tells the patient what to do, based on what his experience leads him to think is best. He does so with an air of absolute knowledge, grimly and tyrannically, and then off he scurries to another patient, thus freeing the owner from the trouble of looking after his sick slaves.*

> *A free doctor generally treats and monitors the ailments of free people. He does this by investigating the origin and nature of the disease, involving both the patient and his friends. He gathers information from the sick person and at the same time keeps him informed, as far as he is able, and he does not give instructions for a cure until he has persuaded his patient to go along with it* (Plato *Laws* 720a).

Julian, the last pagan emperor of Rome, makes much the same point rather more bluntly:

> *Doctors who are free men simply order their patients to follow the necessary course of treatment, but if someone has the bad luck to be a slave and the good skill to be a doctor, he needs to bestow both flattery and treatment on his owner at the same time* (Julian *Against Heraclius* 3).

Doctors tend to exaggerate their own importance by claiming that trivial things are more significant than they are and by overstating dangers (Mimnermus *frg.* 24).

The care of horses and mules has not been regarded as unimportant by either Greek or Latin writers. Just as these animals are inferior only to human beings, veterinary medicine is second only to the treatment of humans. For horses and mules are very useful in war and very attractive in peace. But because the veterinary profession is viewed as being less prestigious than a career in medicine, it has not been followed by the most outstanding people, and books on the subject are not so well written (Vegetius *Mulomedicina* 1 Prologue 1).

BEDSIDE MANNER

A doctor's professional image requires him to look healthy, with a natural fullness of figure, for the ordinary run of people think that if he is not in good physical condition he will not be able to look after anyone else. Personal hygiene is also important, as is dressing well and smelling sweet (but not excessively so). Sick people react positively to such details. If he is wise, a doctor will also pay attention to his moral code, not only by being discreet but also by leading a very well ordered life. This is particularly important for his reputation. He should behave as a gentleman, with both dignity and compassion in his dealings with everyone. Brash glibness can be useful at times, but it is frowned on. . . . A doctor should look serious, but not forbiddingly detached, for that makes him seem arrogant and unsympathetic. But then again, if he laughs a lot and is too cheerful, that is regarded as vulgar, and it is especially important to avoid vulgarity. He should treat everyone fairly, for fairness will help him in tending the sick. Patients have a very close relationship with their doctor, for they put themselves in his hands. At every moment, he comes in contact with women, young girls, and other such precious possessions; it is essential that he should exercise self-restraint in his dealings with them. These then are the qualities necessary in a physician (Hippocrates *The Physician* 1).

When you enter the sick room, bear the following in mind:

> *adopt a good sitting posture*
> *be modest*
> *show decorum*
> *be authoritative*
> *be brief in your speech*

remain calm
be attentive
be diligent
respond promptly to criticism
exercise self-control when faced with difficulties
rebuke anyone who causes trouble
be ready to do your duty

(Hippocrates *Decorum* 12)

Fig. 3.3 Asclepius treating a patient, with Hygieia in attendance.

Asclepiades of Bithynia says that it is a doctor's duty to tend the sick safely, swiftly, and sweetly. That is the ideal to aspire to, whereas excessive haste and undue indulgence of the patient's wishes tend generally to be dangerous (Celsus *On Medicine* 3.4).

If you wish to be a doctor and have managed to find teachers, share your skill generously, practice goodness and love for the rest of mankind. When you are called to see a patient, run; when you enter the sickroom, examine the patient to the best of your ability; commiserate with those who are in pain, and share in the joy of those who have been cured. Regard yourself as a partner in their ailments, and draw on all your expertise for the struggle. Be a brother to patients of your own age, a

son to those who are older, and a father to those who are younger. If
any patient neglects his health, do not imagine you can do the same
(Libanius *Rhetorical Exercises* 7.3).

Some doctors are extremely crass. For example, Callianax the
Herophilean. Zeuxis records that Baccheius wrote this about him in
his Memoirs of Herophilus and his Followers: When a patient asked
Callianax, "Am I going to die?", he replied by quoting ... "Even
Patroclus died, and he was a much better man than you are" [Homer
Iliad 21.107, spoken by Achilles when he is about to kill Lycaon,
one of King Priam's sons] (Galen *Commentary on Hippocrates's*
Epidemics VI 17*b*.145K).

*You must avoid trying to attract patients by wearing elaborate headwear
and refined perfume. Idiosyncrasies, if slight, are regarded as elegant,
but you invite criticism if they are excessive. I am not barring you from
trying to be pleasant, for that is consonant with a physician's dignity*
(Hippocrates *Precepts* 10).

*You should do everything in a quiet and orderly manner, keeping
most things concealed from the patient as you attend to him. . . .
Do not tell him anything about his future or present circumstances,
since doing so has often driven people into a decline* (Hippocrates
Decorum 16).

What doctor can treat the sick with a fleeting visit as he passes by? (Seneca
Letters 40.5).

*I have often used an exchange of letters to treat patients suffering from eye
diseases who lived in foreign countries. People have written to me from
Spain, Gaul, Asia, Thrace, and elsewhere, asking whether I had a reputable medicine I could send them to treat cataracts in their initial stages*
(Galen *The Affected Places* 8.224K).

"Opportunity is our greatest guide in every undertaking": oppor-
tunity means the timely and most advantageous moment for doing
something. Even serious efforts fail, if they are made at an inoppor-
tune time; for example, a doctor discussing the nature of his illness
with a patient when he is in pain, or someone discussing abstinence
with people who are drunk (Sophocles *Electra* 75, with an ancient
commentator's note).

The pulse tends to be quickened by bathing, by exercise, by fear, by anger,
or indeed by any mental agitation. Hence, the patient's pulse-rate is
increased by anxiety about how he will seem to the doctor when he first
arrives. So an experienced physician avoids grabbing the patient's arm
straightaway. He sits down with a cheerful expression and asks him how
he is feeling. If the patient is nervous, he calms him with some appropriate
comments. Only at that stage does he actually touch the patient (Celsus
On Medicine 3.6). "White Coat Syndrome" existed long before doctors wore white coats.

If you are treating a patient for a chronic condition, interrupt the treat-
ment for a while, since it weakens the patient's constitution and becomes
less effective through constant application (Rufus of Ephesus *On*
Melancholy frg. 44).

Criticizing someone sharply and candidly when he is in distress is like
smearing an eye that is injured and swollen with an ointment for
improving the vision: it provides no relief, it merely adds anger to the
pain and annoys the sufferer. A person in good health does not become
at all tetchy or angry at friendly criticism of his sex-life or his drinking
or his idleness or his shirking exercise or his interminable bathing or his
binge eating. But a sick person cannot be expected to tolerate being told
that he only became sick because of his lack of self-control and moral
fiber, or because of his gourmandizing and womanizing; such lectur-
ing would be worse than his actual illness. How tactless you are, man!
Here I am, writing my will, with the doctors preparing castor oil and

scammony [desperate remedies] *for me, and there you are, lecturing me on my shortcomings* (Plutarch *How to Distinguish a Flatterer from a Friend* 69a).

If your mistress is ill, don't fuss over her so much that she is disgusted with you. You should be flatteringly attentive—within reason. Don't prevent her from eating what she wants, and don't hold out cups of bitter medicine for her to drink; let your rival be the one who mixes them for her (Ovid *Art of Love* 2.333–6).

It is the Roman custom ... to bury the emperor's body after a lavish funeral. They then fashion a wax image of the dead man and lay it out on a huge ivory couch with gold-embroidered coverings. The image is pale, like a sick person. For seven days, the whole senate, dressed in black, sits on the left side of the couch, while on the right, without gold ornaments or necklaces, sit the women who share the dignity that is owed to the high status of their husbands or fathers. Doctors come every day, and every day, after supposedly examining the sick man, they declare that his condition is deteriorating. When it is agreed that he is dead, the noblest members of the equestrian order and specially selected young senators pick up the couch and carry it along the Sacred Way to the Old Forum, the place where Roman magistrates lay down their authority (Herodian *History of the Empire* 4.2).

WHEN DOCTORS DISAGREE

We often hear of rival physicians arguing at the sickbed, a scene that no doubt reflects reality; in a world in which a doctor's credentials could not easily be tested, a person who could afford to do so would be very likely to call in several doctors as insurance against a possibly fatal mistake by one of them.

A patient lies there, tossing and turning. A whole gang of doctors comes running, but it is not sympathy for the dying person nor a feeling of common humanity that motivates them; they are all out for empty glory, as if it were a contest at the Olympic Games, with one of them making a fine speech and another one arguing against it, another one constructing a subtle theory and another one knocking it down (Theodore Priscian *Easily Obtainable Recipes* 1 Preface).

The whole art of medicine has such a bad reputation among laymen that it is not thought to be an art at all. Medical practitioners differ so much from one another in their handling of acute illnesses: what one doctor prescribes as being the best treatment a second doctor considers to be bad. Hence laymen might well say that medicine is like prophecy: some soothsayers regard a bird seen on the left to be a good omen, but a bad omen if seen on the right, whereas other soothsayers, seeing the same bird, draw precisely the opposite conclusion (Hippocrates *Regimen in Acute Diseases* 3).

Doctors who meet for a consultation should never bicker or insult one another. I swear, a doctor should not be so confident in his own deductions as to begrudge another doctor his opinions too. That would be a sign of insecurity, the sort of petty behavior one associates more with market-traders than with doctors (Hippocrates *Precepts* 8).

Since it is going to seem that I am frequently contradicting the most eminent anatomists, I thought I had better say something briefly about this. Disagreement among doctors about anatomy did not start with me. It has existed for a very long time, and there are two reasons why this is so: first, because some of those who wrote on the subject made mistakes, and second, because anatomists used different methods of instruction, and so, even if they do not disagree with one another in their interpretation of what they see, they nevertheless convey the impression of disagreement to those who read their books without ever having had any personal experience of observing the things revealed through dissection (Galen *Anatomical Procedures* 2.236K).

THE PATIENT'S COOPERATION

A stubborn patient makes his doctor cruel (Publilius Syrus *Sententiae* C 5).

Doctors need to watch out for patients' tricks, for they often tell lies about whether they are actually taking the prescribed medicines (Hippocrates *Decorum* 14).

Patients who need to be checked in case they are not following medical orders should be seen every day at the same time and place. When the sun has just begun to shine is the best time . . . for that is when a doctor's mind and eyes are at their sharpest (Hippocrates *Prognostics* 2.4).

It is possible to make a diagnosis of a patient's suffering even from his groans, but caution is necessary, since not even that is enough for a complete diagnosis, given that many people lead such soft and delicate lives that they can put on a show of groaning that is every bit as polished as that of actors who groan in tragedies (Rufus of Ephesus *Medical Questions* 41).

Sick people who feel severe pain, if they catch sight of the doctors, no longer feel pain (Philemon *frg.* 108).

There are two points to bear in mind in treating diseases: you should try to help, or at least to do no harm. There are three elements in the medical art: the illness, the patient, and the doctor. The doctor is the servant of the art, but the patient should work with the doctor to counter his illness (Hippocrates *Epidemics* 1.2.5).

No one gains from trying to be cleverer than his doctor, for a doctor's errors do less harm than the trend towards disobeying a doctor's orders (Aristotle *Rhetoric* 1375b).

Few doctors provide proper treatment, and few patients follow medical advice (Galen *Critical Days* 9.830K).

Lack of cooperation from patients was a frequent topic of complaint for Galen, who rather envied the greater clout that Asclepius had in such matters:

> *In my home city of Pergamum, we see people who are receiving treatment from the god acquiescing when he tells them to drink absolutely nothing, often for as much as fifteen days, and yet these same people would never follow a doctor's instructions. The patient's confidence that he is sure to gain some worthwhile benefit goes a long way towards persuading him to do exactly as he is told to do* (Commentary on Hippocrates's Epidemics VI 17*b*.137K). In Galen's time, Asclepius's greatest cult center was in Pergamum.

It is much more reasonable to suppose that patients are incapable of following instructions than that doctors give inappropriate instructions. Doctors are sound in mind and body when they give treatment . . . but patients do not know what is wrong with them or why they are sick. . . . They are in pain in the present and fearful for the future, full of disease but empty of food, more eager to get relief from their disease than a cure that will restore their health, not enamored with death but unable to endure life. In such circumstances, is it more likely that patients should either not follow their doctors' orders and do other things they were not told to do, or that doctors should give inappropriate instructions? (Hippocrates *The Art* 7).

If an illness and its treatment start off on equal terms in the race for health, the illness will not win, but it will win if it is given a head start. Such a head start comes either from the dense nature of our bodies, which allows diseases to lurk unseen, or from negligence on the part of the patients themselves. This negligence is understandable: people ignore illness when it first strikes, and only seek treatment when it has them firmly in its grip (Hippocrates *The Art* 11).

The way to ensure good health is to understand your own body, to observe what is good or bad for you, to exercise restraint in your diet, to forego pleasures that might harm your physical wellbeing, and lastly to make use of the skills of those with expertise in health matters (Cicero *On Duties* 2.86).

Do not be reluctant to ask laymen questions, if it seems that doing so might contribute to a cure. For I believe that this is how the whole of medical science came to be discovered, through the combination into a single entity of all the many individual observations (Hippocrates *Precepts* 2).

Everyone finds it so distressing to disclose details of their health problems, and many people actually die rather than tell a doctor about an ailment that they find embarrassing. Just imagine a great physician such as Herophilus or Erasistratus, or indeed Asclepius himself when he was still a mortal, standing at the door of a house with his medicines and his instruments, asking whether there was anyone inside with an anal fistula, or a woman with a cancer in her womb. Their intrusion would be motivated by a desire to save lives, but everyone, I imagine, would drive such a doctor away for coming to inspect someone else's misery without waiting to be asked. Busybodies try to do these and far worse things, not to offer any treatment, but merely to discover what people have wrong with them. So it is quite proper that they are detested (Plutarch *On Curiosity* 518d).

When doctors want children to take nasty medicine, they start by smearing the rim of the cup with sweet, yellow honey, so as to trick the lips of the unsuspecting children while they swallow down all the bitter medicine (Lucretius *On the Nature of Things* 4.11–6).

When a child refuses to swallow bitter aloes, he should be restrained, face up, with his mouth held open with a soup-ladle, and then, despite his resistance, we inject the aloes as far as possible down his throat by means of a syringe with a sturdy pipe. This is a splendid method of dealing with uncooperative children, and I have often given nourishment in the form of soup to anorexics in the same way (Paul of Aegina *Medical Compendium* 4.57).

It is perfectly easy to restore a broken nose to its original shape, especially if it is treated on the same day as it was broken, or just a short time afterwards. But doctors are slow to act, and handle the nose too gently at first. A finger should be run down either side of the ridge of the nose, exerting downward pressure. In combination with pressure from inside the nose, this sets the nose straight. No doctor is as competent in carrying out this procedure as is the patient himself, using his own index fingers, provided he is willing and brave enough to participate, for using them is the most natural method of treatment (Hippocrates *Joints* 37).

Hephaestion [the close friend of Alexander the Great] *happened to have a fever. Being a young man and a soldier, he could not tolerate a strict diet. As soon as his doctor, Glaucus, went off to the theater, he had breakfast, gobbling up a boiled chicken and draining a large cooler of wine. He felt sick and, after a short interval, died. Alexander showed no restraint in mourning his death. He gave orders that, as a sign of grief, all the horses and mules should have their manes and tails shorn off, and he removed the battlements from the neighboring cities. He also crucified the wretched doctor* (Plutarch *Life of Alexander* 72).

PHYSICIAN, HEAL THYSELF

It's easy to give advice when someone else is in trouble, but doing what you advise others to do isn't easy. As proof of this, I know that doctors all talk earnestly to patients about self-control, but if they themselves have any problem, they do all the things they did not allow their patients to do. Suffering pain is altogether different from merely looking at it (Philemon *frg.* 75).

He is a doctor for other people, but he himself is covered with sores (Euripides *frg.* 1086).

Do not be like those incompetent doctors who claim to understand medicine when they are dealing with other people's illnesses, but cannot cure themselves (Cicero *Letters to and from His Friends* 4.5.5).

A quack doctor was touting a cough remedy guaranteed to work immediately, even though he himself was clearly being tormented with a cough (Lucian *Apology* 7).

DOCTOR JOKES

A teacher whose uvula had been injured was told by his doctor to avoid talking. So he ordered his slave to return the greeting on his behalf whenever anyone spoke to him. Then he himself said to every such person, "Don't take it amiss if my slave replies instead of me; I'm under doctor's orders not to talk" (Philogelos *Joke Book* 7).

After reducing a patient's fever from tertian to semi-tertian, a doctor from Cyme [Cymaeans were proverbially stupid] *asked for only half of the fee* (Philogelos *Joke Book* 175a). The fever now returned every two days, not every four, so he had actually made it twice as bad.

When the patient he was operating on cried out in great pain, a doctor from Cyme reached for a blunter scalpel (Philogelos *Joke Book* 177).

After reading the horoscope of a sickly child, a grumpy astrologer told the boy's mother that he would live for many years. When he asked her for his fee, she said, "Come back tomorrow and I'll pay you then". The astrologer replied, "Does that mean I'll lose my fee if he dies during the night?" (Philogelos *Joke Book* 187).

A man with foul breath went to his doctor and said, "Look, sir; my uvula is drooping". When he opened his mouth wide, the doctor reeled back and said, "Your uvula hasn't drooped; it's your rectum that has moved up" (Philogelos *Joke Book* 237).

Capito the doctor put ointment on Chryses's eyes, when he could see a high tower from a mile away, a man from two hundred yards, a quail from twenty feet, and even a louse from one foot away. Now, Chryses can't see the town from two hundred yards, nor the lighthouse (even when its light is burning) from two hundred feet, he can only just see a horse from six inches, and whereas he used to be able to see a quail, now he can't see a huge ostrich. If Capito manages to give him another dose of ointment, he won't ever again be able to see even an elephant standing right beside him (Strato *Greek Anthology* 11.117).

Socles promised to straighten out the hunchback Diodorus, so he piled three massive stones, each four foot square, on his spine; Diodorus was crushed to death, but he did become straighter than a ruler (Callicter *Greek Anthology* 11.120).

· IV ·

SOME FAMOUS
DOCTORS

HIPPOCRATES

Though he is regarded as the founder of the Western medical tradition, Hippocrates is an extremely shadowy figure. About seventy treatises are attributed to him but, since there are numerous significant contradictions between one treatise and another, they cannot all have been written by the same person. It is in fact quite probable that Hippocrates himself wrote none of them. With this proviso, it is conventional to refer to him as the author of them all.

><

Amazing as it may be, medicine lay in darkest obscurity throughout the time from the Trojan War until the Peloponnesian War [i.e., *from the* end of the thirteenth till the end of the fifth century B.C.]. *Then it was called back into the light by Hippocrates, who was born on the famous and powerful island of Cos, which was dedicated to Asclepius. It was customary for those who had been freed from a disease to record in Asclepius's temple the remedies that would be useful, so that people who suffered from the same illness at a later time might be helped. Hippocrates is said to have copied out these cures and to have used them as the foundation for clinical medicine after the temple burned down* (Pliny *Natural History* 29.4).

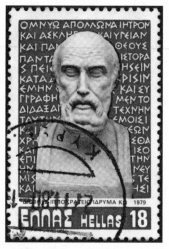 

Fig. 4.1 and 4.2 Ancient sources give some reason to believe that Hippocrates was small in stature, but we do not know what he looked like. He may equally well have been bald (1979) or not (1996).

Life is short, art long, opportunity fleeting, experience uncertain, judgment difficult (*Aphorisms* 1.1). Perhaps the most famous of the sayings attributed to Hippocrates.

Everyone who consults the books written by Hippocrates regards them as preeminent in their understanding of medicine, and welcomes them as the utterances of a god, rather than as words coming from the mouth of a mere mortal (Suda s.v. *Hippocrates*).

Hippocrates traced his ancestry back twenty generations to Heracles, nineteen generations to Asclepius (Soranus *Life of Hippocrates* 1).

Artaxerxes I, the King of Persia, let the people of Cos know he was indignant that Hippocrates refused to be his court physician, on the ground that he was an enemy to Greece:

Great Artaxerxes, the King of Kings, says this to the people of Cos: Hand over to my messengers Hippocrates the doctor, a person of bad character, who has acted outrageously both towards me and towards the Persians. Otherwise, you will learn that you will pay the penalty for initiating wrongdoing. For I shall obliterate your city and hurl your island into the deep sea, ensuring that in future time it will not even be known whether there was an island or city of Cos in that place (Pseudo-Hippocrates *Letters* 8).

Few ancient Greek texts have been as influential in the Western cultural tradition as the so-called Hippocratic Oath. It is included in the Hippocratic corpus, but there is little evidence that it was actually used much in antiquity. The first certain reference to it is not earlier than the first century A.D., in the preface to Scribonius Largus's *Prescriptions*:

A doctor, being bound by the sacred oath of the medical profession, will not give a harmful drug even to his country's enemies, for all that he will attack those same enemies in his capacity as a soldier and a good citizen.

Even in Hippocrates's own family, there would seem to have been no scruples about using drugs in warfare. His son Thessalus appealed to the Athenians to help his homeland of Cos in return for the benefits that their army, afflicted with an infectious disease while conducting a siege, had once received from his ancestor Nebros, "who was universally regarded as the greatest Greek doctor of his time":

The arrival of Nebros in the Athenian camp delighted the god Apollo, who had caused the plague. The soldiers stopped dying and by a divine chance the commander's horse, while rolling in the dust, struck its hoof against the underground pipe through which water was led inside the city wall. Nebros poisoned the water with drugs, and this destroyed the defenders' entrails and contributed significantly to the taking of the city (Pseudo-Hippocrates *The Embassy Speech* 4).

Fig. 4.3 A papyrus fragment of the Hippocratic Oath. The letters in the first line read κ]αιακροησιοσκαι (*k]aiakroesioskai,* "and of [my] lecturing and"), from the section in which the doctor swears to pass on his knowledge free of charge.

HEROPHILUS AND ERASISTRATUS

Herophilus of Chalcedon and Erasistratus of Ceos are the physicians most closely associated with medical studies in Alexandria in the first half of the third century B.C., in the brief period when human dissection was practiced freely.

When someone asked Herophilus for a definition of the perfect doctor, he replied, "The one who is capable of distinguishing between what is possible and what is impossible" (Stobaeus *Anthology* 4.38.9).

Herophilus, that famous doctor (or should I say butcher?), cut up hundreds and hundreds of people so as to pry into nature, and he put aside human feelings for the sake of gaining knowledge. But I doubt whether

Fig. 4.4 The Asclepeion on Hippocrates's home island of Cos.

his investigations of the internal organs were really clear, given that the process of dying changes living organisms, especially when the manner of death is not straightforward, but rather such as to cause distortions during the dissection (Tertullian *On the Soul* 10).

———

When Erastistratus came upon someone who was suffering from a fever but still eating heartily, he asked him what he was doing, and the patient replied, "I'm killing myself with pleasure" (Gnomologium Vaticanum 287).

ASCLEPIADES

In the time of Pompey the Great [i.e., the mid-first century B.C.], *there was a teacher of rhetoric called Asclepiades. Since he felt he was not earning enough from that art, and since his agile wits were actually better suited for any profession other than public speaking, he suddenly turned his attention to medicine. He had never practiced medicine, and knew none of the treatments that can only be learned by personal practical experience. It was therefore inevitable that he rejected all established medical wisdom, and played up to people with his daily torrents of glib and polished oratory. He declared that there were five universal principles in medical treatment: fasting; controlled intake of wine; massages; walking; riding on horseback or in a carriage. Since everyone saw that they could avail themselves of such methods, and since everyone was ready to believe that the easiest way was the true way, Asclepiades soon won over almost the whole human race; it was as if he had been sent down from heaven to help humanity* (Pliny *Natural History* 26.12).

Asclepiades of Bithynia deserves to be regarded as the greatest of all doctors. He founded a school of medicine. He scorned the ambassadors who came with tempting offers from King Mithridates of Pontus. He discovered how to use wine in treating patients. He saved a man's life when his funeral was already under way. But his greatest claim to fame was the wager he made with Fortune, that he should be considered no real doctor if he ever became sick in any way. He won the bet, for he died in advanced old age when he fell downstairs (Pliny *Natural History* 7.124).

At *Natural History* 23.38, Pliny records that *Asclepiades declared that the medicinal benefits to be derived from wine are scarcely equaled by the power of the gods.*

Asclepiades, the greatest of all doctors with the single exception of Hippocrates, was the first to discover the merits of giving wine to sick people (Apuleius *Florida* 19). This assertion is quite incorrect. For example, the merits of giving particular types of wine to patients are discussed by Hippocrates at *Regimen in Acute Diseases* 14.

XENOPHON

Xenophon of Cos, the personal physician of the emperor Claudius, claimed to be a direct descendant of Hippocrates. *When Claudius was served poisoned mushrooms by his wife Agrippina, Xenophon, pretending to help him vomit, tickled his throat with a feather smeared with a fast-acting poison* (Tacitus *Annals* 12.67).

DIOSCORIDES

It is fairly certain that Dioscorides wrote his highly influential *Medical Material* in the middle of the first century A.D. Manuscripts of the work report his name as Pedanius Dioscorides Anazarbeus. From this we learn that he came from the obscure Cilician town of Anazarbus (now in eastern Turkey) and that he may have owed his Roman citizenship to the patronage of the powerful Pedanii family. The most prominent Pedanius at this period was Lucius Pedanius Secundus who, while serving as Prefect of Rome, was murdered by one of his slaves for making homosexual advances to him. By senatorial decree in response to the murder, all four hundred of his household slaves, including women and children, were put to death. It is remarkable to suppose that this Pedanius might well have been the patron of the author of one of antiquity's greatest medical texts.

THESSALUS

During the rule of Nero, Thessalus rose to fame in the medical profession, sweeping aside all received medical wisdom and denouncing all doctors from every epoch with a sort of frenzy. You can get a clear idea of his sense of judgment and his attitude just by looking at his tomb on the Appian Way, where the inscription refers to him by the Greek term iatronikes ("The Conqueror of Doctors"). *No actor or charioteer went out in public accompanied by a larger throng* (Pliny *Natural History* 29.9).

Galen, writing more than a century after Pliny, was still criticising Thessalus for pandering to the Roman élite and promising to teach the art of medicine in six months: *now that medical credentials can be obtained effortlessly, shoemakers, carpenters, cloth dyers, and bronze workers have given up their trades and are scrambling to*

Fig. 4.5 A page from one of the several splendidly illustrated manuscripts of Dioscorides's *Medical Material* surviving in Greek, Arabic, and Latin.

do what doctors do. They set out their sad little stalls and compete for the prize for being the best doctor (*The Therapeutic Method* 10.5K). Galen's own training took ten years, the longest medical education known in antiquity. He got his first job, as physician to the gladiatorial school in Pergamum, at the age of twenty-eight. By contrast, an epitaph survives lamenting the death of a surgeon aged seventeen.

>———

Sitting on his lofty throne with his band of clever followers, Thessalus will have a grand reputation among people who are like sniveling sheep, as he prepares to argue that the same treatment works for every fresh wound, with no inferences drawn from the nature of the damaged part of the body (Galen *The Therapeutic Method* 10.406K).

ROYAL AND IMPERIAL PHYSICIANS

It was Aristotle more than anyone else who implanted a love of medicine in Alexander. He was not attracted simply by the theory of medicine, but actually used to help his friends by prescribing treatments and regimens for them (Plutarch *Life of Alexander* 8).

People suffering from ailments of the spleen fancied that King Pyrrhus helped them: he would sacrifice a white rooster and press down gently with his right foot on the spleen of the afflicted person, who would be lying face up on the ground. No one was so poor or insignificant as not to be granted this treatment on request (Plutarch *Life of Pyrrhus* 3).

Mithridates VI of Pontus was an amateur physician. Some of his courtiers volunteered for surgery and cautery at his hands. This was flattery

Fig. 4.6 Achilles dressing Patroclus's wound, apparently after extracting an arrow (bottom left) from his arm. The two ends of the bandage are both going clockwise round Patroclus's arm. It has been suggested that, mighty warrior though he was and trained in medicine by the Centaur Chiron, Achilles is here represented as an incompetent paramedic. This interpretation is perhaps supported by the way Patroclus is turning his head and extending his left leg.

in action, not just in words, and he regarded their confidence in him as testimony to his skill (Plutarch *How to Distinguish a Flatterer from a Friend* 58a).

When the future emperor Tiberius was on Rhodes, he happened to mention, while arranging his schedule for the day, that he would like to visit the sick people in the city. His staff misunderstood what he meant, and gave orders for all the sick to be brought to a public colonnade and lined up according to the ailments they were suffering from. Tiberius was shocked and surprised, and for a long while was unsure what he should do, but eventually he went round apologizing for the incident to each sick person individually, no matter how lowly and insignificant their status was (Suetonius *Life of Tiberius* 11).

In the period just after his unexpected rise to power, Vespasian still lacked prestige and a certain divinity, so to speak. But he achieved these also. Two lower-class men, one blind and the other lame, came up to him together when he was sitting in court, and begged him to grant them a cure that had been shown to them by the god Serapis during the night. Serapis had said that Vespasian would restore the blind man's sight if he spat in his eyes, and strengthen the lame man's leg if he would deign to touch it with his heel. Vespasian thought that there was little prospect of success, and was therefore reluctant to try. Eventually, however, urged on by his friends, he did try, and was successful in curing them both, publicly in front of a large crowd (Suetonius *Life of Vespasian* 7).

The emperor Commodus loved practical jokes: he named his attendants after male and female private parts; he appointed a man as priest of Hercules because he had an enormous penis; he had human excrement mixed with expensive food at banquets; he pushed the prefect of his Praetorian Guard into a fish pond and made him dance naked in front of his concubines. As the concluding item in the catalogue, we are told that *he even pretended to be a doctor, bleeding people with his deadly scalpels* (Historia Augusta *Life of Commodus* 10).

GALEN (LAST BUT NOT LEAST)

Though well over half of his known works are lost, Galen is by far the most voluminous author to survive from classical antiquity. That is not to say, however, that he altogether deserves the reputation for verbosity he has had imposed on him; see p. 39. Usually, his instinct for ensuring clarity requires him to write at length. There are, however, quite a few exceptions. He devotes several pages at the beginning of *The Function of the Parts of the Body* 3 to establishing that it is not physically possible for Centaurs to exist or function efficiently: the human front half would require different food from the horse back

Fig. 4.7 A Greek stamp honoring Galen. We are no better informed about his actual appearance than we are about that of Hippocrates.

half, and just imagine a Centaur climbing a ladder or rowing a boat or writing a book, and so on and on. But since this passage seems to be a rare instance of Galen attempting humor, perhaps we should be grateful to have it.

>—●

Galen offers many memorable glimpses into life in the Roman Empire. (It should be said, however, that these vivid details are mostly spread rather thinly through his enormous output, and finding them can require considerable patience, since the intervening pages of medical exposition do not always grip the interest of the lay reader.) For example:

> A dead elephant, presumably killed in the arena, attracted a crowd of doctors eager to see it dissected (with the emperor's cooks taking away the heart) (*Anatomical Procedures* 2.619K).

> Good observation is very important, as Galen emphasizes when he rather patronizingly criticizes those who disagree with him about anatomy: *they are like the man who was counting his donkeys but forgot to include the one he himself was sitting on, and so he accused his neighbors of stealing it, or like the man who turned his house upside-down looking for some gold coins that he was holding in his hand* (*The Function of the Parts of the Body* 3.506K).

> Quintus, one of the great doctors of the previous generation, went to visit a rich and powerful patient after dinner. His breath smelled of wine, and the patient asked him to stand farther away, but Quintus arrogantly replied that, since the patient was himself emitting a feverish odor, he should put up with the smell of the wine. Galen then goes on to discuss a doctor with smelly armpits (*Commentary on Hippocrates's* Epidemics VI 17*b*.151K).

> *Alexandria is the best place to learn anatomy. Students unable to travel so far should at least look out for opportunities to examine bone structure – a corpse washed out of its grave by a river in flood, or the skeleton of a highwayman killed by a traveler whom he had attempted to rob* (*Anatomical Procedures* 2.220K).

There are many reasons why people pretend to be ill. So begins Galen's *How to Detect Malingerers*, a very brief treatise (19.1–7K) largely taken up by the case of a slave with a knee so swollen as to appal a layman— but not Galen, who realized that the swelling was self-induced with thapsia (deadly carrot, still used by traditional fishermen to stun fish). Enquiries revealed that the slave was a born liar, and due to leave on a journey, escorting his owner's carriage. One of his fellow-slaves, who disliked him, told Galen that he was reluctant to leave a girl he was in love with. This smug little tale is extracted from Galen's commentary on the second book of Hippocrates's *Epidemics*, where the problem of malingering is discussed at greater length.

Milk is best drawn straight from the nipple, as Euryphon, Herodotus, and Prodicus recommend. Such is their confidence in this method of restoring body weight that they order patients who have wasted away through phthisis to take the woman's breast in their mouth and suck on the nipple. Since most people cannot bear to do that, it is preferable to transfer the milk from the woman's breasts to the patient's stomach while it is still

Fig. 4.8 Galen in discussion with his idol Hippocrates on a twelfth-century Italian fresco.

warm [i.e., by having him drink it from a cup]. *Woman's milk is best because it is from the same species. But most people are put off by the mere notion of having woman's milk given to them as if they were children, so you should give them donkey's milk as if they were donkeys (The Therapeutic Method* 10.474K).

You should give your patient not more than half a pint of donkey's milk, just as you saw me giving it: by having the she-donkey led into the bedroom to ensure there is no time lost between milking and drinking, and by making the patient drink it at once (Galen *The Therapeutic Method* 10.727K).

Elsewhere in the same work (10.468K), we learn that, along with "melka", chilled sour milk, the Romans also enjoyed chilled ἀφρόγαλα (*aphrogala*), which means literally "foam milk", and sounds just like that other drink still popular in Rome, though not in northern Italy, *cappuccino freddo*—but without the coffee, or the sugar, or the ice.

· V ·

ANATOMY

It is not possible to look without strong feelings of disgust at the features that go together to make up a human being—blood, flesh, bones, veins, and so on (Aristotle *Parts of Animals* 645a).

In my opinion, there is no starting point in the body. Every part of the body is the beginning, and likewise every part is the end, just as there is no beginning to a circle. Diseases also arise in all parts of the body indiscriminately (Hippocrates *Places in Man* 1).

In the earliest times, there was no need for manuals on anatomy, since sons practiced dissection under their fathers' supervision, just like reading and writing . . . and there was no fear that anyone who learned that way would forget what he practiced, any more than those who have practiced the letters of the alphabet are likely to forget how to write. . . . When medicine was no longer confined to the clan of the Asclepiads, it deteriorated more and more with each passing generation, and hence the need arose for manuals to preserve knowledge of it (Galen *Anatomical Procedures* 2.280K).

Anyone wishing to observe the works of nature should not rely on books about anatomy, but rather on his own eyes, and either come to me or to one of my colleagues or practice dissection diligently on his own. But so long as he does nothing but read books, he will be relying on earlier anatomists more than on us, for there are so many more of them (Galen *The Function of the Parts of the Body* 3.98K).

><

Apes to be used in dissection should be drowned, so as to avoid the damage caused to the organs in the neck by strangulation (Galen *Anatomical Procedures* 2.423K). In a later part of the same work preserved only in Arabic, he recommends using a goat or a pig for vivisection of the brain, since the expression on an ape's face would be distressing, and since a goat or a pig is more likely to squeal loudly.

>=

Galen castigates doctors who are too eager to put on a display, but he was quite the showman himself. In demonstrating the vocal mechanism, he would tie up the intercostal nerves of a pig (chosen as the animal likely to squeal loudest): the audience would be amazed that the pig was silent, but "they would be even more amazed" when the threads were untied and the pig was once again able to squeal (*Anatomical Procedures* 2.669K).

>•

Since there are pains and various types of disease that arise in the internal regions of the body, people think that no one can administer remedies to them unless they are familiar with those parts of the body. They therefore believe that it is necessary to dissect the bodies of dead people and scrutinize their internal organs and entrails. They maintain that by far the best practitioners of this art were Herophilus and Erasistratus, who performed vivisection on criminals supplied from prison by the Ptolemaic kings of Egypt. While there was still breath in their victims' bodies, they studied things which nature had previously shut off: their position, color, shape, size, arrangement, hardness, softness, smoothness, contact with each other, movement forward or backward, whether one part fits into another or has another part fitting into it. . . . . It is not cruel, as many people claim, to exploit the suffering inflicted on just a few guilty people in the search

for remedies that will benefit innocent people through all ages to come
(Celsus *On Medicine* Preface 23).

*I have never tried to dissect ants, gnats, fleas, or other such tiny creatures,
but I have often dissected animals that creep, such as cats and mice, and
animals that crawl, such as snakes, and many species of birds and fish*
(Galen *Anatomical Procedures* 2.537K).

*The universe is hidden in such darkness that the human intellect does not
possess the sharpness of vision needed to penetrate the heavens or the depths
of the earth. We do not even understand our own bodies, and are ignorant
about the position and purpose of each organ. Doctors, whose business
it is to know such things, have opened bodies up so that their internal
workings may be made visible, but the Empiricist medical sect maintains
that this does not improve our knowledge of the body's organs, since it may
well be that the process of exposing them to view causes them to undergo a
change* (Cicero *Prior Academics* 2.122).

*It is time for anyone reading this book to decide which chorus to join,
the one round Plato and Hippocrates and the others who admire nature's
works, or the chorus of detractors who complain that nature did not design
our bodies in such a way that waste products flow out from our feet. The
person who dared to grumble like that to me was so spoiled by the decadence of his lifestyle that he thought it was a terrible thing that he had to
get up from his couch to relieve himself. In his opinion, a human being
would be better designed if all he had to do was stretch out his foot and
excrete that way* (Galen *The Function of the Parts of the Body* 3.236K).
Galen observes a little later on (3.241K) that *you could not find a better
place on an animal's body to locate its feet than where they are now.*

*The gods imitated the spherical nature of the universe when they enclosed
the two divine courses of the soul in a spherical body, that is to say, in what
we now call the head, the most divine part of the body and the one which
rules over all the other parts . . . and, to prevent it from rolling around on*

the ground, they provided the head with the body as a convenient means of transportation (Plato *Timaeus* 44*d*). This notion of more or less free-ranging heads is not quite so bizarre as Empedocles's vision of creation before evolution ensured the survival of the fittest: *Many heads grew without necks, and arms roamed about naked, lacking shoulders, and eyes wandered alone, deprived of foreheads (frg. 57).*

Empedocles was wrong when he said that many of the characteristics of animals are a result of accidental occurrences in the course of their development, as for instance when he claimed that the backbone is the way it is because it happened to be broken down [into vertebrae] *when the fetus twisted about* [in the womb] (Aristotle *Parts of Animals* 640*a*).

Expert craftsmen often show off their skill when they are making a doorbolt, or a shield, or a sword handle, or a bowl by adding some decoration or ornament that transcends the object's utilitarian value—ivy or vine tendrils or a cypress branch or something like that. Likewise, nature in its abundance ornaments all body parts, especially in humans. In many areas of the body the decoration is obvious, but sometimes it is obscured by the brilliance of the functional aspect. It is obvious with the ears and also, I suppose, with the skin at the end of the penis, the part that people call the prepuce. But it is also true of the flesh on the buttocks, for if you look at an ape you will appreciate how ugly that part of the body would be if it were exposed (Galen *The Function of the Parts of the Body* 3.898K).

There are some external features of the body put there for appearance alone, but serving no practical purpose: for example, men's nipples and beards. Beards are purely ornamental, not intended for protection, as is proved by the smoothness of women's faces; they are the weaker sex, so they should have the greater protection (St. Augustine *City of God* 22.24).

The hair on a man's chin does not merely give a covering to his cheeks; it also contributes to his elegant appearance. For men look more dignified, especially as they get older, if they have a fine covering of hair on their faces. . . . But women have no need of any special covering to ward off the cold, since they generally spend their time at home (Galen *The Function of the Parts of the Body* 3.899K).

Nature herself seems to have applied a marvelous logic in designing our bodies. She placed in clear sight any attractive looking part of our anatomy, whereas she covered up and hid away those parts which have an essential function but would be ugly and unpleasant to look at (Cicero *On Duties* 1.126).

Most of the external parts of the body have specific names, and familiarity with them makes them well known. The opposite is true of the internal organs; the inner parts of a human being are largely unknown, and hence we have to inspect the various parts of other animals with a nature comparable to ours (Aristotle *History of Animals* 494*b*).

Men and women alike have thick veins in both breasts that make the greatest contribution to a person's intelligence (Hippocrates *Epidemics* 2.6.19).

The greatest experts report that there is a vein linking the eyes with the brain. I think there is also a vein linking the eyes with the stomach; at any rate, it is a fact that no one has ever suffered a blow to the eye without vomiting (Pliny *Natural History* 11.149).

The arteries are without sensation, for they are also without blood, and not all of them contain the vital spirit. When an artery is cut, only that part of the body is paralyzed. Birds have neither veins nor arteries, nor do snakes, tortoises, or lizards, and these creatures have very little blood. The veins are dispersed over the whole of the skin, leading eventually to filaments that are so extremely fine that the blood can progress no farther. Nor can anything else, except the moisture that arises in these filaments in countless droplets and is called sweat.

The veins have a central meeting point at the navel (Pliny *Natural History* 11.220).

Males have more teeth than females. This applies to humans, cattle, goats, and pigs (Pliny *Natural History* 11.167).

The teeth should be counted among the bones, even though some authorities disagree. If they do not allow us to call them bones, it is only fair that they should give us some other name for them. Quite obviously, it would not do to call them cartilage, or arteries, or veins, or nerves, and it would be even less appropriate to call them fatty tissue, or hair, or flesh, or glands, or indeed any other part of the body at all. So, if I omit them from my exposition on the nerves, the muscles, and the internal organs, as well as from the discussion of bones that I am now beginning, I will not refer to them at all. And so we should bid the experts farewell (Galen *Bones for Beginners* 2.752K).

Human teeth contain a sort of poison; baring one's teeth in front of a mirror dulls its brightness, and it also kills fledgling pigeons (Pliny *Natural History* 11.170).

The liver is congealed blood, and that is why it is hot by nature (Macrobius *Saturnalia* 7.4.19). The liver was regarded as the seat of the passions, especially love. Highly unromantic as it may seem to us, that notion stayed in vogue until very recently.

The spleen does nothing and has no function (Rufus of Ephesus *On the Anatomy of the Parts of the Body* 31).

The spleen is so called because it fills up [as if the Latin term *splen* were derived from *supplementum*] *the part opposite the liver, to ensure that the space is not empty* (St. Isidore *Etymologies* 11.1.127).

A patient suffering from pain in the spleen should be given the root or the crushed leaves of a tamarisk to drink in vinegar. Should you wish to assess the effectiveness of this treatment, feed a pig for nine days on tamarisk leaves and roots. If you then kill the pig, you will find it has no spleen (Marcellus *On Medicines* 23.49).

The diaphragm is the main center for hilarity. This can be appreciated especially through tickling the armpits, which are linked directly to the diaphragm. Nowhere else is the human skin thinner, and the pleasure of scratching is therefore particularly immediate there. The association of hilarity with the diaphragm is also why, whether in battle or at a gladiatorial show, a wound in the diaphragm brings laughter as well as death (Pliny *Natural History* 11.198).

The creators of the human race knew that we would not exercise restraint in drinking and eating, and that our gluttony would make us consume much more than was reasonable and necessary. So, to prevent acute diseases from destroying us, bringing the mortal race to a rapid end before it had achieved anything, the creators, foreseeing what would happen, made what is called the lower belly as a receptacle for superfluous food and drink, and they wrapped the entrails round and round to ensure that our food did not pass quickly through and force the body to request more food right away. That would have caused insatiability, making the whole human race, because of gluttony, an enemy to philosophy and the Muses, unresponsive to the most godlike element in our nature (Plato *Timaeus* 72e).

THE PULSE

Herophilus had such confidence in the frequency of the pulse as a reliable indicator of a person's health that he constructed a water-clock containing specific amounts of water calibrated to correspond to the normal pulse-rate at the various stages of a person's life. He would go to see a patient, set up his water-clock, and take the patient's pulse. The extent to which the pulse-rate exceeded the normal rate for emptying the water-clock revealed the extent to which the pulse was too rapid, that is to say, it measured the intensity of the patient's fever (Marcellinus *On Pulses* 11).

Some of the terms used to describe variations in the pulse, many of which were coined by Herophilus and Archigenes and their followers, seem rather imprecise. "Ant-like" is often mentioned in conjunction with "gazelle-like" and "worm-like." Note also, for example:

agitated
disrupted
hectic
intermittent
mouse-tailed
quivering
running backwards
spasmodic
wave-like

The "ant" pulse is so called because it resembles the creature known as the ant. Some say it gets this name from its small size, others from the way it moves, as is the case with the "worm" pulse and the "gazelle" pulse (Galen *The Different Kinds of Pulse* 8.553K). That Galen gives us two quite different reasons for the name of a pulse shows up one of the difficulties with Herophilus's oversubtle definitions.

Precisely because they had a confused and inarticulate notion about pulses, these doctors all followed the same authority, the one who was the first to fall into error. And then they wrangled bitterly, not only among themselves, but also with Herophilus, about issues that have no relevance to the art of medicine, either for better or for worse (Galen *Diagnosis by the Pulse* 8.868K).

When King Antigonus heard that his son Demetrius was sick, he went to see him. At his bedroom door, he met a beautiful woman. Going in and sitting down, he took his son's pulse. Demetrius said, "The fever has left me now", and Antigonus replied "Of course it has, my son. I met it myself just now at the door as it was leaving" (Plutarch *Life of Demetrius* 19).

THE HEART

In arguing that the physiology of the human body shows nature's marvelous handiwork, Cicero stops short of detailing the processes of excretion "for fear that this might be rather unpleasant," and goes on to describe the respiratory system:

> *Air drawn into the lungs by our breathing is warmed first by the act of breathing and then by contact with the lungs. It is then partly breathed out again, but some of it goes to the part of the heart called the ventricle, beside which there is another similar chamber, into which the blood flows from the liver through the vena cava. From these chambers the blood flows out to all parts of the body through the veins and breath flows out through the arteries* (On the Nature of the Gods 2.138).

Some people, it is said, are born with a hairy heart. They are thought to be outstandingly brave. Aristomenes the Messenian, for example. After killing three hundred Spartans, he was wounded and taken captive, but escaped from imprisonment in the quarries by following paths taken by foxes through a cave. He was captured again, but when his guards fell asleep, he rolled over to the fire, and burned through his bonds, even though he himself also suffered burns. When he was captured a third time, the Spartans cut open his chest while he was still alive and found his hairy heart (Pliny *Natural History* 11.185). King Leonidas, the commander of the three hundred Spartans who held the Persians back at Thermopylae in 480 B.C., was also found to have a hairy heart.

They say that the heart of someone who has died of heart disease cannot be burnt, and the same applies to those killed by poison (Pliny *Natural History* 11.187).

THE HEART RULING THE HEAD?

We hear that the ancient Greeks wore a ring on the finger of the left hand that is next to the smallest finger, and they say that the Romans generally adopted the same practice. In his Egyptian Books, *Apion gives the following reason for this: When human bodies were cut up and laid open, as was the custom in Egypt (the procedure that the Greeks call "anatomy"), it was discovered that a very fine nerve runs all the way to the heart from the finger I have just mentioned, and from no other finger. So it seemed reasonable for that finger to be honored with such a decoration, since it apparently has a close connection with the heart, the organ that rules the body* (Aulus Gellius *Attic Nights* 10.10).

There was little consensus among philosophers, physicians, and other scientists about the location of the *hegemonikon* (literally, "the leading thing"), the part of the body that controls all the other parts. The heart and the brain were the main contenders for the honor, but there were others: the entire head or chest, the space between the eyebrows, the breath around the heart, the stomach.

Such influential physicians as Praxagoras and Phylotimus of Cos could maintain that, whereas the soul is located in the heart, *the brain is just some sort of superfluous growth, an offshoot from the marrow in the spine* (Galen *The Function of the Parts of the Body* 3.671K).

Aristotle found at least some use for the brain: *The function of the brain is to regulate the temperature of the blood* (Aristotle *Parts of Animals* 653b).

A syllogism by Zeno of Citium, the founder of Stoicism:

> *Voice comes through the windpipe*
> *If it came from the brain, it would not come through the windpipe*
> *Voice comes from the same place as speech does*
> *Speech comes from reason*
> *Therefore reason is not in the brain*
> (Galen *The Doctrines of Hippocrates and Plato* 2.5.8)

Chrysippus, also a Stoic, offered etymological proof of the heart's supremacy, pointing out that the word for "heart" is *kardia*, which has an alternative form, *kradia*, and that is almost the same as *kratia*, which does not exist in isolation, but is found in such compounds as *demokratia*, "rule by the people" (Galen *The Doctrines of Hippocrates and Plato* 3.5.27). Galen had focused on Chrysippus earlier in the same work when he declared, "etymology is an unreliable witness for it often testifies to the truth of things that are the direct opposite of the truth" (2.2.7).

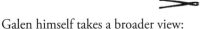

Galen himself takes a broader view:

> *The brain is situated in the head the way the King of Persia lives in a citadel, but it does not inevitably follow that the element that rules the soul is located in the brain. Just because the brain has the senses settled round it like bodyguards, and just because, one might even say, the head is the equivalent in the human body to what heaven is to the whole universe, it does not inevitably follow that the brain is the home of reasoning just as heaven is the home of the gods. Arguments like this in favor of the brain being the ruling part of the body are far more plausible than arguments in favor of the heart, but even so they are not reliable (The Doctrines of Hippocrates and Plato 2.4.17).*

The stomach deserves to be called the body's paterfamilias (head of household), *as if it alone controlled the whole animal. For if the stomach becomes ill, life is endangered because the passage for nourishment falters; and nature has granted to the stomach the power to decide whether to accept or refuse food, as if it were capable of rational thought* (Macrobius *Saturnalia* 7.4.17).

Those who maintain that the stomach is the king of the whole body seem to rely on true reasoning. For if the stomach is strong it strengthens all the limbs, but if it is in pain they are all affected. It is even said that, if good care is not taken of the stomach, it can harm the brain and upset our otherwise healthy senses (Serenus Sammonicus *The Medical Book* 17.300).

· VI ·

SEX MATTERS

Penile erection is caused by air. This is an obvious inference from the speed with which swelling and detumescence occur. No liquid could cause such a rapid change. Since this is so and since dissection reveals that the arteries that enter the penis are rather large for such a small part of the body . . . what other conclusion can we draw if not that, when the penis increases in size, it is filled with vaporous air that flows in from the arteries? (Galen *The Affected Places* 8.441K). Once it is established that an erection is caused by air carried in by the arteries, it does not take much to determine that priapism, involuntary erection, is caused by flatulence (Galen *Causes of Symptoms* 7.267K).

>

It is perfectly clear that reasonable people do not engage in sexual intercourse for the sake of pleasure, but rather to relieve a troublesome urge (Galen *The Affected Places* 8.419K).

➤

An uncontrollable flow of semen is not fatal, but it is unpleasant and disgusting even to hear about. . . . Even young people who have had this problem inevitably come to appear old, for they are sluggish, enervated, lacking in vitality, hesitant, dull, feeble, shriveled, inactive, pale, white, and womanish. They have no appetite, they are sensitive to cold, their

limbs are heavy, and their legs are numb, they have no control over them-
selves, and they are entirely apathetic. In many cases this affliction leads to
paralysis (Aretaeus *On the Causes and Symptoms of Acute Diseases* 2.5.1).

As for those who derive their pleasures from the belly, indulging excessively
in eating, drinking, and sexual intercourse, for all such people pleasures
are slight and fleeting—just the time they spend eating and drinking—
but pains are many (Democritus *frg.* 235).

The testicles of castrated mules, roasted and then mixed with the juice
of the willow tree boiled in water, act as a contraceptive (Aëtius *On*
Medicine 16.17).

Men with large penises are not as fertile as men with average-sized penises,
for sperm is unproductive if it is cold, and sperm that has too far to travel
turns cold (Aristotle *Generation of Animals* 718a).

Sterility may be due to the man, not just to the woman, or to both. . . . For
example, if a man looks like a eunuch and has only a very small penis, so
that he cannot ejaculate far into the vagina. Excessive corpulence can also
be the cause of the problem; obese men are prevented from ejaculating deep
in the vagina (Aëtius *On Medicine* 16.26).

Men's semen is tested for fertility in water. If it is thin and cold, it spreads out
on the surface, but if it is fertile, it sinks to the bottom, since what is ripe is
hot, and what is firm and thick is ripe. Women are tested both with pessa-
ries, to see if smells permeate upwards from below to the breath they exhale,
and also with dyes smeared on their eyes, to see if these color their saliva. If
these results are not obtained, it shows that the passages through which excess
fluids should be secreted are blocked and shut. The region round the eyes is
the part of the head that has most to do with the generative process. Two facts
prove this: the eyes are the only part of the body that is visibly altered during
sexual intercourse, and those who indulge frequently in intercourse have
remarkably sunken eyes (Aristotle *Generation of Animals* 747a).

The Scythians [a nomadic people of the northern steppes] . . . *are not particularly eager for sexual intercourse, because of their moist constitution and their soft, cold stomachs, characteristics that are particularly unconducive to passion. Moreover, their constant bouncing around on horseback reduces their sexual capabilities. These are the things that affect the men. With the women, it is their fat, moist flesh. Their wombs cannot seize hold of the sperm, and their monthly period is not as it should be, for it is little and late in coming. The mouth of their womb is closed with fat, and does not admit the sperm. The women themselves are obese and unused to hard work, and their stomachs are cold and soft. It is for these reasons that the Scythian race is inevitably not very fertile. Their slave women offer clear proof of this, for they no sooner go to a man than they are pregnant, and this is because they are lean and used to hard work* (Hippocrates *Airs, Waters, Places* 20).

Fig. 6.1 It is perhaps hard to imagine this magnificently mustachioed Scythian being anxious about his capabilities, sexual or otherwise.

Here is how the Scythians treat themselves for impotence. At the onset of the affliction, they open the vein behind each ear. When the blood flows out, they become weak and sleep overcomes them. When they wake up, some are cured, others not (Hippocrates *Airs, Waters, Places* 22).

At *Easily Obtainable Recipes* 2.34, Theodore Priscian devotes a whole chapter to the treatment of impotence. After recommending moderate exercise, massage by feminine hands especially of the lower parts of the body, the use of various ointments, foods, and drinks, lots of rest in a comfortable bed during the day as well as at night, and the acquisition of attractive young slaves, he concludes with the suggestion that one should read literature that turns one's mind towards pleasure through the seductive narration of erotic stories.

A man who becomes bald is of a phlegmatic nature. During sexual intercourse, the phlegm in his head is tossed around and heats up, and when it encounters the epidermis, it burns the roots of the hairs, which then fall out. It is for this same reason that eunuchs do not become bald, for they do not undergo this strong movement that takes place during intercourse, and hence the phlegm does not heat up and burn the hair roots (Hippocrates *The Nature of the Child* 20). On phlegm (literally "heat" in Greek) and the other humors, see p. 229.

According to Hippocrates, women derive less intense pleasure from sexual intercourse than men do, but it lasts longer (*Procreation* 4). This same issue is debated by Jupiter and Juno in the third book of Ovid's *Metamorphoses*, and resolved by Tiresias, more famous as the blind prophet who advised the rulers of Thebes and later Odysseus in the Underworld than as a sex counselor:

> *When he was relaxed with nectar, Jupiter said to Juno: "You women definitely enjoy sex more than men do." She disagreed, and they decided to seek the opinion of Tiresias, since he was familiar with sex both as a man and as a woman. He had seen two huge snakes copulating in a green wood and had struck them with his stick. As a result, he spent seven*

*autumns changed into a woman, but in the eighth he saw the snakes
again and said, "If striking you has such great power as to change the
striker's sex, I shall strike you again now". He struck those same snakes
and his former appearance returned, the one he was born with.* As ref-
eree of the lighthearted argument, he confirmed what Jupiter had said
[but Juno was angry and blinded him, so Jupiter compensated for the
loss of his sight by granting him the power of prophecy. Elsewhere,
Tiresias is more specific, ruling that women enjoy sex nine or ten
times as much as do men (Apollodorus *The Library* 3.6.7)].

Sex changes were known in real life also:

*There was a person in Epidaurus, who seemed to be a girl. She had lost
both parents, and her name was Callo. The orifice that women have in
their genitalia was, in her case, without an opening, but, beside the so-
called pubes, she had had from birth a pipe through which she excreted
liquid waste. When she reached adulthood, she lived with a man. She
lived with him for two years, but could not have sex the way women
usually do; instead, she had to endure unnatural intercourse. At the end
of this time, a swelling appeared on her genitals and she suffered terrible
pains. Several doctors were called in, but none of them was willing to take
on the responsibility of treating her. However, a drug seller promised to
cure her. He cut into the swollen area, and out fell a set of male genitalia,
testicles and a penis lacking a perforation. While everyone else stood in
amazement at this strange occurrence, the drug seller started to fix the
remaining defects. First, he made an incision at the head of the penis and
bored a passage to the urethra, and started draining off the liquid waste
by inserting a silver tube. Finally, he scarified the perforated area, thus
making the various parts grow together.*

*After curing her in this way, he demanded a double fee, saying that he
taken on a sick woman and restored a healthy young man. Callo laid
aside her loom-shuttles and the rest of her instruments for working wool,
started to dress and behave like a man, and changed her name to Callon
by adding the letter "n" at the end. Some people say that she had been a
priestess of Demeter before her sex change, and that, because he/she had
seen things that were not to be seen by men, he/she was put on trial for
impiety* (Posidonius *frg.* 85).

Perhaps the least surprising application of the electric ray (see p. 160) mentioned by Pliny is the use of its gall, smeared on the genitalia, as an antaphrodisiac (*Natural History* 32.139).

Osthanes claims that a woman loses interest in sex if her sides are smeared with the blood of a tick pulled off a black wild bull or if she drinks the urine of a he-goat, mixed with nard to disguise the awful taste (Pliny *Natural History* 28.256).

A lizard drowned in a man's urine acts on him as an antaphrodisiac; so also do snails and pigeons' droppings drunk with olive oil and wine. The right-hand section of a vulture's lung worn as an amulet in a crane's skin is a powerful aphrodisiac, as is consuming the yolks of five dove's eggs mixed with a denarius *of pig fat and honey, or sparrows or sparrows' eggs, or wearing as an amulet a rooster's right testicle wrapped in ram's skin* (Pliny *Natural History* 30.141).

For those who have no enthusiasm for sex and are depressed about it. . . . Burn a gecko and grind the ashes to a fine powder, pour on some olive oil, smear the big toe of your right foot with the mixture, and then have intercourse. If you want to stop, wash the mixture off your toe (Paul of Aegina *Medical Compendium* 3.58).

That sexual intercourse might be thought to have medicinal advantages will not have seemed all that strange. Already in the Hippocratic corpus, it had been advocated fairly often and in a matter-of-fact sort of way. For example: *It is good for patients to bathe in warm water, to sleep in a soft bed, also to get drunk once or twice (but not excessively so), to have sexual intercourse, and to ease up on exercises other than walking* (Hippocrates *Diet* 3.85).

Sexual intercourse gives relief to a man who has been bitten by a snake or stung by a scorpion, but it harms the woman who is his partner (Pliny *Natural History* 28.44).

In the winter, Timochares suffered from catarrh, especially nasal catarrh. It dried up completely after sexual intercourse (Hippocrates *Epidemics* 7.72).

Uninhibited fornication cures dysentery (Hippocrates *Epidemics* 7.122).

The benefits to be derived from sexual intercourse are as follows:

> *It provides relief from indigestion caused by overeating*
> *It makes the body lighter, more masculine, more likely to grow strong*
> *It dissipates anxiety and uncontrollable rage*
> *It is the best possible cure for depression*
> *It gives a degree of rationality to the insane*
> *It is a powerful remedy to combat phlegmatic disorders*
> *It restores the appetite*
> *It suppresses erotic dreams.*
>   (Paul of Aegina *Medical Compendium* 1.35)

Sexual intercourse is good for lower back pain, for weakness of the eyes, for derangement, and for depression (Pliny *Natural History* 28.58). As Celsus says, *it is better to try a risky remedy than no remedy at all* (*On Medicine* 2.10).

When he stood trial on a charge of using magic to induce a wealthy older widow to marry him, Apuleius argued that she had married him for the sake of her health: *Pudentilla decided that she should not remain a widow any longer. Even though she could endure the dreariness of solitude, she could not endure the physical illness. She was a deeply respectable woman, who had lived as a widow unscathed by scandal or gossip for so many years. But she was sickening because of her lack of a husband and the long neglect of her insides, wasting away to the point of death with the agonies that arose from the destruction of her womb. The doctors and midwives were in agreement that her illness had been brought on by her not being married, that the trouble was getting worse every day, and that marriage, while she still retained some of her youth, would be the best medicine* (*Defence Speech* 69).

The same treatment features in the eleventh book of Martial's *Epigrams*, which is especially rich in obscenities of all sorts:

> *Leda told her little old husband that she was suffering from a disordered womb, and complained that she needed to be fucked. But she wept and she groaned, saying that her health was not worth that much, and that she had decided she would rather die. Her husband begs her to live and not to abandon her young years, and he allows to be done what he himself cannot any longer do. Straightaway in come the gentlemen doctors and out go the lady doctors. Up go her legs: oh, what serious medical treatment!* (11.71).

Fig. 6.2 Martial's Leda has an evocative name. The Spartan queen Leda, after mating with Zeus in the guise of a swan, laid two eggs from which were hatched Helen and Clytemnestra, Castor and Pollux, one daughter and one son from each egg. Zeus's immortality was passed down in only one egg: Pollux and Helen were immortal, but not Castor or Clytemnestra, who famously came to a bad end, killed by her son, Orestes.

I recommend that young women suffering from a blockage of their monthly flow should live with a man as soon as possible, for if they give birth they will regain their health. Otherwise, right at the time of puberty or very soon after they will be beset with this ailment or some other. Among married women, those who are infertile are more prone to suffer in this way (Hippocrates *Young Girls* 1).

Mares that have not been mated run faster than those that have, and sows that have had their wombs cut out are bigger, better nourished, stronger, and as firm fleshed as boars. The same principle clearly applies to humans also. Just as men who abstain from sexual intercourse are more robust and bigger than other men and lead healthier lives, so it follows that by and large virginity is correspondingly healthy for women also. Pregnancies and childbirth use up women's bodies and cause them to waste rapidly away, whereas virginity spares them such damage and should therefore be considered healthy (Soranus *Gynecology* 1.30).

Some men are enfeebled by sexual intercourse right from an early age, whereas others, if they do not have sex frequently, suffer from heaviness of the head, nausea, fever, loss of appetite, and poor digestion (Galen *The Affected Places* 8.417K).

It is better to have sexual intercourse infrequently, though it revitalizes sluggish athletes, restores a husky voice, and cures back pain, dull vision, mental problems, and depression (Pliny *Natural History* 28.58).

Why is it that those who indulge frequently in sexual intercourse and eunuchs, who never do, suffer equally from blurring of the vision? (Pseudo-Aristotle *Problems* 875*b*).

Some doctors recommend sexual intercourse as a cure for jaundice, on the theory that it is desirable to relax the patient's flesh. But this also disturbs the nerves and diminishes the body's strength, which needs rather to be built up when one is ill (Caelius Aurelianus *Chronic Diseases* 3.78).

Some doctors have actually recommended sexual intercourse as a cure for sciatica, at least in cases in which the problem seems not to have been brought on by sexual intercourse (Caelius Aurelianus *Chronic Diseases* 5.22).

Sexual intercourse relieves those afflicted with melancholy or madness, since it restores the patient's reason and distracts him from his obsession. This treatment is effective even if intercourse is not with the person whom the patient loves (Rufus of Ephesus *On Melancholy frg.* 58).

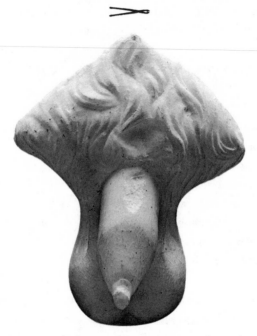

Fig. 6.3 It is uncertain whether sexual diseases were as widespread in antiquity as now, but votive offerings of this type have survived in large numbers.

It is not at all surprising that people who indulge immoderately in sexual intercourse end up being rather feeble, given that the whole body thereby loses the purest part both of the semen and of the spirit of life. Apart from that, there is also the pleasure that comes with sex; even on its own, that is sufficient to destroy the vital tone. People have died of too much pleasure before now (Galen *Semen* 4.588K).

· VII ·

WOMEN AND CHILDREN

WOMEN PATIENTS

Men have more sutures in their skulls than do women, because their bigger brains need more ventilation (Aristotle *Parts of Animals* 653b).

Men have often been observed using both their hands as if they were right hands. This is not so with women, because of the weakness of their nature. Some men can do this because of the strength in their nerves and muscles, but women inevitably cannot do it, and have to be satisfied with making moderate use of their right hands alone (Galen *Commentary on Hippocrates's* Aphorisms 18a.148K).

Fig. 7.1 Medea killing one of her sons. The uniformity of the battle line ensured that no soldier would hold his sword in his left hand. With his shield in his right hand, he would be leaving both himself and his comrade to the left exposed.

If a woman does not conceive, and you wish to ascertain whether she ever will, wrap her in blankets and fumigate her lower body. If it appears that the smoke passes up through her body to her nose and mouth, you may be sure that she is not infertile (Hippocrates *Aphorisms* 5.59). Fumigation (odor therapy) in this context involves having the woman squat over a smoking fire; see p. 96. The learning curve for this tricky procedure was presumably quite steep.

It helps relieve a swollen vulva to smear it with a mixture of oil and the dung of a wild boar or a domestic pig. The powder of the dried dung sprinkled on a drink is even more effective, and can be given even to pregnant women and nursing mothers (Pliny *Natural History* 28.249).

Fig. 7.2 A woman with a mirror, c. 430 B.C.

Women do not generally suffer from hemorrhoids or nosebleeds or any other such affliction, unless their menstrual flow stops. If they ever do suffer from them, their menstrual flow is reduced, as if the secretion were transferred to the other location (Aristotle *Generation of Animals* 727*a*).

Treating pimples, spots, and freckles is more or less a waste of time, but there is no way to stop women from fussing over their appearance (Celsus *On Medicine* 6.5).

It is said that those who organize cremations burn one woman along with every ten men, for women's bodies contain a resinous and fatty substance that ensures that the flames catch hold (Plutarch *Table Talk* 651b).

Galen states that women's periods are regulated by the moon (*Critical Days* 9.903K). Aristotle says less comprehensively that menstruation has a tendency to happen when the moon is waning (*Generation of Animals* 738a, 767a). Soranus disagrees: *Every woman has her period according to her own personal schedule. It is not true … that all women have their period at the same time, when the moon is waning* (*Gynecology* 1.21).

THE WANDERING WOMB

Men's genitals are by nature disobedient and self-willed, like some living animal that won't listen to reason, goaded by its desires to try to control everything. Likewise in women and for the same reasons, the womb is like a creature shut in and longing to produce children, and whenever it remains unproductive for a long time beyond its due season, it complains and takes it hard. It wanders about everywhere through the body, blocking the channels needed for breath and thus preventing respiration. In so doing, it engenders extreme distress and causes all sorts of diseases (Plato *Timaeus* 91b).

Hysterical suffocation. The womb is an organ found in women. It lies between a woman's sides, and is very like a living creature, in that it moves of its own volition to both the right and the left side. It can also move upwards to the floating ribs or laterally towards the liver or the spleen. It can also move straight down. The womb is altogether erratic. It enjoys pleasant smells and rushes towards them, but it is bothered by foul smells and tries to avoid them. A woman's womb is generally like an animal within an animal (Aretaeus *On the Causes and Symptoms of Acute Diseases* 2.11).

Soranus flatly contradicts this notion: *the womb does not come rushing out like a wild animal from its den* (*Gynecology* 3.29).

If the womb has wandered upwards and is causing suffocation, apply fomentations and burn foul-smelling substances in gradually increasing amounts under the patient's nose. If they are burned in large quantities all at once, the womb is displaced to the lower regions and that causes trouble. Give the patient beaver juice and fleabane to drink. Conversely, if the womb has been drawn downwards, burn disgusting substances beneath the patient, and fragrant substances under her nostrils (Hippocrates *Women's Diseases* 125).

A fourth-century A.D. lead phylactery contains the following spell in Latin to guard against the wandering womb: "Womb, I say to you, 'sit in your place' [. . .] I adjure you in the name of Iao and of Sabao and of Adonai, do not hold on to her side, but sit in your place and do not harm Cleuomedes, the daughter of [A . . ." (*Zeitschrift für Papyrologie und Epigraphik* 115 [1997] 291–4).

PREGNANCY

You should not treat what women say about childbirth with skepticism, for they always say the same, and they are talking about something they know. They could not be persuaded either by fact or by argument to believe anything other than what they know is going on in their own bodies (Hippocrates *The Eight-Month Child* 4).

As an aid to conception, Hippocrates recommends "fat little puppies, well boiled, and cuttlefish boiled in very sweet wine" (*Women's Diseases* 217, also *Superfetation* 29).

To ensure conception, have the woman nibble on half-cooked cuttlefish, roasted over a flame, as hot as possible (Hippocrates *Epidemics* 2.29). In his commentary on this passage, surviving only in Arabic, Galen records rather discursively and with great relish how Philistion, a contemporary doctor and fellow-citizen of Pergamum, charged a very inflated fee for this treatment. He supposed that the cuttlefish, having suckers on their tentacles, would encourage the semen to adhere to the walls of the womb. When his patient chewed on the cuttlefish, she felt sick and protested: "No dog would eat what you are giving me to eat, to say nothing of a woman like me from a decent and prosperous household, living on fine and pure food." But she persisted with the treatment, this second time vomiting and falling unconscious. Then she and her maids threw Philistion out of the house and he lost both his fee and his reputation.

According to Aristotle, women find gestation and childbirth more difficult than do the females of other animals, which tend to be fitter. But he adds that there are some women who attain their best physical condition during pregnancy, when all their excess body mass is used up in supplying nourishment to the fetus (*Generation of Animals* 775a).

Soranus is among the most admired of ancient physicians nowadays, clear-headed, practical, and sympathetic, so it is hard to credit that he expressed the following opinion:

> *Just as food swallowed reluctantly and without appetite is not properly assimilated or digested, so likewise the man's seed cannot be taken up or, if it is taken up, it cannot result in pregnancy unless there is enthusiasm and appetite for intercourse* [on the part of the woman]. *It is possible to maintain even in the case of women who become pregnant through rape that they at least felt the urge, but that it was obscured by their mental choice* (*Gynecology* 1.37).

You should find out which of a woman's breasts is bigger, for the embryo will be on that side. It is the same with the eyes; the eye on the side on which the breast is bigger will also be bigger and altogether brighter within the eyelid (Hippocrates *Superfetation* 19).

If a woman is pregnant with twins and one of her breasts shrivels up, she loses one of the children, the boy, if it is the right breast, the girl, if it is the left one (Hippocrates *Aphorisms* 5.38).

A pregnant woman has a good complexion if the baby is a boy, but a bad complexion if it is a girl (Hippocrates *Aphorisms* 5.42).

A pregnant woman has a better complexion and an easier delivery if the child is a boy, whereas the fetus is hard to carry and her legs and groin swell slightly if it is a girl (Pliny *Natural History* 7.41).

The following story is found in the books of the very ancient and very experienced doctor Hippocrates. A woman was to be punished on suspicion of adultery because she had given birth to a baby boy who was very handsome and quite unlike either parent. But her doctor understood the real reason, and suggested looking to see if there happened to be a picture of a handsome boy in the woman's bedroom; such a picture was found and the woman was freed from suspicion (St. Augustine *Questions on the Heptateuch* 1.93). Augustine cites this story as a parallel to Jacob's trick to make Laban's sheep and goats produce offspring with variegated fleeces and hides (*Genesis* 30.25ff.).

How is it that children sometimes look like people other than their parents? Most doctors think this happens by mere chance since, when the seed both of the man and of the woman is chilled, children do not resemble their parents. Empedocles's view is that children are shaped by the woman's imagination at the time of conception, and it often happens that a child is born looking like a statue or picture with which its mother has fallen in love (Pseudo-Plutarch *On the Opinions of Philosophers* 906e).

What are we to make of the fact that the condition of the soul causes changes in the appearance of the child being conceived? For example, while they were having intercourse some women saw monkeys and produced children who looked like monkeys. Because he was deformed, the king of the Cypriots made his wife look at very handsome statues during intercourse, and he became the father of good-looking children. Horse trainers make pedigree stallions stand in front of mares that are being mated. A woman should be sober during intercourse, so that the child that is conceived may not be made ugly, for the soul experiences strange imaginings through inebriation (Soranus *Gynecology* 1.39).

Apart from women, few animals have sexual intercourse during pregnancy, and superfetation is extremely rare. There is a recorded case of twelve babies being stillborn after a single miscarriage. But if there is a short interval between the conception of the first and second child, both can be brought to term, as was the case with Hercules and his brother Iphicles, or with the woman who had twins, one of whom resembled her husband, the other her lover. Likewise the slave-girl who produced one child like her owner and one like his bailiff, after having had intercourse with both of them on the same day, and the woman who had one child after five months, the other at the normal time (Pliny *Natural History* 7.48). It was also said that Apollo was born a day later than his twin sister Artemis.

MIDWIVES

By giving drugs and making incantations, midwives can bring on birth pangs and make them less painful if they wish. They can also help women having a difficult labor to give birth, and if an abortion seems desirable they perform it (Plato *Theaetetus* 149d). The speaker is Socrates, who has just said that he himself is the son of the midwife Phaenarete (which happens to be the name of Hippocrates's mother as well).

A midwife must not be greedy for money, for fear that she might wickedly procure an abortion for payment (Soranus *Gynecology* 1.2). Abortion was not illegal in antiquity.

The child should be extracted from the womb from a higher to a lower plane. But having the midwife kneel, as some authorities recommend, is undignified and impedes her work. The same applies to having her stand in a hole in the ground so as not to work with her hands from a higher level; Heron approved that method, but it is not merely unseemly, it is actually impossible in a room on an upper storey (Soranus *Gynecology* 2.5).

Fig. 7.3 Attendants at childbirth are all but exclusively women.

The midwife should be careful not to look intently at the genitals of the woman in labor, for fear that her body might contract through embarrassment (Soranus *Gynecology* 2.6).

The best implements for cutting are made of iron. But most midwives think that it is ill-omened to use iron to cut the umbilical cord. They prefer to use a piece of glass or pottery, or a reed or the crust of a loaf, or else they bind it up tight with a linen thread. This is perfectly ridiculous; after all, crying is ill-omened, and that's the first thing an infant does in its life (Soranus *Gynecology* 2.11).

At *Lives of the Philosophers* 463, Eunapius gives an interesting vignette of a woman in Rome who runs a bar, but is also a skillful midwife. She is pouring wine for a typically obnoxious Egyptian stranger (Eunapius suggests that Egyptians are trained in rude behavior before they go abroad), when she is called away to attend a kinswoman who is having a difficult labor. She rushes off without serving the Egyptian hot water to

Fig. 7.4 The chair has handles for the mother to grip, but otherwise does not seem particularly well suited to its purpose here.

dilute his wine. After delivering the child, she washes her hands [!] and returns to her customer, who is peevish about the slow service. He calms down when she tells him why she left, and, being an astrologer, bids her to go back to the mother and tell her she has just given birth to a child who will one day be the second most powerful man in the Empire (Ablabius, a corrupt official at the court of Constantine the Great).

CHILDBIRTH

The philosophers [in this context, fifth-century B.C. Greek scientists] *proposed different theories about the factors that determine a child's sex:*

> *Alcmaeon: the child is of the same sex as the parent who provides more copious seed*
>
> *Hippon: the child is a girl if the seed is thinner, a boy if it is thicker*
>
> *Democritus: the child is of the same sex as the parent whose seed reaches the receptacle first*

Parmenides: the child is of the same sex as the parent whose seed wins a struggle for supremacy

Anaxagoras and Empedocles: the child is a boy if the father's semen comes from the right side of the body, a girl if from the left (Censorinus *The Birthday Book* 6.4).

Pregnant women with pimples on their face give birth to a girl. Those who retain a good complexion generally give birth to a boy. If the mother's nipples are turned upwards, it is a boy, if downwards, a girl. Take some of the mother's milk and mix it with meal, make a small loaf, and bake it on a gentle fire; if it is completely burned up, she will have a boy, but if it splits open, a girl. Roll up the same mixture of milk and meal in leaves and bake it; if it solidifies, she will have a boy, if it melts, a girl (Hippocrates *Barrenness* 4).

If a woman wishes to have a son, she should tie to her right foot a white ribbon of the sort that children wear, but a black one to her left foot if she wishes to have a daughter. . . . A woman who wishes for a son should smear her body with goose grease and resin from the terebinth tree for two days. She will conceive a son if intercourse takes place on the next day. Alternatively, to father a son, the man should have his right testicle bound up during intercourse, but if a daughter is desired, his left testicle. . . . To determine whether an unborn child is male or female: place some parsley on a pregnant woman's head without her noticing, and she will give birth to a boy or a girl, depending on the sex of the first person she talks to. This method is infallible. Alternatively, collect a sample of the pregnant woman's urine, then dig two little holes and put barley seeds in one and wheat seeds in the other. Pour the urine into the holes and cover them with soil. If the wheat sprouts first, she will produce a son, if the barley, a daughter (Pseudo-Galen *Readily Available Remedies* 14.476K).

A male child tends to make its first movement after about forty days, and usually on the right side of the womb, whereas with a female child this

*usually happens after about ninety days and on the left.... After birth,
however, females pass more rapidly than males through youth, maturity,
and old age, especially if they bear many children* (Aristotle *History of
Animals* 583b).

To test whether a woman is pregnant, give her a drink of honey
and water at bedtime on an empty stomach. If she has an attack
of colic, she is pregnant, but otherwise she is not (Hippocrates
Aphorisms 5.41).

*Which part of the body is the first to be fully formed in the womb?
The Stoics think the whole body is formed at the same time. Aristotle
thinks the lower back, just as the keel is the first part of a ship to be laid
down. Alcmaeon think the head, since it is in command. Some doctors
think the heart, with its veins and arteries. Others think the big toe,
and still others think the navel* (Pseudo-Plutarch *On the Opinions of
Philosophers* 907e).

You said that, when you went to Liburnia, you saw mothers carrying
wood and nursing children at the same time, sometimes one, sometimes
two. Those women show how weak and worthless are our pregnant
ladies, who lie for many days under mosquito netting.... In Illyria it
often happens that, when the time for her delivery comes, a pregnant
woman moves off a little way from where she is working, gives birth,
and carries her child back with such little fuss that you might suppose she had simply found it, rather than given birth to it (Varro *On
Farming* 2.10).

*The most curious thing about Corsica has to do with childbirth. When a
woman gives birth, no concern is shown for her or the delivery of the child,
but her husband falls down as if he were ill, and he goes into labor, as it
were, for a fixed number of days, with his body ostensibly suffering great
pains* (Diodorus Siculus *The Library* 5.14).

Fig. 7.5 An al fresco accouchement, under the shade of a leafy tree. In pre-microbe times, there was no reason to prefer a more sterile environment.

Gorgias of Epirus slipped from his mother's womb during her funeral and his unexpected crying forced the pallbearers to halt.... So it was that, at the same moment, a woman whose life was over gave birth, and a child was carried out for burial before he was born (Valerius Maximus *Memorable Deeds and Sayings* 1.8 ext. 5).

It is said that if someone takes a stone or some other missile that has slain three living creatures—a human being, a wild boar, and a bear—at three blows, and throws it over the roof of a house in which there is a pregnant woman, she will immediately give birth, however difficult her labor may be (Pliny *Natural History* 28.33).

Any plants that grow up through a sieve that has been thrown away in a hedge, if worn by a pregnant woman as an amulet, will ensure that she gives birth quickly (Pliny *Natural History* 24.109).

When a woman is having a difficult labor, fumigating her with the fat from a hyena's lower back will ensure immediate delivery.... Placing a hyena's right paw on a woman in labor makes delivery easy, but even moving a left paw over her is deadly (Pliny *Natural History* 28.102).

><

If delay in giving birth becomes life-threatening, news should be brought suddenly to the pregnant woman that a family member, whether her husband, or her father, or her mother, or her brother, or her son, has died or been murdered (Theodore Priscian *Easily Obtainable Recipes* Additions 2, p. 341).

><

Infant mortality occurs mostly before the seventh day. That is why a child is not named until then, when the parents are more confident that it will survive (Aristotle *History of Animals* 588a).

><

In most countries women generally give birth to a single child per pregnancy, but twins are frequent in many parts of the world, especially in Egypt. Sometimes triplets and even quadruplets are born, in some countries more than others. The largest number of children at one birth is five, as has been observed to happen on numerous occasions. There was a woman who produced twenty children at four births, five at a time, and most of them grew to adulthood (Aristotle *History of Animals* 584b).

><

Among the decorations for his theater, Pompey the Great included statues of celebrities, sculpted carefully by great artists. These included Eutychis [whose name means "Lucky Woman"], *who was carried to her funeral pyre by her twenty children, also a woman who had thirty children, and Alcippe* [whose name means "Strong as a Horse"], *who gave birth to an elephant* (Pliny *Natural History* 7.34).

><

Megasthenes says that there are women living in India who give birth when they are six years old (Phlegon *Marvelous Things* 33).

><

If childbirth causes a woman's breasts to swell, they can be restored to their normal size with a drink of mouse droppings in rain water (Pliny *Natural History* 30.124).

Fig. 7.6 A touching but melancholy domestic scene, for it is carved on a funerary monument.

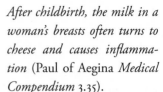

After childbirth, the milk in a woman's breasts often turns to cheese and causes inflammation (Paul of Aegina *Medical Compendium* 3.35).

Most children are subject to convulsions, especially if they are given abundant rich milk from a plump nurse. Wine makes this malady worse, and red wine more so than white, particularly if it is undiluted. Constipation and most things that cause a child to have wind are also harmful (Aristotle *History of Animals* 588a).

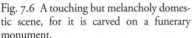

The polytheistic nature of Roman religion is nowhere more obvious than in the vast array of gods and, far more numerously, goddesses with responsibility for some aspect of childbirth. This list of deities and their spheres of interest is long, but not comprehensive:

Juno, Diana, Lucina	childbirth in general
Vitumnus, Sentinus	animating the fetus
Alemona, Fluvionia, Mena	feeding the unborn child
Levana, Partula	delivery
Nona	ninth-month births
Decima	tenth-month births
Antevorta, Postvorta	position of the child in the womb

Parcae	the Fates who control the child's lot in life
Rumina	milk supply
Edusa	suckling
Ossipaga	strong bones
Cuba	lying down
Vagitanus	crying
Abeona, Adeona	walking
Potina	drinking
Cunina	sleeping
Paventia	driving away fear

NURSING

A fairly typical contract drawn up in Alexandria on March 29, 13 B.C. (*Berliner Griechische Urkunden* 4.1058) for the hiring out of a slave girl as a wet nurse for two years includes the stipulations that she should:

take good care of herself and the child
ensure that her milk does not spoil
refrain from sexual intercourse and avoid pregnancy
nurse no other child in addition.

The children of the wealthy were regularly given over to wet nurses. In the second book of his *Gynecology*, Soranus makes the following recommendations:

A wet nurse should be between twenty and forty years old and have had two or three children of her own.
She should be self-controlled, sympathetic and even-tempered, Greek, tidy.
She must not be superstitious.
She must not allow the diaper to get smelly.

Fig. 7.7 A well-to-do Roman lady feeding her child while her husband looks on. Her status is assured by her elaborate hairdo and by her fine dress. It is, moreover, improbable that a husband would commission a representation in marble of himself ogling a wet nurse.

She should not drink alcohol, because the psychological and physical damage done to her by wine spoils her milk; she may lapse into a stupor, and then neglect or fall over the child; the wine's characteristics are passed into the milk, and this can make the child slow and drowsy, sometimes even apoplectic, just as sucking piglets become slow and drowsy if the sow has eaten plants with narcotic qualities.

We should not heed those doctors who believe that girls should be weaned six months later than boys on the ground that they are less robust. They fail to observe that some female infants are stronger and plumper than male ones.

PEDIATRICS

Under the heading "How to tell whether an infant is worth rearing," Soranus gives the midwife a handy checklist of points to look out for:

The mother should have been healthy during the pregnancy
The baby should be born full-term
It should cry immediately and vigorously
It should be perfect in all its parts and all its senses
All the passageways in its body should be free from obstruction
Its limbs should move quickly and strongly
Its joints should bend and stretch easily
It should be of the proper size and shape
It should react appropriately to stimuli

(*On Gynecology* 2.10)

The most admirable custom among the Egyptians is that they rear all the children that are born to them (Strabo *Geography* 17.2).

A Spartan father did not have the authority to decide whether or not to rear his child. He took it to where the elders of the tribes sat. They examined the infant and, if it seemed sturdy and vigorous, they ordered him to rear it, and granted it one of the nine thousand allotments of land. But if it was weak and deformed, they sent it away to the place called Apothetae ("Disposal"), a precipitous spot under Mt. Taygetus, on the principle that it was not in the interests of the child itself nor of the state that it should be allowed to live if nature did not ensure right from the start that it would grow up strong. For the same reason, Spartan women used to bathe their children, not in water, but in wine, as a way to test their constitution; it is said that the undiluted wine caused children who were epileptic or sickly to become disoriented and to have seizures, whereas healthy children were toughened and made stronger by it (Plutarch *Life of Lycurgus* 16).

If a nursing infant has a fever and you lay him down to sleep surrounded by cucumbers of the same length as the child, he will be cured immediately, since all the heat will drawn off from him into the cucumbers (Anonymous Byzantine *Farm Work* 12.19).

The bones of the skull are fixed firm later than all the other bones. That is why it is so thin and weak at the front that the movement of a newborn child's brain can be detected, not just when we touch it but even when we are merely looking at it (Galen *The Shaping of the Embryo* 5.673K).

Generally speaking, a doctor should not treat children suffering from fever in the same way as he treats adults. As with other illnesses, children must be treated less rigorously. Drawing off blood is tricky, and so is giving enemas, and it is not appropriate to torture children with wakefulness, with hunger, or with thirst (Celsus *On Medicine* 3.6).

Teething and the itching that this causes are relieved if you smear butter on the child's gums, either by itself or mixed with honey. The broiled brains of a hare, rubbed on and then swallowed, are equally effective. Eating a boiled house mouse also helps. Mice moreover stop children drooling if they are put in their mouths alive (Dioscorides *Medical Material* 1.71). His recommendation for dealing with infant drool is marginally less repellent in the next book: *House mice, chopped up and applied to the wound, give relief to those who have been bitten by a scorpion. If roasted and eaten, they dry up the drool in children's mouths* (2.69).

A cure for teething. Nature sends mankind into the world naked at first. She then afflicts us with torture when she arms us with snow-white teeth. So bind round your child's soft neck a horse's teeth, the first teeth that fall out as a foal grows bigger. Or smear the child's tender gums with the brains of a pig or of a hare, or with the snow-white milk of shaggy she-goats (Serenus Sammonicus *The Medical Book* 58.1029). Paul of Aegina suggests that *massaging the gums with bird fat or a hare's brains is best carried out when the child is in the bath* (*Medical Compendium* 1.9).

It is an observable fact that children in Rome have a particular tendency to be bow-legged. Some people attribute this to the cold water that flows under the city and chills people's bodies. Others attribute it to the frequency with which women have sexual intercourse, or to their having intercourse while drunk. The real reason is lack of experience in child *rearing. Women in Rome are not so attached to their children as to be careful about every detail of the nurturing process, the way Greek women are* (Soranus *Gynecology* 2.44).

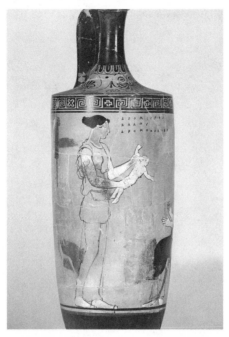

Fig. 7.8 A slave-woman handing a baby to its mother on a Greek vase of c. 450 B.C. I have seen Greek shepherds handling newborn goats just like this.

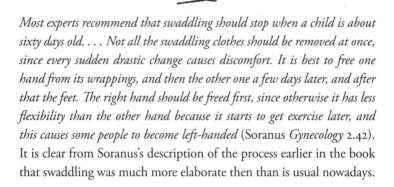

Most experts recommend that swaddling should stop when a child is about sixty days old. . . . Not all the swaddling clothes should be removed at once, since every sudden drastic change causes discomfort. It is best to free one hand from its wrappings, and then the other one a few days later, and after that the feet. The right hand should be freed first, since otherwise it has less flexibility than the other hand because it starts to get exercise later, and this causes some people to become left-handed (Soranus *Gynecology* 2.42). It is clear from Soranus's description of the process earlier in the book that swaddling was much more elaborate then than is usual nowadays.

If a boy's right testicle descends first at puberty, he will father sons, if the left, daughters (Hippocrates *Epidemics* 6.4.1). How many men recall their passage through puberty clearly enough to endorse or challenge this statement? Perhaps the greater prevalance of male nudity in ancient Greek society made it easier to keep track of such things.

It is good for all children, especially the very young, to be nursed and carried about as much as possible both at night and during the day; ideally, they should live as if they were sailing in a ship (Plato *Laws* 790d).

Moistening a child's skull with a cold sponge and then tying a frog to it belly up is a very effective treatment for heatstroke (Pliny *Natural History* 32.138).

· VIII ·

PREVENTIVE MEDICINE

Dream-interpreters advise us to take precautions to ensure that no harm befalls us, but they do not teach us how to go about taking precautions. They merely instruct us to pray to the gods. Praying is all well and good but we should also take action ourselves, and not just ask the gods for help (Hippocrates *Diet* 4.87).

People pray to the gods to grant them health, not realizing that they have within themselves the power to obtain it. They betray their own health through their cravings, self-indulgently working against it (Democritus *frg.* 234).

What a person eats is not sufficient to ensure his good health, if he does not also exercise. Food and exercise have opposite qualities, but they work together to ensure health, for it is in the nature of exercise to use up resources, of food and drink to replenish what has been depleted (Hippocrates *Diet* 1.2).

The only way to ensure the health of both the body and the soul is by not moving the soul without the body nor the body without the soul, for that guarantees that they keep each other in check and are balanced and healthy. A mathematician or anyone engaged in any other intense mental activity should take time to exercise his body through physical training, and likewise a person who is devoted to physical development should take time to exercise his soul by studying music and the whole range of intellectual pursuits. This applies to anyone who intends to earn a reputation as a gentleman (Plato *Timaeus* 88*b*).

Why is it that we make the children of those who die of consumption or edema sit with their feet in water till after the corpse has been cremated? It is thought that this prevents the disease from being passed on to them (Plutarch *On the Delaying of Divine Vengeance* 558*d*).

It is more ridiculous that god should punish the children of the wicked than that a doctor should give medicine to a child because his father or grandfather is sick. In some ways the comparison is valid, but in others it is not. Treating one person does not stop another person from being ill—no one suffering from an eye disease or a fever ever got better through seeing someone else being given eye ointment or a poultice.... On the other hand, it is necessary and helpful, not bizarre and ludicrous, to prescribe exercise, diet, and medicines for the children of people who suffer from seizures, or depression, or gout—not because they are ill, but to prevent them becoming ill. For someone who inherits a weak constitution from his parents may not deserve punishment, but he does deserve treatment and preventive care (Plutarch *On the Delaying of Divine Vengeance* 561*c*).

Many people think that having one's hair cut on the seventeenth or the twenty-ninth day after the new moon prevents baldness and headaches (Pliny *Natural History* 28.28).

Medical advice for sea voyages. It is neither easy nor useful for a person making his first sea voyage to try to resist vomiting, since that usually brings relief. After he has vomited, he should not eat much, nor be offered the usual sort of food. He should eat either beans, soaked in vinegar and boiled with a little pennyroyal, or pieces of bread in wine with a fine bouquet that has been well diluted. He should drink only a little, either very well diluted wine or a mixture of vinegar and honey. . . . Use the aroma of quinces, thyme, or pennyroyal to counter disagreeable shipboard smells. It is important that the sufferer should look at the sea as little as possible until he has become acclimatized to life on board, and he should also be careful to ensure that his drinking water is neither cloudy, nor foul smelling, nor brackish (Dieuches *frg.* 19).

Single-minded devotion to our goals in life brings disappointment more often than pleasure, and is hostile to our health. So I commend moderation rather than excess (Euripides *Hippolytus* 261–5).

The Romans used to worship the other gods in order to receive benefits from them, but they honored the goddess Fever with temples in order to limit the harm that she did them (Valerius Maximus *Memorable Deeds and Sayings* 2.5).

DIET

Wild animals live on a simple diet of one type of food only, and are healthier than humans. Animals that are kept in enclosures are susceptible to diseases and easily develop problems with their digestion because of the varied and sweetened fodder they are given. Moreover, no doctor is so adventurous and hell-bent on innovation as to give a variety of different dishes to a fever patient, rather than simple and easily digested food without sauces (Plutarch *Table Talk* 661a).

If the same food, drink, and other dietary measures were appropriate for the sick as for those in good health, if there were no preferable alternative, the art of medicine would not have been invented, and no such researches would have been undertaken, for they would not have been necessary (Hippocrates *Ancient Medicine* 3).

Even nowadays, there are still people, not just barbarians but also some Greeks, who have nothing to do with medicine. When they fall ill, they persist in indulging in the same diet as when they were healthy, and refuse to abstain from anything they fancy, or to exercise any restraint (Hippocrates *Ancient Medicine* 5).

There are some foods which appease hunger and thirst and conserve strength even if taken in very small amounts: for example, butter, cheese made from mare's milk, and licorice. Excess is very dangerous in any aspect of life, and this is particularly true with regard to our bodies. It is better somehow to reduce anything that is burdensome (Pliny *Natural History* 11.284).

Most people live to gratify their stomach, and yet it is the cause of more trouble than any other part of the body. Sometimes it does not let food pass through, sometimes it does not retain it, sometimes it overflows with it, sometimes it does not digest it. Our habits have degenerated to the point that most people die because of their food. The stomach is the most bothersome part of the body, demanding payment from us several times a day, like a creditor. More than anything else, it is to appease the stomach that greed has become so insistent; it is for the stomach that luxury seasons our food with expensive spices; it is for the stomach that our fleets sail to the ends of the Empire; it is for the stomach that the depths of the sea are explored. No one is led by the nastiness of its end product to realize how disgusting the stomach actually is. And so it is that medical attention is focused particularly on the stomach (Pliny *Natural History* 26.43).

People cater to their gluttony with whatever is produced by the earth, the depths of the sea, and the unmeasurable breadth of the sky. . . . Their appetites know no boundaries. . . . That sort of person seems to me to be nothing but a set of jaws. . . . They are addicted to their gourmet food, which ends up in a little while on the dunghill (St. Clement of Alexandria *Paedagogus* 2.1.3).

Gluttons are easy to spot, for they are more like hogs or dogs [there is a similar sound play in the original (ὑσὶν ἢ κυσὶν, husin e kusin)] than human beings, so eager to cram themselves full that they load up both cheeks at once, with their blood vessels standing out and sweat pouring down their faces. They are dominated by their insatiable greed, panting with indigestion, as they stuff their food into their bellies with antisocial urgency, as if they were packing for a journey, not for digestion (St. Clement of Alexandria *Paedagogus* 2.1.11).

><

What need is there to list all the nasty and painful indignities that come pouring in upon us as we go through the troublesome and disgusting process of digestion? I think Homer has this in mind when he uses their not taking nourishment as proof that the gods do not die: "they do not eat bread, nor drink sparkling wine, and hence they are bloodless and are called immortal" [Iliad 5.341–2]. *What he means is that food not only gives us life but also leads us to death, for it is from food that illnesses arise; they feed on the same nourishment as do our bodies, for which repletion is no less unhealthy than deprivation* (Plutarch *Banquet of the Seven Wise Men* 160a). As Plutarch himself notes (*On the Face in the Moon* 938b), the gods are elsewhere said to feast on ambrosia (literally "immortality") and nectar. For Demeter, distracted by the abduction of Persephone, taking a bite from the shoulder of Pelops, see p. 187.

>——◀

Having observed at *On Abstinence from Animal Food* 1.17 that vegetarians miss out on remedies attainable from the meat of many different animals, such as eating a viper to cure blindness or stop drastic weight loss, Porphyry goes on to argue with rather more conviction later in the same book (1.47) for the benefits of vegetarianism:

If we get used to being satisfied with a very modest diet, we shall free ourselves from countless evils:

> *vast expenditure*
> *slaves to wait on us*
> *elaborate eating utensils*
> *drowsiness*
> *frequent serious illnesses*
> *the need for medical assistance*
> *sexual stimuli*

massive flatulence
excessive excrement
the burdensome bonds of our corporeal nature
forceful incitements to wrongdoing

A simple vegetarian diet, such as is easily available to everyone, will free us from an Iliad of evils and grant us serenity and a healthy outlook, for it is the meat-eaters, not the bread-eaters, who turn out to be thieves and brawlers, blackmailers and tyrants.

Galen begins one of his treatises on nutrition by observing that most fruit and vegetables are taken off to the towns, leaving country folk with very little. They sustain themselves through the winter mostly on leguminous plants, but by spring they are reduced to eating twigs and buds of bushes and trees, tubers and roots of indigestible plants, and wild herbs and grass (*Good Humor and Bad Humor* 6.749K).

Pork is more nourishing than any other food derived from four-footed animals, since it is the meat that tastes and smells most like human flesh, as some people have discovered when they tasted human flesh unawares (Paul of Aegina *Medical Compendium* 1.84).

The lightest meats for the body to digest are well-boiled dog, poultry, and hare (Hippocrates *Affections* 52).

Dog flesh warms and dries the body, and is strengthening, but it is not easy to excrete. Puppy flesh moistens the body, and is easy to excrete, but it is more diuretic (Hippocrates *Diet* 2.46).

The flesh of foxes and bears is slimy, but at a certain period in the fall it becomes firmer and then it is at its best. As for carnivores, wolves and lions and all such creatures, those who have eaten that sort of meat say that it is heavy and hard to digest, and likely to cause colic. That of tree mice causes evacuation of the bowels and is not very nutritious, while as for house mice, mountain tortoises, field lizards, and other such creatures,

one might say that those who eat them are not squeamish (Mnesitheus
frg. 39).

*Wine mixed with sea water is particularly bad for the stomach, the nerves,
and the bladder* (Pliny *Natural History* 23.46).

*In Western Locri, it was a capital offence to drink undiluted wine, unless
prescribed by a doctor for medical reasons* (Athenaeus *Wise Men at
Dinner* 10.33).

*It is firmly established that wine should not be given to fever patients
unless they are elderly, and even then not until the crisis has passed. If
the fever is acute, wine should be allowed only to patients who are definitely in remission, and the risk is only half so great if the remission takes
place at night, when wine may be used to facilitate sleep. Wine should
not be given to women just after childbirth or an abortion, or to those
suffering from:*

> *over-indulgence in sexual intercourse*
> *headaches*
> *any ailment that involves chilling of the extremities*
> *fever accompanied by coughing*
> *shaking*
> *pains in the sinews*
> *pains in the throat*
> *pains in the groin*
> *hardening of the thoracic organs*
> *violent throbbing of the veins*
> *muscle spasms*
> *tetanus*
> *hiccups*
> *breathing difficulties accompanied by fever*
> *fixed or bulging eyes*
> *weak or heavy eyes*
> *abnormally bright eyes*
> *eyelids that do not fully close*
> *bloodshot or rheumy eyes*
> *a thick and furry tongue*

dysuria
susceptibility to sudden fright
spasms
bouts of torpor
nighttime emissions

(Pliny *Natural History* 23.48)

After a meal, you should drink water in which a blacksmith has dipped red-hot iron, for it is particularly effective in reducing the spleen. It has been observed that animals reared in smithies have very small spleens (Celsus *On Medicine* 4.16).

To ensure that its milk is first rate, you must provide a she-donkey with suitable fodder and exercise it appropriately. If it is suckling any foals, they should be removed. As is obvious to everyone, it is important that it should be in the prime of life. You also have to ensure that its milk is as easy as possible to digest, and pay no heed to those who scoff at the idea of putting she-donkeys on a diet (Galen *The Therapeutic Method* 10.477K).

Food and drink that is slightly inferior but more palatable should be given preference over that which is better for the patient but less palatable (Hippocrates *Aphorisms* 2.38).

Plutarch's monograph *Advice on Preserving One's Health* is largely devoted to dietary concerns:

> *From time to time, we should sample the sort of food that is served to sick people, so that we become familiar with it while we are healthy, and not shudder in disgust at that kind of diet, as little children would. We should gradually get used to such food so as to ensure that, when we actually are sick, we do not grumble at our food as if it were medicine, and refuse to tolerate it just because it is simple and short on savor and flavor* (123*b*).

> *Cheaper foods are always better for the body. It is particularly important to guard against overindulgence in food and drink when we are getting ready for a festival or a visit from friends, or when we are anticipating*

a banquet for a king or an important government official, or some other unavoidable social occasion. We should, as it were, brace ourselves for stormy winds and waves while the weather is still fair, by ensuring that our bodies are trim and light. When people are cheerfully socializing, it is really rather difficult to observe our normal moderation without giving everyone present the impression that we are dreadfully unpleasant, tiresome, and disagreeable (123d).

Ship owners who are led by greed to overload their ships soon find themselves spending all their time bailing out sea water. We must not follow their example, stuffing and overburdening ourselves, and then resorting to purges and enemas. We should keep our bodies trim, so that, if they are ever pressed down, their lightness will bring them up again, like corks (127c).

It is difficult to argue with one's stomach because, as the elder Cato was fond of saying, it has no ears. We have to devise a way to make the bulk of what we eat less burdensome, by monitoring the types of food we choose. We should be careful with solid and very nourishing foods—meat, for example, and cheese, and dried figs, and boiled eggs. It is, of course, difficult always to decline such dishes, but we should focus on light and less substantial food—most vegetables, for example, and poultry, and fish with a low fat content. A diet like that satisfies the appetite without overloading the body. The indigestion caused by eating meat is especially dangerous, for meat not only weighs us down as soon as we eat it, but it also leaves a nasty, lingering residue. The best policy is to accustom our bodies not to crave meat at all (131e).

Even if they could not otherwise restrain their appetites and ensure that they did not attack their food like dogs or wild beasts, academics have many fine ways to distract and entertain themselves at the dinner table with conversation on scholarly topics. By contrast, athletic trainers and gymnastic coaches regularly assert that intellectual talk at meal times spoils the food and causes headaches. . . . Medical authorities recommend leaving an interval between dinner and sleep, and that is precisely what academics do. . . . The time spent on after-dinner discussions is just the right amount of time needed to allow the digestive process to gain control over the food as it gradually settles and coalesces in the stomach (133b).

It is best to adopt a moderate and sensible diet, to ensure that the body functions efficiently without any extraneous help with regard to filling and emptying the stomach. But, if the need for vomiting should ever arise, induce it without drugs and without fuss, disturbing the body no more than is necessary to avoid indigestion by removing excess food immediately and painlessly. For, just as linen sheets that are washed with soap and salts wear out more quickly than those washed in water alone, so the use of drugs to induce vomiting causes ruinous damage to the body (134d).

EXERCISE

Gymnastics and medicine are opposites, for medicine needs to cause changes, but gymnastics does not. A person in pain is benefited by changes from his existing condition, whereas a healthy person is not (Hippocrates *Places in Man* 35).

Socrates *Do you think people keep their bodies fit through intensive training or through moderate exercise?*

Anonymous Speaker *I think, Socrates, as the saying goes, even a pig knows that it is moderate exercise that keeps our bodies fit.*

(Plato *The Lovers* 134a)

That ball-playing was a significant part of physical training may be inferred from the statue of the doctor Herophilus, since he is portrayed with a ball, along with other exercise equipment, lying beside him (Suetonius *On Children's Games among the Greeks* 1).

Galen devoted a short treatise to playing ball games as an inexpensive and safe way to keep fit. In *Exercise with a Small Ball* (5.905K), he expressed his conviction that *most gymnastic exercises, by contrast, are counterproductive, leading to fatty deposits such as can even inhibit breathing. People who exercise that way are not likely to be good military or political leaders; it would be better to give such responsibilities to a pig.*

A healthy person who is fit and free to do whatever he pleases should not feel bound to follow any particular regime or to have his own doctor or masseur. He should have a varied lifestyle, sometimes in the countryside, sometimes in the city, but he should spend most time on his farm. He should go on voyages, hunt, and relax, but he should also devote a lot of his time to exercising. Idleness dulls the body and brings a premature old age, whereas work strengthens the body and prolongs youth (Celsus *On Medicine* I.I).

Daily exercise of the voice through speaking aloud is a wonderful way to ensure not just health but also strength. I am not referring to the strength that wrestlers have, the sort that merely adds flesh and makes the outside of the body solid, the way walls support a house. I mean strength that gives deep-seated vigor and real energy to the most vital and important parts of the body. . . . Even so, one has to guard against vehement and convulsive shouting, since the uneven and strained expulsion of the breath causes ruptures and spasms (Plutarch *Advice on Preserving One's Health* 130b).

It is essential to take care not to strain your voice too harshly on a full stomach or after sexual intercourse or when exhausted. This happens a lot

Fig. 8.1 Ball-playing on a fourth/fifth-century A.D. mosaic at a villa near Piazza Armerina in southern Sicily.

to politicians and professors, when they are drawn into a debate at an inappropriate time, whether for glory and ambition, or for financial rewards, or in political controversies (Plutarch *Advice on Preserving One's Health* 130f).

MEDICINE AND LIFESTYLE

We rely so much on medicine because our modern lifestyle is so indulgent and extravagant (Ammianus Marcellinus *History of Rome* 22.18).

When self-indulgent people fall sick, they do not summon the best doctors, whom they never showed any enthusiasm to select when they were healthy. They call in the doctors they are most accustomed to, and these are in fact the doctors who are particularly eager to flatter them. Such doctors will give their patients cold water whenever they ask for it, and permit them to bathe whenever they are commanded to give permission. They will offer them wine chilled with snow, and follow every order, just like slaves—the complete opposite to the Asclepian doctors in the old days, who thought they should rule their patients as generals rule their soldiers and kings their subjects. . . . So it is not the better doctor that decadent people pick, but rather the one who is the more accomplished at flattery; everything is made available and accessible for him, and all doors are open for him, he quickly becomes rich and influential, and has many students, his ex-lovers when they have lost the bloom of youth (Galen *The Therapeutic Method* 10.4K).

There are people who make themselves ill through their harmful way of living, but they are reluctant to give it up because they lack self-control. What a fine life such people live! They consult doctors, but that achieves nothing—other than making their ailments more serious and more complicated. They're always hoping to be cured by whatever drug anyone happens to recommend. . . . Isn't it altogether charming that what they hate most is the person who tells them the truth, namely that, until they stop their drinking and gorging, their sexual excesses and their lazy habits, neither drugs nor cautery nor surgery nor incantations nor amulets nor anything like that will be of any use to them? (Plato *Republic* 425e).

A few days after the seventy-third day of the siege of Amida, the tribune Discenes calculated that the Persian King Sapor had lost thirty thousand men. It was that much easier to differentiate between the Persian and the Roman dead because the Roman corpses split open and rotted so quickly that within four days their faces were quite unrecognizable, whereas the bodies of the dead Persians dried up like tree trunks, without their limbs wasting away or putrefying, a consequence of their more frugal lifestyle and the dry heat of their homeland (Ammianus Marcellinus *History of Rome* 19.9).

The younger Seneca was one of the richest men in the ancient world, but the denunciation of modern decadence is a constant theme in his writings. His vigorous attack on the disastrous consequences of gluttony in *Letters* 95 is a fine example:

Fig. 8.2 Seneca in his plumper days, but he is punching well above his philosophical weight on this bust, which twins him, rather flatteringly, with Socrates; see p. 22.

Medicine once amounted to nothing more than familiarity with a few plants to stop bleeding and to heal wounds. It gradually evolved into today's complex system. It is hardly surprising that medicine had less to do then, when people still had sound and robust bodies, and their food was easy to digest and had not been tainted with decadent sophistication. . . .

Only a hungry person could enjoy the sort of food available in the old days. That is why there was no need for such vast teams of doctors or such a range of medical instruments and pillboxes. People's health was simple then for a simple reason: it takes a plethora of dinner-courses to create a plethora of diseases. Just look at the vast range of things that, by plundering land and sea, luxury has mixed all together, destined to pass down one single person's throat. It is inevitable that such diverse foods should disagree with one another; they are gulped down and difficult to digest, as they struggle for supremacy in the stomach. It is no wonder that the illnesses arising from ill-matched foods are unstable and complex, and that stuffing the belly with unnatural combinations leads to a reaction. That is why nowadays there are as many ways to be ill as there are to live. . . .

Hippocrates, the supreme doctor and founder of the science of medicine, stated that women neither go bald nor suffer from gout, and yet nowadays they do go bald and they do suffer from gout. Their physique has not changed, it has been overwhelmed. They rival men in self-indulgence, and so they rival men in the consequent afflictions. They stay up just as late as men, they drink as much as men do, they challenge men to wrestling-bouts, and they drink strong wine. They bring up all their food again from their guts, which cannot tolerate it, and they measure out their wine again in their vomit. They gnaw at ice as much as men do, as a way of soothing their heaving stomachs. They don't even give ground to men in their sexual passions—may the gods and goddesses damn them! . . .

Nowadays, people are ashamed of eating foods separately. All the various flavors are blended together. What should happen in the stomach happens already during the dinner. It is only a matter of time till food is served up already chewed. We have almost reached that stage, with shells and bones removed and the chef performing the function naturally allotted to our teeth. . . .

Bring on all the courses at the same time, with the delicate flavors of many dishes blended. . . . Oysters, sea-urchins, shellfish, mullet, cook them all together and serve them up all together. The food that people vomit could not be more mixed up. The complexity of such dishes is matched by the illnesses to which they give rise: complex and diverse diseases, defying analysis and taking many forms. Medicine has begun to arm itself to combat them, with many sorts of treatment and much research.

Seneca practiced the frugality that he preached so vehemently. Actually, he rather overdid it, for when Nero forced him to commit suicide, he had considerable difficulty in killing himself:

Seneca and his wife opened the veins in their arms with a dagger at the same moment. Since his aged body was wasted by his spare diet, allowing his blood to escape only slowly, he severed the veins in his legs and behind his knees as well. . . . His death dragged slowly on, so he asked his trusted friend, Statius Annaeus, who had medical experience, to give him hemlock that had been prepared earlier, the poison used to execute condemned people in Athens. He drank it, but it had no effect, for his limbs were already chilled and his body resisted the effect of the poison. In the end, he got into a pool of hot water . . . From there he was carried to a bath, the steam from which suffocated him (Tacitus *Annals* 15.63). His wife's wound was bound up, and she lived on for several years, but without fully recovering.

Who would not be justified in criticizing our modern values? Extravagance and luxury have made our lifestyle more expensive. Life has never been longed for more than it is now, nor cared for less. We think that our health is other people's responsibility, that other people should look after it even without instructions from us, and that our doctors should see to everything on our behalf. We ourselves live our lives and enjoy our pleasures by putting our trust in other people—nothing could be more shameful than this attitude (Pliny *Natural History* 22.14).

Do you remember what people say when they are sick? . . . That nothing is sweeter than good health. This escapes their notice before they are sick (Plato *Republic* 583c).

A sick person is beyond all hope of recovery if his doctor urges him to live with no regard for moderation (Seneca *Letters* 123).

People should not make a practice of vomiting as part of a decadent life-style. Experience, however, leads me to believe that it can contribute to good health, provided that no one who wishes to live to a healthy old age makes a daily habit of it (Celsus *On Medicine* 1.3).

Vomiting was not an inconvenient consequence of a bout of hard drinking, it was part of the process:

> *Three points to bear in mind when you are drinking a lot: do not drink cheap wine; do not drink undiluted wine; do not eat snacks during drinking bouts. When you have drunk enough, do not go to bed without vomiting as much as you can. When you have vomited enough, have a short bath and then rest. If you cannot empty your system satisfactorily, have a longer bath, soaking in a tub of warm water* (Mnesitheus *frg.* 40).

Contrary to popular belief, there is no evidence that either the Greeks or the Romans had a special room designated for vomiting during banquets. Roman *vomitoria* were the exits through which spectators exited en masse from the amphitheater. If *vomitoria* had existed in Roman houses, they would have been a mark of great decadence. Since they did not exist, we should assume an even greater level of decadence, with banqueters remaining in situ. It was not for nothing that the Roman architect Vitruvius recommended that dining rooms be equipped with drains and an absorbent layer of charcoal under the floor (*On Architecture* 7.4.5).

HEALTH AND THE ENVIRONMENT

They say that, although he was aware of the damage it might do to his physical health, Plato nevertheless deliberately chose to found his school

Fig. 8.3 A slave steadies a drunken diner's head as he vomits into a conveniently placed bowl. The scene is portrayed, appropriately enough, at the bottom of a drinking cup, made in Athens during or just before the city's glory days, when the Persian invasions were repulsed in the early fifth century B.C.

in the Academy, a pestilential region near Athens. His purpose was to prune away excessive physical comfort, rather as overproductive vines are cut back. I myself have heard doctors say that being at the peak of good health is actually a dangerous thing (St. Basil *On Reading Pagan Literature* 9.80).

In marshy regions, you have to be on your guard against little airborne creatures, so tiny as to be invisible. They enter the body through the mouth and nose, and cause serious illnesses. Fundianus asked: "What can I do to reduce the chance of disease, if I inherit a farm like that?" Agrius replied: "Sell it for as much as you can get or, failing that, just abandon it." But Scrofa suggested: "Make sure the farmhouse does not face the direction from which the wind usually brings the infection, and build it high up rather than in a valley, so that anything harmful can be blown away that much more easily. A location that gets the sun all day is healthier, since any little creatures that are bred nearby are carried off by the wind or die quickly because of the lack of humidity (Varro *On Farming* 1.12).

It is said that Vesuvius used to rumble once every hundred or more years, but that this has been happening with much greater frequency in more recent times. People assert that, whenever the volcano happens to belch forth ash, the region is sure to flourish with crops of all sorts. The air on the mountain is very light and more conducive to good health than anywhere else in the world. Doctors have been sending consumptive patients there for very many years (Procopius *On the Wars* 6.4). The eruption in A.D. 79 buried Pompeii and Herculaneum.

Fig. 8.4 Vesuvius has not erupted since March 23, 1944, when the Allied invasion of Italy was in full swing. The next eruption in this densely populated area is perhaps overdue.

The philosopher Anaxarchus instructed his baker to wear gloves while kneading dough, so as to prevent sweat running off his hands, and also to put a mask over his mouth to avoid breathing on the cakes he was making (Athenaeus *Wise Men at Dinner* 12.70). Of course, we only hear about this precursor to modern rules of hygiene because it was unusual enough to be remarked on.

People with weak constitutions—most city dwellers and practically everyone who is keen on literature belong in this category—need to monitor their health more carefully than other people, so that by taking precautions they may compensate for the deficiencies in their physical wellbeing or in their environment or in their activities (Celsus *On Medicine* 1.2).

Fig. 8.5 A Roman earthenware pot, not particularly artistic, but safe.

Sores of all kinds heal very quickly near copper mines (Pliny *Natural History* 34.100).

Much of the Romans' water supply was channeled through lead pipes. (The English word "plumbing" is derived from the Latin term *plumbum* "lead.") It has been suggested that infertility caused by lead poisoning contributed to the eventual fall of the empire. The Romans, however, were fully aware that water conducted through terracotta pipes was healthier and better-tasting (Vitruvius *On Architecture* 8.6.10–1).

A more dangerous source of lead poisoning would have been cauldrons and cooking pots made at least partially of lead: *grape juice should be boiled down in pots made of lead rather than of copper, since copper pots give off rust during the cooking process, and this spoils the flavor* (Columella *Country Affairs* 12.20).

· IX ·

PROGNOSIS AND DIAGNOSIS

PROGNOSIS

It is impossible to restore every sick person to health. That would be prefer-able to simply being able to anticipate how things will turn out. . . . But, by devoting attention to prognosis, a doctor is quite justifiably admired and regarded as a good physician. For he can thereby give the appropriate treatment to those whom it is possible to save, planning well ahead for every eventuality; moreover, if he finds out early and makes known in advance which patients will live and which will die, he avoids being held liable for what happens (Hippocrates *Prognostics* 1).

It is a fatal sign if the right testicle is retracted and cold (Hippocrates *On Sevens* 51).

If a patient suffering from consumption is losing his hair, and has in fact already become almost bald because of his illness, and if his sputum has a heavy odor when he spits on coals, you should tell him that he is

going to die within a short time, and that diarrhea is what will kill him
(Hippocrates *Diseases* 2.48).

*Never tell a patient anything about either his present or his future state of
health. Many patients have been pushed into a decline this way, through
hearing a prognosis about their condition* (Hippocrates *Decorum* 16).

*If you want to find whether or not a sick person is going to recover, wash him
for three days in water infused with the juice of the chameleon plant; if he survives this treatment, he will recover* (Theophrastus *History of Plants* 9.12.1).

*A tick from a dog's left ear, worn as an amulet, soothes all kinds of pain.
It is also considered an indicator of life and death. When a person brings
the tick in and stands at the foot of a sick person's bed and asks about
his ailment, if the patient gives some reply it is a sure sign that he will
pull through, but he is certain to die if he does not. The dog from which
the tick is plucked must be entirely black* (Pliny *Natural History* 30.83).

The way to make predictions based on when a patient takes to his bed
is as follows:

Step One:

*Find out the number of days between the new moon before the person was
born and his birthday.*

Divide that number by four.

Make a note of the number of days left over after the division.

Step Two:

*Find out the number of days between the equivalent new moon and his
birthday in the current year.*

Divide that number by four.

Make a note of the remainder.

Step Three:

*Find out the number of days from the new moon before he took to his bed
and the day on which he took to his bed.*

Divide that number by four.

Compare the remainder with the remainders in the previous two calculations.

If all the three numbers are the same, the crisis is fatal; if they are different, the patient will survive, whatever the nature of his illness may be.

(Vettius Valens *The Astrological Anthologies* 339)

In the prediction of chronic diseases, particular signs of the zodiac match particular parts of the body:

Aries	head
Taurus	neck
Gemini	shoulders
Cancer	hands and chest
Leo	sides and heart
Virgo	belly and spine
Libra	bladder
Scorpio	genitalia and buttocks
Sagittarius	thighs
Capricorn	knees
Aquarius	legs
Pisces	feet

(Dorotheus *Carmen Astrologicum* [Arabic Version] 4.1)

Not even a doctor can tell whether someone who says he has a headache actually does have a headache. But he will treat him on the assumption that he does. This uncertainty does not undermine the validity of medicine as a science (Quintilian *Education of the Orator* 2.17.39).

Even expert doctors say that we should pay close attention to dreams (Aristotle *On Prophecy through Sleep* 463a).

Galen records that, when he was still a young man, he was persuaded by dreams to draw off a large quantity of blood from his right hand and this immediately cured a chronic pain between his liver and his diaphragm (*Treatment by Bloodletting* 11.314K). When Galen was sixteen his father had a dream that made him decide that his son should be a doctor (*The Order of My Own Books* 19.59K).

A doctor should ask his patient whether he slept or not, and about his usual sleep pattern, and whether he had any visions or dreams, for a doctor can make a diagnosis even from such information (Rufus of Ephesus *Medical Questions* 29).

A man dreamed that Asclepius, the god of medicine, wounded him in the stomach with a sword and that he died. A tumor subsequently developed in his stomach, but he was cured by surgery (Artemidorus *The Interpretation of Dreams* 5.61).

PHYSIOGNOMY

A fat stomach does not produce a subtle mind (*Anonymous Fragments of Greek Comedy* 1234) is quoted or alluded to with approval several times in the medical corpus.

Aristotle not only believed that there are signs in our actual physical bodies predicting our future lives, he even published his opinions on such matters. I find this amazing and consider such notions preposterous, not to be proposed without hesitation, in case anyone should try anxiously to discover such indications of the future in his own body. Even so, I shall mention them, given that such a great scientist as Aristotle did not scorn them. He lists the following as indicative of a short life: having few teeth or very long fingers or a leaden complexion or numerous short lines on one's hand; as indicative of a long life: having more than thirty-two teeth or sloping shoulders or big ears or just one or two long lines on one's hand (Pliny *Natural History* 11.273).

The first thing Pythagoras did when young men applied to enroll in his school was to "physiognomize" them. This word means assessing a person's character and disposition through inferences drawn from his facial appearance and expression and from the form and bearing of his body as a whole (Aulus Gellius *Attic Nights* 1.9).

If the distance from the lowest point of a person's chest to his navel is greater than that to where his neck starts, he is greedy and gluttonous. Praise a large and firm chest. A chest that is thin and weak indicates a petty soul and cowardice; a fleshy chest indicates ignorance and clumsiness. Anyone with a big chest covered with wobbly and pendulous flesh is lecherous and a drunkard (Adamantius *Physiognomonica* 2.15).

Body Feature	Significance
Big ears	insensitivity
Small ears	criminal tendencies
Really small ears	stupidity
(that look as if they have been trimmed)	
Good-sized square ears	sensitivity and bravery
Hollowed-out ears	quick wits and intelligence
Ears not hollowed and too round	lack of intelligence
	(Adamantius *Physiognomonica* 2.29)

An irritating person has a pinched face, a wrinkled forehead, twisted eyebrows, and tense eyelids, and he moves like someone who has been purged too vigorously (Adamantius *Physiognomonica* 2.51).

In talkative men, the upper body is much more developed than the rest of the body from the groin downwards; such people have irregular facial features and a hairy stomach (Anonymous *Physiognomonica* 111).

People who gamble have short arms, like weasels, and enjoy dancing (Pseudo-Aristotle *Physiognomonica* 808*a*).

Sharp and bony buttocks indicate strength, fat and fleshy buttocks indicate softness, buttocks that are scrawny, as if they had been rubbed bare, indicate a bad character—as with apes (Pseudo-Aristotle *Physiognomonica* 810*b*).

People with small faces have small souls, like cats and monkeys (Pseudo-Aristotle *Physiognomonica* 811*b*).

People with large faces are slow-witted, like cows and donkeys (Pseudo-Aristotle *Physiognomonica* 811*b*).

Red-haired people are very devious, like foxes (Pseudo-Aristotle *Physiognomonica* 812*a*).

Fig. 9.1 Gamblers painted on the wall of a tavern in Pompeii. Neither seems to have particularly short arms.

If a man has a mole close to his nose and a ruddy complexion, he will be sexually insatiable (Pseudo-Melampus *On Moles* 3).

HOPELESS CASES

Whatever drugs do not cure, surgery cures; whatever surgery does not cure, cautery cures; whatever cautery does not cure must be reckoned to be incurable (Hippocrates *Aphorisms* 7.87).

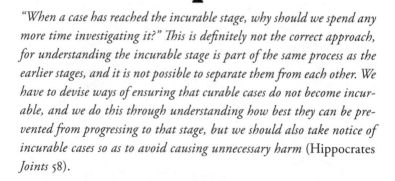

I shall begin with a definition of what I consider medicine to be: it consists of freeing patients from their diseases, dulling the intensity of diseases, and not taking on hopeless cases, since medicine can do nothing for them (Hippocrates *The Art* 3). This rather ruthlessly pragmatic attitude to hopeless cases was hardly universal. When the Great Plague struck Athens in 430 B.C., doctors were among its first and most frequent victims, and we may suspect that devotion to their calling led to the deaths of many doctors at all periods.

Some people criticize the medical art because of doctors who refuse to take on hopeless cases. They claim that those they do take on would recover by themselves, while they do not touch those who do need help. If medicine really is an art, they assert, it should cure all alike. . . . But, whenever someone suffers from a disease that is too strong for the resources available to medicine, there should be no expectation that such an affliction can be overcome through medicine (Hippocrates *The Art* 8).

"When a case has reached the incurable stage, why should we spend any more time investigating it?" This is definitely not the correct approach, for understanding the incurable stage is part of the same process as the earlier stages, and it is not possible to separate them from each other. We have to devise ways of ensuring that curable cases do not become incurable, and we do this through understanding how best they can be prevented from progressing to that stage, but we should also take notice of incurable cases so as to avoid causing unnecessary harm (Hippocrates *Joints* 58).

You should try to avoid cases of complicated fracture, as long as you can make a decent excuse not to get involved. There is little hope of recovery in such cases, and many risks. If a doctor fails to set the bone, he is regarded as incompetent, whereas, if he does set the bone, he brings the patient closer to death than to recovery (Hippocrates *Fractures* 36).

It is better not to treat cases of internal cancer: treatment merely hastens death, whereas, if such people are left untreated, they go on living for a long time (Hippocrates *Aphorisms* 6.38).

Above all else, a doctor should know which wounds are incurable, which are difficult to treat, and which are relatively easy. A shrewd doctor will not go near a person who cannot be saved, for fear of seeming to have caused the death of someone who was destined to die anyway. When there is some hope, but still a high risk that a patient will die, the doctor should make it clear to the relatives that there is hope, but also risk. This way, if the injury gets the better of his medical skill, he will not seem to have been ignorant or to have made a mistake. This is how a careful doctor should act. Only

Fig. 9.2 Philoctetes, the archetypal hopeless case. On the way to Troy, he was bitten on the foot by a snake. The smell from the festering wound was so bad the Greeks left him on the island of Lemnos for ten years. This is not the only malodorous myth associated with Lemnos. Either for neglecting her worship or for murdering their menfolk, Aphrodite caused the women of the island to stink.

a mere showman exaggerates the seriousness of a patient's illness in order to make his achievement seem all the greater (Celsus *On Medicine* 5.26).

If a doctor wishes to straighten the limbs of someone suffering from tetanus, he can only do so by cutting and breaking a living person. Since he can no longer treat sufferers overwhelmed by the disease, he can only sympathize. This is the doctor's great misfortune (Aretaeus *On the Causes and Symptoms of Acute Diseases* 1.6).

With all his limbs twisted and broken, he could only look at his vast wealth, and was unable to move even in his bed without the help of other people. He even —this is such a sad and pitiable thing to say—he even had to have his teeth cleaned by someone else and, when he was complaining about the indignities he suffered because of his infirmities, he was often heard to say that he had to lick his slaves' fingers every day [Romans ate with their fingers]. *But he lived on, and wanted to live on, largely through the support he received from his wife* (Pliny *Letters* 8.18).

I shall not kill myself to escape from my illness, so long as it is curable and does not impair my mind. I shall not lay hands on myself on account of the pain, for dying that way is a defeat. If, however, I find that I must endure pain constantly, I shall depart—not because of the pain itself, but because it will impede my reason for living. Anyone who kills himself because he is in pain is feeble-minded and cowardly, and anyone who goes on living just to endure pain is a fool (Seneca *Letters* 58.36). Seneca did, in fact, commit suicide, when ordered to do so by Nero; see p. 127.

· X ·

PARTICULAR AILMENTS AND CONDITIONS

WOUNDS

A doctor is worth as much as many other men together, since he is an expert at cutting out arrows and spreading gentle drugs on wounds (Homer *Iliad* 11.154–5).

At *On Medicine* 5.2, Celsus lists substances used in closing wounds. For example:

> *boiled honey*
> *egg white*
> *frankincense*
> *myrrh*
> *glue (and specifically fish glue)*
> *gum (especially gum arabic)*
> *snails (ground up with their shells)*
> *spiders' webs (for slight wounds)*

Fig. 10.1 Aeneas receiving treatment for a wound. Whereas his son, Ascanius, is weeping and his anxious mother, Aphrodite, has come down from Olympus to oversee the surgery, he himself seems quite nonchalant.

Nothing hinders the healing process more than frequent changes of medication. A wound never closes if the doctor experiments with different ointments (Seneca *Letters* 2.3).

Arzes, one of Belisarius's bodyguards, was hit by a Gothic archer between his nose and his right eye. The point of the arrow went in as far as the back of his neck, but without coming out again, and the rest of the shaft projected from his face, quivering as he rode along. . . . The doctors wanted to draw the missile out of Arzes's face, but for a long time they hesitated anxiously. They were not concerned about his eye, which they assumed could never be saved; rather they were afraid of causing the death of an important member of Belisarius's retinue by boring through all the many membranes and sinews in that part of his head. But then Theoctistus, one of the doctors, exerted pressure on the back of Arzes's neck to try to find out if he felt acute pain there. When Arzes said that he did, he announced "Then you'll recover, and your eye won't be damaged." He based this assertion on the fact that the point of the arrow had penetrated so far that it was very near the skin. He cut off as much of the arrow as was sticking out, and threw it away. Then he cut open the skin at the back of Arzes's neck, at the spot where the pain was the most intense, and extracted the point of the arrow without any difficulty, bringing out the rest of the missile, including the three barbs that were now projecting from the back of his neck. And so Arzes was saved from any lasting injury, with not even a scar on his face (Procopius *On the Wars* 6.2).

One of the barbarians shot Trajan [a Roman officer, not the emperor of that name, who ruled four hundred years earlier] *in the face, above his right eye, close in towards his nose. The whole of the missile's iron head, even though it was big and quite long, stuck so deeply inside his skull that it could not be seen at all. The rest of the weapon dropped to the ground straightaway, without anyone pulling at it. (I suppose the iron head had not been fixed securely to it.) Trajan was not distracted by the wound: he kept right on pursuing and killing the enemy. But five years later the tip of the iron appeared of its one accord, sticking out from his face. It has now been working its way out gradually for three years. The entire head of the weapon will presumably come out, though not for quite some time yet. Trajan has never been bothered by it at all* (Procopius *On the Wars* 6.5).

When a wound caused by a mad dog is not properly treated, the patient usually develops a fear of water (what the Greeks call hydrophobia), and he is tortured simultaneously by thirst and by fear of water. There is little hope for a victim of this condition. The only remedy is to throw him suddenly into a swimming pool. If he does not know how to swim, he is left to sink and drink, then pulled to the surface, the process being repeated more than once. If he can swim, he is pushed under several times, so that he is filled up, however reluctantly, with water. By this means, both his thirst and his fear of water are relieved (Celsus *On Medicine* 5.27).

Apply finely ground niter and honey to crocodile bites, till the wounds are cleansed. Then fill the wounds up with honey, butter, deer's marrow, and goose fat. Galen claims to know of people bitten by crocodiles who derived great benefit from the application of fat from the actual crocodiles who bit them (Paul of Aegina *Medical Compendium* 5.25).

As regards injuries to the toes, especially injuries caused by a blow, in the case of slaves and peasants who were going off on a journey where there was no doctor, I have often treated such injuries with urine. I put a pad over the wound, securing it by wrapping a linen thread round it, and then I tell the patients that, whenever they want to urinate, they should point the urine stream at their toe, and not remove the pad till the wound is fully healed (Galen *The Mixtures and Properties of Simple Medicines* 12.286K).

MENTAL ILLNESS

Whenever a doctor went to visit a patient, and found him lying in bed, groaning, and refusing food, if he then examined him and determined that he did not have a fever, he said "Mental illness" and went away (Plutarch *On Desire for Wealth* 524d).

How is the following to be explained? We are made up of a mind and a body. The art of healing and preserving the body has been intensely sought after and, because it is so beneficial, its invention has been attributed to the immortal gods. But it is different with medicine for the mind: no one felt the need for such a thing before it was discovered, and now that this type of therapy has come to be known, it is rather neglected; not many people appreciate it and approve of it, indeed quite a number are suspicious of it and detest it. Could the reason be that we use our mind to assess bodily disorders and pains, but is it not by means of the body that we perceive mental illness? And hence the mind only makes an assessment of itself when the very faculty by means of which the assessment is being made is itself weakened by illness (Cicero *Tusculan Disputations* 3.1).

In the old days, patients suffering from mental disorders were usually kept in darkness, in the belief that darkness helped to keep them calm. But

Asclepiades said they should be kept in the light, since the darkness terrified them. Neither treatment is universally applicable. Some patients are more disturbed by light, others by darkness, and there are some on whom light and dark have no discernible effect (Celsus *On Medicine* 3.18).

><del>=

I once examined a woman who had bound up her middle finger very tightly because she was suffering from a delusion that she was holding the whole universe on it. She kept weeping for fear that she would bend her finger, causing the collapse of the universe and the immediate destruction of all things (Alexander of Tralles *Therapeutics* 1.605).

━━◀▶━━

Varicose veins are very useful, since they help those who suffer from melancholy, and mania, and every chronic ailment that afflicts the head; they also work against heaviness and humps in the lower back, and any affliction caused by tension in that part of the body (Rufus of Ephesus *On Melancholy frg.* 74).

For men and women alike it is a warning sign of the onset of insanity if blood collects in a person's breasts (Hippocrates *Epidemics* 2.6.32).

><del>=

Do not let your patient suspect that he is suffering from melancholy. Pretend to treat him just for indigestion; help him combat his excessive grief, terror, and joy, and keep him from thinking too much (Rufus of Ephesus *On Melancholy frg.* 40).

━━◀▶━━

An account of phrenitis. A person's intelligence is derived mostly, some people would say exclusively, from the blood. So when bile is stirred up and enters the blood in the blood vessels, it alters the blood's normal consistency and motion, intensifying its movement, making it serous, and heating it. When the blood is heated, it heats all the rest of the body. Because of the strength of his fever and the blood's serum content and abnormal movement, the patient becomes deranged and is no longer his usual self (Hippocrates *Diseases* 1.30).

A man who was mentally unbalanced kept going to the theater in Abydus day after day, and he would applaud, as if he were watching a play. When he recovered his sanity, he said that that had been the most enjoyable period in his whole life (Pseudo-Aristotle *On Marvelous Things Heard* 832b). Likewise, when an Athenian was cured of the delusion that all the ships in the Piraeus were his, he said he had never been as happy as when he saw them sailing safely into harbor (Aelian *Miscellaneous History* 4.25).

In his fictional treatise *The Disinherited Son*, Lucian imagines a scenario in which, foreseeing that his father might become insane, a young man who had been disinherited trained to be a doctor. His father did become insane, and the young man cured him and was reinstated as heir. His stepmother then became mad, but he refused to treat her, saying that he did not have sufficient expertise. He was disinherited again, and took his father to court.

Antiphon devised a way to abolish grief, comparable to the treatment available from doctors to counter physical ailments. He set up an office near the marketplace in Corinth, and displayed a notice saying that he could treat those who were in distress by talking to them. By enquiring about people's depression, he was able to console them. But, thinking this profession beneath his dignity, he gave it up and turned to politics (Pseudo-Plutarch *Lives of the Ten Orators* 833c).

Doctors want people not to be ill, and, if they are ill, they want them to be aware that they are ill. But lack of awareness is typical of all sicknesses of the soul. Those who act in a silly, outrageous, or unjust manner do not think they are doing anything wrong, and indeed some such people think they are doing something useful. No one calls fever "health," nor consumption "good condition," nor gout "swiftness of foot," nor pallor "a rosy complexion," whereas many people do call anger "manliness," and lust "affection," and envy "rivalry," and cowardice "caution." Those with physical ailments send for doctors (for they are aware who it is they need to

*deal with the problem), but those whose souls are sick avoid philosophers,
for they imagine they are making a success of precisely those issues in which
they are going wrong* (Plutarch *Whether Illnesses of the Mind or of the
Body Are Worse* 501a).

*In the treatment of patients suffering from insanity, every case must be
considered separately:*

> *Sometimes, you have to relieve groundless fears; for example, a very rich
> person who was anxious about starvation was told from time to time
> about fictitious legacies he had inherited.*

> *Sometimes, you have to restrain violent patients, some of whom actually
> need to be kept under control with floggings.*

> *Sometimes, you have to resort to curses and threats to stop patients laugh-
> ing for no reason.*

> *Sometimes, you have to snap patients out of depression. Music, cymbals,
> and indeed any sort of noise helps in such cases.*

> *It is more often necessary to agree with a patient than to contradict him.
> You should bring him back slowly and subtly from irrational utterances
> to a better frame of mind.*

> *Sometimes, it is necessary to provoke a patient's interest and attention.
> A book can be read to people who are fond of literature; it should be read
> correctly, if they are enjoying it, but badly, if that irritates them, for by
> correcting mistakes they start to divert their mind.*

> *Patients should be urged to recite anything they know by heart.*

> *Placing them in among the diners at a banquet has even induced some
> insane people to eat when they had no desire to do so.*

(Celsus On Medicine 3.18)

*A lunatic is not to be allowed out in public in the city. His family must
keep him at home by whatever means they know how, or else they must
pay a fine* (Plato *Laws* 934c).

If their relatives are incapable of keeping them under control, the pro-
vincial governor should resort to the solution of confining insane people
in prison. In the case of parricide, the point to determine is whether the
perpetrator was merely pretending to be insane or whether he genuinely
was insane when he committed the crime; if he was merely pretending, he
should be punished, but if he was insane, he should be kept in confine-
ment (Justinian's *Digest* 1.18.13).

We need not doubt that Galen sympathized with his patients suffering
from mental afflictions, but it also seems fairly clear that some of the
cases he mentions are chosen for their curiosity value. For example:

> *One patient thought he had turned into a snail, so he used to get out the*
> *way of anyone he met, for fear of being crushed. Another patient, every*
> *time he saw roosters crowing, used to beat his arms against his ribs the*
> *way they flap their wings before they crow, and then he would imitate*
> *their crowing. Another patient was afraid that Atlas would get tired of*
> *holding up the world and drop it, crushing him and killing everyone else*
> *along with him* (*The Affected Places* 8.190K).

EPIDEMICS

When an epidemic of one single disease strikes a community, it is clear
that the cause lies not with people's widely differing lifestyles, but with the
air we all breathe. For it is also clear that the air gives off some pestilential
exhalation. Here is the advice you should give people at such times: ...
They should reduce to a minimum the amount of air breathed in through
the mouth, and do their best to ensure that the air is as different as pos-
sible, by moving as far as they can from the source of the epidemic. They
should also lose weight, for then they would not need to breathe so fre-
quently and so deeply (Hippocrates *The Nature of Man* 9).

It was apparently fated that the emperor Verus should bring destruction on
all the provinces he passed through during his return march from the East,
and even on Rome itself. The epidemic is said to have arisen in Babylonia,

when a pestilential vapor escaped from a golden casket that a soldier happened to smash open in the temple of Apollo. From there, it spread over Parthia and the whole world (Historia Augusta *Life of Verus* 8). When the Roman army returned from campaigning in the East in A.D. 165, it brought back a disease, quite possibly smallpox, which raged through the Roman world for twenty-five years, and may have carried off as many as six million people, which was perhaps a tenth of the population of the empire. The emperor Marcus Aurelius himself probably died of it, as did nearly all of the slaves that Galen owned in Rome (*Avoiding Distress* 1).

The pestilence first attacked the mules and the swift dogs [Iliad 1.47]. *Homer's representation of the onset of the epidemic in this way is very scientific. Experts in medicine and philosophy know from detailed observation that the first signs of infection appear among four-footed animals. The most important reason for this is that humans breathe air that is purer because it is higher up, and so they are less rapidly affected by the disease, whereas animals, being prone on the ground, are more vulnerable to drawing in the pestilential vapors that arise from the earth* (Heraclitus *Homeric Questions* 14).

He frequently ate camels' heels and crests of roosters cut off while they were still alive, as well as the tongues of peacocks and nightingales, for it was said that anyone who ate them would be safe from the pestilence (Historia Augusta *Life of Elagabalus* 20). After an outrageously decadent rule of four years (A.D. 218–22), Elagabalus was killed, when he was perhaps just nineteen years old, not by any disease, but by his own troops. (Assassination by one's own soldiers was to be by far the commonest form of death among the many emperors throughout the rest of the third century.)

POISONS

Wounds are aggravated if a person who has ever been bitten by a snake or a dog comes near. Such people also cause hens' eggs to addle and cattle to abort. There is sufficient residue from the poison in the bite they have suffered that they themselves become poisonous to other creatures.... Similarly, anyone who has ever been stung by a scorpion is never afterwards stung by a hornet or a wasp or a bee. This will seem that much less amazing if one is aware that garments that have been worn at a funeral are not attacked by moths (Pliny *Natural History* 28.32).

Hippopotamus testicles, dried, then ground to a powder and drunk with wine, are a good antidote for snakebite (Dioscorides *Medical Material* 2.23).

The tricks with snakes performed by traveling showmen do not depend on any particular expertise. They require merely confidence born of experience and a willingness to take risks. Snake venom, like some poisons used in hunting, does no harm if swallowed, but is very dangerous in a wound. It is safe to eat the actual snake, but its bite is fatal. If anyone puts his finger into the mouth of a snake that has been drugged (a trick played by itinerant show folk), its saliva is not harmful provided it does not actually bite. This is why it is safe to save someone's life by sucking out the venom from a snakebite. There is just one vital precaution necessary: the person who sucks out the poison must make sure he has no open sores on his gums, or on his palate, or anywhere else in his mouth (Celsus *On Medicine* 5.27).

Although the quantity of poison employed by spiders and scorpions is extremely small, it is so powerful that its effect is massive. The same characteristic can be observed also in torpedo fish [see p. 160]. *The shock they emit is so strong that it even runs along the trident used by fishermen and numbs their whole hand immediately* (Galen *The Affected Places* 8.421K). Pliny attributes even more impressive powers to a little snake called the basilisk:

> *It destroys bushes without even touching them, but merely by breathing on them, and it burns up grass and splits rocks, such is its malign power. It is believed that a horseman once killed a basilisk with his spear, but*

that its destructive force ran up along the spear and killed both horse and rider (Natural History 8.78).

Dog's blood is thought to be the best remedy for arrow-poison (Pliny Natural History 29.58).

If a person whispers in a donkey's ear that he has been stung by a scorpion, the affliction is immediately transferred to the donkey (Pliny Natural History 28.155).

WEIGHT PROBLEMS

Fig. 10.2 Depictions of massage are rare in Greek and Roman art.

At *On Medicine* 1.3, Celsus lists various ways to control one's weight:

For Weight Gain:

> *Moderate exercise*
> *frequent siestas*
> *massage*
> *bathing after lunch*
> *tightening the bowels*

exposure to moderately cold winter weather
sufficient sleep, but not too long
a soft bed
freedom from anxiety
very sweet and fatty food and drink
frequent meals, as substantial as you can digest

For Weight Loss:

Bathing in hot water, especially if salty
bathing on an empty stomach
exposure to scorching sun, or any kind of heat
worry
late nights
too much sleep
too little sleep
a hard bed in summer
running
walking a lot
any sort of strenuous exercise
vomiting
purging
dry and bitter food
eating just once a day
habitually drinking unchilled wine on an empty stomach

>———

Since I included them among the methods used for losing weight, I should say something specific about vomiting and purging. I am aware that Asclepiades rejected vomiting in his book entitled On Maintaining Health. *I do not criticize him for doing so, if he was concerned about habitual daily vomiting as a way of increasing one's capacity for over-eating. He went a step further when he likewise ruled out purgings in the same book; they are indeed detrimental, if brought on too vigorously by medications (Celsus* On Medicine *1.3).*

———►

Because of his luxurious lifestyle and his daily gourmandizing, Dionysius, the tyrant of Heracleia, gradually became so overweight that his obesity made it hard for him to breathe. So his doctors had needles made, thin and of varying lengths, that were to be pushed into his sides or his belly if he ever happened to fall into an unusually deep sleep. Since his flesh

Fig. 10.3 and 10.4 Nero (ruled AD 54-68) just before he became emperor (left) and towards the end of his reign, by which time he had grown most uncommonly fat.

had been desensitized by fat, the needles would penetrate a certain distance without him noticing them, but, if a needle ever reached a spot that had not been affected, he woke up. If anyone wanted to have an audience with him, Dionysius would put a box in front of his body, leaving only his head showing over the top while he discussed matters with his visitors (Athenaeus *Wise Men at Dinner* 12.72).

Lucius Apronius Caesianus, consul with Caligula in A.D. 39, had a son who was so fat that he could not move; he was cured by a primitive liposuction procedure (Pliny *Natural History* 11.213).

Those who are by nature very fat are more likely than thin people to die quickly if they contract a disease (Hippocrates *Aphorisms* 2.44).

Whatever anxious thoughts a person has, his soul is disturbed by them, and consequently it heats up and dries out. As the soul uses up moisture, it exerts itself and depletes the flesh, thereby making the person thin (Hippocrates *Diet* 2.61).

THE SACRED DISEASE

The "sacred disease" was a euphemism for ἐπιληψία (*epilepsia*, literally "condition of being seized upon"). The Greek term is rather less specific than "epilepsy," and could refer to a range of sudden seizures.

In my opinion, the first people to claim a divine origin for seizures were no different from magicians, purifiers, wandering priests, and charlatans nowadays, imposters who claim to be very pious and to have special knowledge. Alleging a divine origin is just a way to cover themselves, intended to disguise their inability to suggest anything that might help sufferers. They called the affliction sacred to prevent their total ignorance from being made obvious (Hippocrates *The Sacred Disease* 1).

Those who suffer from seizures and are already familiar with their affliction can tell when an attack is imminent. They run away from other people: if their home is close by, they go there, but if not, they go to the most isolated place, where only a very few people are likely to see them when they have fallen down, and there they hide away. They do this because they are ashamed of having the disease, and not, as the masses imagine, because they are afraid of some divine spirit. Little children, when they first have seizures, fall down wherever they happen to be, for they have no familiarity with their affliction. But, after several attacks, when they realize that they are about to have a seizure, they run to their mothers or to some other person whom they know well. They do this through fear and panic at what they are suffering, but since they still only children, they have no concept of shame (Hippocrates *The Sacred Disease* 12).

Hippocrates, a man who possessed godlike knowledge, regarded sexual intercourse as part of that appalling disease which we call epilepsy. His very words are on record: sexual intercourse is a minor seizure (Aulus Gellius *Attic Nights* 19.2). This statement is not, in fact, to be found in the surviving corpus of Hippocratic writings. Galen (*Commentary on Hippocrates's* Epidemics III 17*a*.521K) and St. Clement of Alexandria (*Paedagogus* 2.10) attribute it to the philosopher Democritus, whereas Stobaeus (*Anthology* 3.6) credits Eryximachus, the doctor in Plato's *Symposium*.

The Romans called seizures *morbus comitialis*, the assembly disease, because political meetings were adjourned if someone in attendance had a seizure, such an attack being considered a bad omen.

At Trapezus on the Black Sea, the honey from box-trees has an oppressive smell. They say that it drives healthy people insane, but is an infallible cure for seizures (Pseudo-Aristotle *On Marvelous Things Heard* 831*b*).

It is said that seizures can be prevented by eating the brains of a vulture, the uncooked heart of a seagull, or a domestic ferret. I have not tried any of these remedies, but I did once see people drinking the blood of a person who had just been killed, putting a cup to the wound. Oh, what a terrible, urgent necessity, to countenance treating an evil with such an evil curse! No one can tell me for sure whether they were actually cured by this treatment. There is another story, of a person's liver being eaten. But let those who could bear to take such measures write about them! (Aretaeus *On the Treatment of Chronic Diseases* 1.4).

Some people who suffer from seizures even drink the blood of gladiators, from living cups, as it were. It is a dreadful sight to see wild animals drink the blood of gladiators in the arena, and yet those who suffer from seizures think it the most effective cure for their disease, to absorb a person's warm blood while he is still breathing and to draw out his actual living soul straight from his wounds, for all that it is not human to apply one's lips even to the wounds of wild beasts. Others seek a cure through eating the leg marrow and brains of infants (Pliny *Natural History* 28.4).

Human blood, regardless of which part of the body it is taken from, is very effective against tonsillitis, if smeared on the patient. If it is applied to the mouth of someone who has fallen down in convulsions, he gets back on his feet again immediately. Some authorities claim that seizures should be treated by pricking the patient's big toes and smearing his face with the drops of blood that come out. Another remedy is to have a young girl touch the patient with her right thumb, and this is why it is thought that people

prone to seizures should eat the meat of animals that have never mated
(Pliny *Natural History* 28.43).

The following prevent seizures:

> *mare's milk*
>
> *a horse's chestnut* [the growth on the inside of the leg] *in sweetened vinegar*
>
> *goat's meat roasted on a funeral pyre (as recommended by the Magi)*
>
> *goat fat boiled down with an equal weight of bull's gall, and stored in a gall bladder to prevent it touching the ground; the patient drinks this in water while standing upright*
>
> (Pliny *Natural History* 28.226)

The goat is thought to be more susceptible to seizures than any other animal, and to pass the infection on to anyone who eats its flesh, or touches it when it is suffering an attack. The reason is said to be that its breathing passages are narrow and often become blocked. This is an inference from the thinness of its voice. People who happen to speak while having convulsions do in fact make a sound very like a bleat (Plutarch *Roman Questions* 290a).

Quails really enjoy eating poisonous seeds, and that is why they are barred from dining tables. It is customary to spit when one sees a quail; this is a precaution against seizures, an affliction suffered only by quails and humans (Pliny *Natural History* 10.69).

In his *Medical Material*, Dioscorides refers to almost fifty substances thought to prevent, control, or cure epilepsy and other such conditions. His focus is primarily on plants, but he also mentions, for example:

weasel's blood and stomach
donkey's hoof
rennet from a seal's stomach
iron filings scraped on a whetstone from the island of Naxos
amulets of stones found in a swallow's stomach when the moon is
    waxing

GOUT

Marcus Agrippa [who radically influenced the course of Western history by defeating Antony and Cleopatra at Actium] *suffered dreadfully from gout during the last years of his life. When he could tolerate the pain no longer, he decided that it was worth being without the use of his legs and losing all feeling in them, provided that he could also be without the awful agony; and so, trusting in the appalling expertise of one of his doctors, but without the emperor Augustus knowing anything about his intention, he plunged his legs into hot vinegar during an exceptionally severe attack* (Pliny *Natural History* 23.58).

Caelius said he could no longer endure the bother of running all round Rome to pay his early morning respects to the mighty, and so he began to pretend to have gout. He tried so hard to make it seem that the affliction was genuine, by smearing ointment on his perfectly healthy feet, and binding them with bandages, and walking with a painful limp! Oh, the power of subtly faked pain— Caelius has stopped merely pretending to have gout (Martial *Epigrams* 7.39).

When your patient has a gout attack, you should have him stand on the seashore—not the dry beach, but at the water's edge—with his feet on a black electric eel. He should do this till he feels numbness in his whole foot and his leg as far as the knee. This not only stops the pain on this particular occasion but also prevents it recurring in the future. Anteros, the emperor Tiberius's freedman responsible for inheritances, cured himself using this method (Scribonius Largus *Prescriptions* 162).

This cure, like several others in Scribonius's collection, is not a drug prescription. He had already included the electric ray as a cure for headaches, no matter how severe and persistent. The ray should be attached to the part of the body suffering pain (i.e., the head), and kept there till the pain ceases and that part of the body grows numb. Scribonius advises having several rays to hand, since two or three are sometimes scarcely enough for the treatment to work (*Prescriptions* 11).

Men's urine is an effective remedy for gout, as is proved by the fact that launderers do not suffer from that affliction (Pliny *Natural History* 28.66). Urine, collected from jars set up in public places and sometimes channeled directly from toilets, was used as a bleaching agent in laundries.

Fig. 10.5 Its five *ocelli* (dorsal dots) identify the bottom fish as a common torpedo (*Torpedo torpedo*), a type of electric ray still widespread in the Mediterranean.

BLADDER STONES

There are thousands of diseases that every single mortal must fear. To determine which of them are the most serious might seem to be a stupid thing to try to do, since everyone thinks the illness from which he personally is suffering at the time is the most devastating. Even so, the experience of generations has concluded that the fiercest torments are caused by bladder stones, second place going to stomach pains, and third place to pains in the head. Hardly any other diseases cause people to commit suicide (Pliny *Natural History* 25.23).

Women suffer less than men from stones in the bladder because, in their case, the urethra leading from the bladder is short and wide, so that the urine is forced out easily, and because they do not rub their genitals with their hand the way men do (Hippocrates *Airs, Waters, and Places* 9).

A particularly effective remedy for bladder stones is obtained from the genitalia of ferrets (Pliny *Natural History* 11.109).

The wren comes highly recommended as a cure for kidney stones. . . . Pickled and eaten raw, it causes stones that are already formed to pass out with the urine, and it prevents further stones from forming in the future. The same result is achieved if it is burnt alive, wings and all, and its ashes are then drunk in honey wine, either on their own or mixed with pepper and a leaf from the [unidentified] *tree* (Paul of Aegina *Medical Compendium* 3.45).

SPORTS MEDICINE

The way of life of athletes is sluggish and creates health risks. Or don't you see that they sleep their lives away and, if they depart ever so slightly from the regimen drawn up for them, they contract serious illnesses? (Plato *Republic* 403e).

Athletes live just the way pigs do, except that pigs do not overexert or force-feed themselves (Galen *Exhortation to Study the Arts* 1.28K).

Even while athletes are still active, their bodies are vulnerable to many injuries, but when they retire the risks are much worse. Some of them die soon, others manage to live a bit longer, but even they do not usually reach old age; if that ever does happen, they are like the Homeric goddesses of repentance—lame, wrinkled, and squinting. Walls that have already been thoroughly battered by siege-engines collapse easily at the slightest attack, . . . and likewise the bodies of athletes, rotten and weakened by the blows they have received as an occupational hazard, are susceptible to illnesses brought on by even the most trivial cause (Galen *Exhortation to Study the Arts* 1.30K).

Fig. 10.6 and 10.7 This Minoan fresco of c. 1500 BC suggests that boxing was then a rather gentle affair. Things had changed by classical times, when boxers began to wear gloves of stiff leather with metal fittings. Even so, despite his broken nose and cauliflower ears, the veteran fighter on the right seems to be bearing up fairly well.

Now that we have discussed the greatest of physical advantages, namely health, let us turn to other points. When it comes to good looks, not only do athletes not derive any such thing from their exercises, but quite the opposite happens even to many of those who are naturally well proportioned: trainers get control of them and fatten them up, stuffing them with blood and meat (Galen *Exhortation to Study the Arts* 1.32K).

The least successful athletes, those who have never won anything, suddenly call themselves trainers and squeal stridently and incomprehensibly—just like pigs. Some such people even try their hand at writing about massage, fitness, health, or exercise, and have the audacity to attack and contradict experts of whose works they are entirely ignorant (Galen *Thrasybulus* 5.894K).

A sufferer from gout won a race at the Olympic Games during a period of remission of the disease (Aretaeus *On the Causes and Symptoms of Acute Diseases* 2.12).

On medical advice, as a preventive measure against a disease of the spleen, Laomedon of Orchomenus took up long-distance running. This treatment was so effective that he entered for the great games [Olympian, Pythian, Isthmian, Nemean] *and became one of the top long-distance runners* (Plutarch *Life of Demosthenes* 6).

Fig. 10.8 A fragmentary list of fifth-century B.C. Olympic victors, in their own day among the greatest celebrities in the Greek world, but now mostly lost to history. Perhaps the unknown gout-afflicted athlete's name appears here.

The statues of the athletes Polydamas and Theagenes, the former at Olympia and the latter on the island of Thasos, cure people who are suffering from fever (Lucian *The Council of the Gods* 12).

If a man is not interested in having children, but is keen on winning victory crowns at the games or is engaged in some other such pursuit to which he recognizes that sexual intercourse is detrimental, then nothing would be of greater benefit to him than castration. It is time therefore for us to cut off the testicles of Olympic athletes (Galen *Semen* 4.571K).

Men who train as athletes or singers from a very young age and refrain from sexual activity, keeping themselves entirely free from all thoughts and fantasies about sex, tend to have small shriveled penises, just like old men (Galen *The Affected Places* 8.451K).

I once observed a trainer putting a lead sheet under an athlete to prevent him from having wet dreams (Galen *Matters of Health* 6.446K).

If a man is restrained in emitting semen, he will be strong, courageous, and as mighty as any wild beast. Athletes who control themselves prove this point, for through indulgence those who are naturally superior become far inferior to their inferiors, whereas through restraint those who are naturally inferior become superior to their superiors (Aretaeus *On the Causes and Symptoms of Acute Diseases* 2.5.4).

SEASONAL COMPLAINTS

The dry seasons of the year tend to be healthier than the rainy ones, and to cause fewer deaths (Hippocrates *Aphorisms* 3.15).

Later in the same book of *Aphorisms*, Hippocrates relates particular ailments to particular seasons:

Ailments associated with spring:

> *madness*
> *melancholy*
> *seizures*
> *blood fluxes*
> *sore throat*
> *runny nose*
> *hoarseness*
> *coughing*
> *leprosy*
> *pustules*
> *scaly skin*
> *cracked skin (mostly with lesions)*
> *tumors*
> *arthritis*

Ailments associated with summer:

> *some of those associated with spring, and also*
> *continual burning fever*
> *vomiting*
> *diarrhea*
> *ophthalmia*
> *earache*
> *mouth ulcers*
> *mortification of the genitals*
> *heat spots*

Ailments associated with fall:

> *most of those associated with summer, and also*
> *irregular malarial fever*
> *enlarged spleen*
> *edema*
> *tuberculosis*
> *urinary hesitancy*
> *undigested food in stool*
> *dysentery*
> *sciatica*

sore throat
asthma
intestinal problems
seizures
mania
melancholy

Ailments associated with winter:

pleurisy
pneumonia
runny nose
hoarseness
coughing
chest pains
pains in the sides
pains in the lower back
headache
dizziness
apoplexy

When thinking about one's health, it is important to take account of the season of the year:

In winter, it is appropriate to eat more, and drink less wine, though not so diluted as at other times. Lots of bread, and meat, preferably boiled; vegetables in moderation. Only one meal a day, unless suffering from constipation. If anyone eats lunch also, it should be a very small meal, dry, without meat and without wine. In winter, all food and drink should either be hot or produce heat in the body. Sexual intercourse is not as harmful in winter as at some other times of year.

In spring, eat slightly less, but drink more wine, diluted rather more than in winter. More vegetables, and more meat, but switching gradually from boiled to roast dishes. This is the safest time of year for sexual intercourse.

In summer, our bodies require food and drink more frequently. So we should take lunch as well as dinner. Both meat and vegetables are appropriate in summer. Wine should be diluted as much as possible, to relieve thirst without heating the body. Cold baths, roast meat, food that is either cold or cools the body. Since we need to eat more frequently, the amount of food at each meal should be very modest.

In fall, the changeability of the weather is very dangerous. You should never go out without a coat and stout shoes, especially on chillier days. Do not sleep out of doors or, if you must do so, wrap up well. Eating more food is permissible now, with less wine, though not so diluted. . . . Sexual intercourse is good for us neither in summer nor in the fall, but it is easier to tolerate in the fall; in summer, if it can be managed, total abstinence is best.

(Celsus On Medicine 1.3)

———▶

Those afflicted with the disease known as cynanthropy or lycanthropy go out at night in the month of February and behave exactly like wolves or dogs. They are to be found particularly in the vicinity of tombs, where they linger till dawn. Here are the symptoms of this affliction:

sallow complexion

vacant expression

dry, tearless, and hollow eyes

dry tongue

absence of saliva

excessive thirst

incurable ulcers on the legs (caused by frequent falls and dog bites)
(Aëtius On Medicine 6.11)

GERIATRICS

The years seven and nine and their multiples, for reasons that are both natural and mysterious, affect people all through their lives with various dangerous crises. Hence the sixty-third year, which is the multiple of these two numbers, is called the androclas *("man-breaker"). Nine times seven years is sixty-three, and likewise seven times nine years is sixty-three. Since the courses of both numbers coincide then, the sixty-third year always brings the risk of serious danger* (Firmicus Maternus *Astrology* 4.20.3).

My dear Gaius, my sweetest little donkey, goodness knows I always miss you when you are away from me. But especially on days like today my eyes long for my Gaius. Wherever you are today, I hope you are celebrating my 64th birthday in health and happiness. As you see, I've passed the crisis that all old men face, the 63rd year. Whatever time is left to me, I pray to the gods that we may enjoy it in safety and prosperity, as you and your brother act like men and prepare to take over my position (Aulus Gellius, *Attic Nights* 15.7.3). This letter, sent to his grandson on September 23 A.D. 2, shows that even Augustus, the first Roman emperor, whose success was built on unscrupulous deviousness, had a softer side.

Ctesias says that no Indian suffers from headaches, eye problems, toothache, mouth ulcers, or any kind of abscess. They live for one hundred and twenty years, or one hundred and thirty, or one hundred and fifty, some even for two hundred years (Photius *The Library* 72.47a).

There is some justification for the view that illness is an old age we acquire for ourselves, whereas old age is a natural illness. It is at any rate true that some diseases have the same effect as old age (Aristotle *Generation of Animals* 784b).

Menander mentions a law that was apparently once passed on the island of Ceos: "The Ceans' law is a good one. Anyone who can't live a healthy life should not live an unhealthy one" [*The Lyre-Player frg.* 12]. *It seems that this law ordained that everyone over sixty years of age should be given hemlock to drink, to ensure that there was enough food for the rest of the population. On one occasion, when they were being besieged by the Athenians, they voted to put to death the most elderly among them, and fixed a particular age; but the Athenians gave up the siege* (Strabo *Geography* 10.5.6).

The Stoics unanimously maintain that old age is brought on by shortage of heat. . . . According to Asclepiades, the Ethiopians are old by the age of thirty because their bodies are exposed to excessive heat and they are scorched by the sun, whereas the Britons live for a hundred and twenty years because their country is so cold, and they keep the fiery heat inside their bodies. The Ethiopians have more delicate bodies, relaxed by the sun's heat, but the bodies of people in northerly regions are densely compacted, and therefore they live for many years (Pseudo-Plutarch *On the Opinions of Philosophers* 911*b*).

For a young person, having a large body is splendid and attractive, whereas, for an old person, it is uncomfortable and less desirable than being small (Hippocrates *Aphorisms* 2.54).

Craterus, the brother of King Antigonus, claims to know of a person who, all within a period of just seven years, turned from a boy into a young man, then into an adult, then into an old man, and finally died. During that time he married and fathered children (Phlegon *Marvelous Things* 32).

To all the other perils of living to an advanced age add fires, falling buildings, shipwrecks, and the tearing apart of our bodies by doctors, as they gather up our bones while we are still alive [rather than after cremation]*, and thrust their whole hands deep down into our entrails, and inflict exquisite pain on us while treating our innermost parts* (Seneca *To Marcia, On Consolation* 22).

During the Roman period, life expectancy at birth was not much more than twenty-five years, and most children who survived the perilous first five years might hope to live for about forty more. Nevertheless, longevity was not uncommon. In the census records for one district of Italy in A.D. 74, Pliny (*Natural History* 7.164) had no difficulty in finding many people claiming to be of impressively advanced years:

Age	Number of people
100	54
110	14
125	2
130	4
135 or 137	4
140	3

We hear very little about doctors working to alleviate the suffering of the terminally ill, and likewise they seem not to have concerned themselves much with euthanasia in the modern sense of the term. (In antiquity, euthanasia "dying well" referred above all to a heroic death in battle.)

NEW DISEASES

The races of mankind once lived on the earth far removed from evils, from hard toil, and from painful illnesses, which bring death to mortals. But Pandora took the lid off the jar and scattered the contents, thus causing mankind dreadful sorrows. . . . The land is full of evils, and the sea is full of evils. Diseases come to mankind spontaneously by day and by night, bringing evils to mortals in silence (Hesiod *Works and Days* 90–104). Note the term "jar." The expression "Pandora's box," universal nowadays, stems from an error in translation by Desiderius Erasmus, perhaps the greatest of all Renaissance scholars. (He shows several times elsewhere that he knows perfectly well what the Greek word means.)

Even though people in the old days had no resources to help them against illnesses, they were probably healthy for the most part, because their way of life was free from the corrupting influences of idleness and luxury. These two factors first weakened people's physical health in Greece, and they have subsequently assailed the Romans as well. Medicine has been developed to a level of sophistication needed neither by our ancestors nor by foreign peoples nowadays, and yet it is scarcely able to ensure that any of us reaches even the threshold of old age (Celsus On Medicine Preface 4).

Was it not bad enough that mankind was already exposed to so many diseases—more than three hundred of them—without having new ones to be afraid of? (Pliny *Natural History* 26.9). Pliny is thinking of new afflictions that the Romans associated with the decadent affluence denounced by Celsus (see above) and Seneca (see p. 125). It would be interesting to have a catalogue of his three hundred and more diseases, with a description of each.

Philon the doctor insisted that the affliction known as leprosy had only recently become known. His argument was that none of the ancient physicians had mentioned it, even though they had a tendency to expatiate on trivial, pedantic, and obscure points. In support of Philon's contention, I cited the philosopher Athenodorus, who records in the first book of his Epidemics *that not only leprosy, but also hydrophobia, first appeared in the time of Asclepiades. Everyone was amazed at the thought of new diseases arising then for the first time, but they regarded it as every bit as astounding that such symptoms might have escaped notice till then. Most people were inclined to accept the latter view, that the diseases existed but had gone unnoticed, since it is more convenient for mankind to suppose that nature does not welcome change and does not strive to craft new troubles for the body in the way that civil unrest afflicts communities* (Plutarch *Table Talk* 731a).

It is not likely that all diseases came into being simultaneously, the way runners start out together when the barrier falls. They probably arose one after another, each at its own particular time. It is a reasonable assumption that our bodies were first afflicted by illnesses caused by deficiencies, or by heat, or by cold. Gluttony, indulgence, and luxurious living came along subsequently, accompanied by indolence and idleness made possible by the abundance of life's necessities. This engendered harmful excess, which brought with it all sorts of new diseases with endless permutations and complexities (Plutarch *Table Talk* 732d).

Xenocrates has shown that the number of syllables that can be formed by making combinations of the letters of the alphabet is one hundred million, two hundred thousand. This being so, how is it surprising if . . . the complex range of influences to which our bodies are subjected should sometimes cause new and unfamiliar diseases? (Plutarch *Table Talk* 733a).

Plutarch goes on to catalog new and unfamiliar diseases:

> *The Great Athenian Plague. The birds and animals that scavenge off carrion refused to touch the corpses of those who died of the plague, and Thucydides infers* [History 2.50] *that it must be a previously unknown disease.*
>
> *An outbreak of pestilence by the Red Sea, the never previously recorded symptoms of which included little snakes that ate their way out of a person's legs and arms; if the snakes were touched, they went back in again and caused intolerable inflammations by wrapping themselves round the victim's muscles.*
>
> *A person who had suffered for a long time from difficulties in micturation voided a barley stalk with knots in it.*
>
> *A man in Athens ejaculated, along with a great quantity of semen, a hairy little creature that could move fast with its many feet.*
>
> *A woman hibernated for two months every year in a cave in Cilicia, her breathing being the only clear vital sign.* (This is reported on the authority of Aristotle, but does not appear in his surviving works.)

A person with liver disease watched intently for house mice, and chased them. (This is also reported on the authority of Aristotle; in this case the reference is specifically to his lost work addressed to Menon the physician.)

➤

So many dreadful diseases arise in the body that they are not all included in the medical books (St. Augustine *City of God* 22.22).

· XI ·

TREATMENT AND CURES I

In my opinion, the present state of medical knowledge represents the complete discovery of the art, for it is able to give precise instructions about the nature of diseases and explain the essential aspects of their treatment (Hippocrates *Places in Man* 46).

Many aspects of treatment in antiquity were very stressful and unsophisticated (Pliny *Natural History* 26.16).

SURGERY

It is not easy to explain surgical procedures in writing (Hippocrates *Joints* 33).

Some people dread surgery so much that they cannot even think about the pain to come without fainting (Galen *Commentary on Hippocrates's Surgery* 18b.686K).

Imagining something terrible is worse than actually experiencing it. For example, it sometimes happens that people who undergo surgery or some other such procedure can bear the pain, whereas those who are standing round them faint at the very thought of what is going on (Sextus Empiricus *Outlines of Pyrrhonism* 3.236).

A doctor performing trephination should take the saw out frequently and dip it in cold water, to prevent the bone from heating up. For the saw becomes hot as it moves round, thus heating and drying the bone, and this results in more of the bone round the hole coming away than is intended (Hippocrates *Head Wounds* 21).

In cases of skull fracture involving lesions in the dura mater, if the patient is in distress, we use fetters during surgery. The attendants should sit close to the operating table, with one of them holding the patient's head, and the other seeing to whatever arises during the procedure. The patient's ears should be blocked with wool, to prevent him from being alarmed by the noise of the bone being chipped away (Oribasius *Medical Compilations* 46.11).

Many people are cowards when they have to face treatment with the iron blade, and fear the pain involved in the cure more than they fear the harm that will come if they do not receive attention. So, come on then, let us give some comfort to those made hesitant by the thought of pain, and let us make those who are suffering better able to face the treatment bravely. Let the surgeon have a light hand, so that he can make the incision easily, and let him also have a sharp blade, for bluntness is a cause of great pain. . . . It is good to anoint the iron blade that inflicts the wound before thrusting it into the wound. We should say "Ta Ta" three times and also spit and recite a certain Latin phrase included in the fifth pentagon facing the signs of the chromatic scale, a tipped-over alpha followed by a mark and a reversed gamma followed by two marks. The pain will then stop. Let the sons of doctors take care of the wound, since the patient will offer himself unflinchingly to their touch (Julius Africanus *Kestoi* 1.4).

Anyone who wants to practice surgery should go on campaign with an army of mercenaries (Hippocrates *The Physician* 14).

A wise doctor does not chant magic spells when faced with an ailment requiring surgery (Sophocles *Ajax* 581).

If he delays and gives it time, a doctor cures an illness more often than he does by operating on it (Euripides *frg.* 1072).

New recruits scream even when their wounds are trivial, and they fear the surgeon's hands more than they fear the sword. But veteran soldiers, even when their wounds are deep, submit to treatment patiently and without a groan, as if their bodies were not their own (Seneca *To Helvia, His Mother* 3.1).

A surgeon should be fairly young, with strong and steady hands, ambidextrous, with good eyesight, eager to cure his patient, but detached enough not to want to hurry or to cut less than is necessary. He has to perform his task as if the patient's screams had no effect on him (Celsus *On Medicine* Preface 7).

A doctor was once called on to treat a king's daughter, and could not do so without surgery. So, while putting a dressing on a swelling on her breast, he applied a scalpel that he had hidden in a sponge. The girl would have resisted the treatment if it had been administered openly, but she tolerated the pain because she was not expecting it. Sometimes, deception is the only way to achieve a cure (Seneca *On Anger* 3.39).

There are three reasons why a doctor should conceal his treatment. It should be kept from the view of spectators when the spectacle is disgusting or when some moribund part is being amputated, lest the sight of the amputation distress the family or the servants of the patient. The third reason for concealment is when the patient is cowardly and weak. Then you should dissemble and say: "I will operate tomorrow, but now I am going to foment the part or to treat it with hot water or with sponges dipped in hot pitch". Make him think that that is what you are going to do and then take him

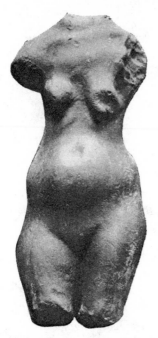

Fig. 11.1 A votive offering displaying a breast tumor.

unawares as you make your incision. In no other cases should concealment be used (From the notes by Ali ibn Ridwan to Galen's *Commentary on Hippocrates's Surgery* 18*b*.686K).

Marius's wisdom and bravery are both well attested. His attitude to surgery is a good example. He was apparently plagued with unsightly varicose veins in both legs, so he decided to put himself in a doctor's care for treatment. He presented one leg, without being tied down, without flinching, and without even a groan, and tolerated extreme agonies in silence during the surgery, with a fixed expression on his face. But, when the doctor turned to the other leg, Marius did not present it this time, saying that he could see that the cure was not worth the pain it entailed (Plutarch *Life of Marius* 6). Gaius Marius was a leading military and political figure in early first-century B.C. Rome. Cicero claims that he was the first person to submit to surgery without being tied down, and that other people followed his example (*Tusculan Disputations* 2.53).

Although the medical writers frequently discuss varicose veins, Cicero himself is the only other person in antiquity known to suffer from them. By an odd coincidence, Marius and Cicero came from the same home town and were distantly related by marriage. Was there something in the water? As extreme examples of tolerance of pain Seneca refers to an anonymous patient who continued reading a book while his varicose veins were removed and a victim of torture who kept on smiling at his torturers (*Letters* 78.18). Galen observes that some doctors refuse to perform phlebotomy because patients had been known to die of fright even before the procedure began (*Bloodletting, Against Erasistratus* 11.151K).

The entrails sometimes roll out as the result of a wound to the stomach.... If the smaller intestine is pierced, there is nothing that can be done. The larger intestine can be sutured: there is no great likelihood of success, but an uncertain hope is better than certain hopelessness (Celsus *On Medicine* 7.16). After describing the procedure to be adopted, which, in the absence of properly effective anesthetics, must have been excruciating, he concludes: *when he puts the entrails back in, the surgeon must always reverse the*

Fig. 11.2 A rather oversized leg with varicose veins as a votive offering to Asclepius.

sequence in which they fell out. When the entrails are all inside again, the patient is to be shaken gently, so that each coil may return of its own accord to its proper position and settle there.

It is not the act of a friend, but of a crafty cheat, to enhance one's reputation by profiting from other people's mistakes, making oneself look good to bystanders, behaving like those surgeons who perform operations in the theaters as a way of drumming up custom (Plutarch *How to Distinguish a Flatterer from a Friend* 71a).

A fragmentary second-century A.D. inscription from Ephesus (*Inschriften aus Kleinasien* 14 1162) records the various medical contests at the Grand Festival of Asclepius: Therapeutics, Surgery, Case Studies, and Surgical Instruments.

PROCEDURES

It is easier to cure people suffering from edema if they are slaves than if they are free. Being cured involves enduring hunger, thirst, and countless other troublesome measures over a long period. It is therefore easier to help those who can be forced to undergo the treatment than those whose freedom does them no good (Celsus *On Medicine* 3.21).

How to deal with tattoos, from the works of Archigenes: you can remove tattoos by smearing on them a mixture of very sharp vinegar and the stuff that sticks to the sides of a chamber pot (Paul of Aegina *Medical Compendium* 4.7).

Suppuration occurs with ulcers, and this is relatively easy to treat. It also occurs on the outside of the lung, most commonly as a result of a rupture or tear. Pus collects there. When this happens, and the patient is shaken, it splashes about and makes a noise: that is the spot for cauterizing (Hippocrates *Places in Man* 14).

Fig. 11.3 Bleeding cups and a folding case containing medical instruments. Such a case would have been very handy, especially since doctors made house calls much more then than nowadays, and might well need surgical instruments in the patient's home.

Doctors seem to be able to help prevent pestilential diseases by lighting a large blazing fire, since that makes the air thinner. This thinning is more effective if they burn pleasant-smelling types of wood, such as that of the cypress, the juniper, and the pine. At any rate, they say that Acron the doctor earned a fine reputation at the time of the Great Plague in Athens, since he helped very many people by giving instructions to keep a fire burning beside those who were suffering. Aristotle says that the fragrant exhalations of perfumes, flowers, and meadows contribute to health just as much as to pleasure, for they gently pour their smooth warmth over the brain, which is by nature cold and frigid (Plutarch *On Isis and Osiris* 383c).

Burn off all the hemorrhoids, without leaving a single one uncauterized. You will recognize the hemorrhoids without difficulty, for they project on the inside of the rectum like dark grapes, and when the anus is forced out they spurt blood. The patient's head and arms should be held firmly, so that he does not move, but let him scream during the cautery, for that will make his rectum protrude all the more (Hippocrates *Hemorrhoids* 2).

If a polyp develops in the nose, swelling out sideways from the nostril, you remove it by dragging it with a noose from the nose into the mouth. It can also be withered with drugs (Hippocrates *Affections* 5).

There are people who are unable to speak because they were born with their tongue fused with the flesh under it. The procedure to follow is to grasp the tongue with a forceps, and then cut through the membranes beneath it, taking great care not to damage the surrounding veins or to allow excessive bleeding to harm the patient. . . . As soon as they have recovered from the operation, most people can speak. I know someone who had the operation and could stick his tongue right out over his teeth, but still could not speak. This illustrates the point that, in medicine, even when the procedure to follow is always the same, the results are not always the same (Celsus *On Medicine* 7.12).

Fig. 11.4 Cosmas and Damian, the patron saints of medicine, replacing a patient's infected leg with the healthy leg of a person who had recently died. The patient seems miraculously oblivious to the procedure. We are not told how he reacted when he woke up to find that his legs were now of different colors.

The most effective treatment for a person who has been whipped is to have the newly flayed skin of a sheep wrapped round him while it is still warm; he will feel better within a day and a night (Paul of Aegina *Medical Compendium* 4.12).

◆━━━━━━

When people are eating, they often swallow fish bones and other such things, which then stick in various parts of the throat. Any bones that are visible can be extracted with a purpose-made forceps, but other methods are needed for bones stuck farther down in the gullet. Some doctors recommend swallowing rather large pieces of food, such as a lettuce stalk or a bit of bread. Others bid the patient swallow a small piece of soft, clean sponge tied to a thread, and then, holding on to the thread, they draw it back up as often as necessary, till the bone sticks to the sponge and comes up with it (Paul of Aegina *Medical Compendium* 6.32).

Swallowing a lead pill is beneficial to many people suffering from intestinal blockage, for by its weight it pushes against and thrusts out whatever is causing the obstruction (Caelius Aurelianus *Acute Diseases* 3.17.160).

A man was in pain because he thought his head had been cut off as a punishment for setting himself up as a tyrant. The doctor Phylotimus cured him by putting on his head a close-fitting cap made of lead. The patient felt the weight of the cap and supposed that his head had been restored (Alexander of Tralles *Therapeutics* 1.607).

Someone who is so drunk that he loses his voice recovers his health if he becomes feverish straightaway; if he does not, he dies on the third day. If you come across a person in this condition, wash him in copious warm water and bathe his head with sponges dipped in warm water, then peel onions and put them in his nostrils (Hippocrates *Diseases* 2.22).

One of the many cures for warts recorded by Pliny: *at the new moon, people touch the warts (whatever the type) with chickpeas (one single chickpea to each individual wart), then they tie the chickpeas in a little linen bag and throw it behind them, thinking that this will dispose of the warts* (*Natural History* 22.149).

The experts say that it is vital that a poultice for an abscess should be applied by a naked virgin when both she and the patient have been fasting. The girl should touch the patient with the back of her hand and say "Apollo says that no one's disease can grow worse if a naked virgin checks it." She should say this three times with her hand turned over, and both she and the patient should spit three times (Pliny *Natural History* 26.93).

As regards the cylindrical box that some doctors fit round broken legs, I am unsure what advice to give. It is not as beneficial as those who use it imagine, for it does not immobilize the leg ... and the patient feels rather uncomfortable with pieces of wood attached to his leg in this way, unless some padding is inserted. But it is very useful when bedding has to be changed, or the patient has to go to the bathroom. With or without the box, treatment can be good or bad. Ordinary folk have more confidence if a box is used, so a doctor is more likely to escape criticism if he uses one. That said, it is not really sound medical practice (Hippocrates *Fractures* 16).

I find that medical authorities state that there is no better way to perform cautery than by using a ball of crystal that catches the rays of the sun (Pliny *Natural History* 37.28).

In treating scrofula, it is beneficial to eat the middle section of snakes, with both the head and the tail cut off, or to burn them in a new earthenware pot and then drink their ashes. It is particularly efficacious if the snakes have been killed by being run over between the ruts made by cart wheels (Pliny *Natural History* 30.37).

Millipedes are used in treating asthma: thrice seven millipedes dissolved in Attic honey and sucked through a reed (Pliny *Natural History* 30.47). The phrasing, "thrice seven" rather than "twenty-one", shows the influence of magic.

BLOODLETTING

An experienced practitioner can let blood very speedily, but the procedure is extremely difficult for those without experience (Celsus *On Medicine* 2.10).

Galen acknowledges that some people had actually died after bloodletting or even at the prospect of undergoing the procedure, and that there were those who asked what the difference was between unregulated phlebotomy and murder (*Bloodletting, Against Erasistratus* 11.151K).

Fig. 11.5 Bloodletting, while the doctor's next patients wait their turn to be seen.

Bloodletting [cures] *flatulence* (Hippocrates *Epidemics* 2.5). A laconic dictum, untypical of the Hippocratic corpus.

Leeches are able to suck out diseased blood while leaving the purer blood alone (Julian *Against the Galileans* 198).

When there is a significant loss of blood from a wound in a part of the body that has neither sinews or muscles, such as the forehead or the top of the head, the best thing to do is to apply a cupping-glass to some other part of the body, to divert the flow of blood there instead (Celsus *On Medicine* 5.26.21).

BANDAGES

The man gave a description of bandaging, since he thought that it was important to practice that skill right at the start. Bandaging can be practiced either on pieces of wood carved in the shape of a person or, failing that, on the bodies of children (Galen *Commentary on Hippocrates's Surgery* 18*b*.630K). Notice that Galen refers to Hippocrates simply as "the man" (τἀνδρός, *tandros*) as a tribute to his distinction.

When doctors bind up wounds, they do it carefully, not casually, so that the bandage, as well as being serviceable, may also be elegant (St. Augustine *On Christian Doctrine* 1.14).

Have nothing to do with showy and ostentatious bandages, for they are useless, vulgar, and utterly pretentious; indeed, they are often likely to cause the patient harm. A sick person does not want to be made to look nice; he wants to be helped (Hippocrates *The Physician* 4).

The doctors who make mistakes are the ones who rely too much on theory. Fixing a broken arm is not difficult; practically any doctor can do it. But I feel compelled to write on this subject at some length because I am aware that there are doctors whose methods of bandaging broken arms have gained them a reputation as great experts, when in fact those very methods should have exposed their ignorance. This sort of faulty judgment affects many other aspects of medical science. People prefer the bizarre to the obvious, and enthuse over the exotic, before they know if it is effective, whereas they ignore the familiar, which they know to be effective, and weird ideas are more highly regarded than straightforward ones (Hippocrates *Fractures* 1).

You should clearly understand that bandaging a broken jaw efficiently does little good, and bandaging it inexpertly does great harm (Hippocrates *Joints* 32).

Those who devote themselves to pointless displays of manual skill are always delighted when they happen to come across a broken nose to bandage. For a day, or perhaps two days, the doctor preens himself on his handiwork, and the patient is happy with his bandage. But then the patient quickly becomes irritated, for the bandage is uncomfortable. Even so, the doctor is content, for he has shown that he knows how to put a complicated bandage on a person's nose (Hippocrates *Joints* 35).

In his *On Bandages*, Soranus catalogues and describes sixty types of bandage. Quite a few are not known from elsewhere. Some of the more interesting names give little or no indication of that particular bandage's specific function. For example:

Axe
Little boat
Charioteer
Thunderbolt
Tortoise
Hawk or Eagle
Hare with ears
Hare without ears

PROSTHETICS

Tantalus chopped up his son Pelops and offered him to the Olympian gods to eat. But the appalling deed was detected; Pelops's body was reconstituted and he was revived. Demeter, however, had absent-mindedly eaten part of his shoulder, so that was replaced with an ivory prosthesis. Pliny tells us that the artificial shoulder used to be

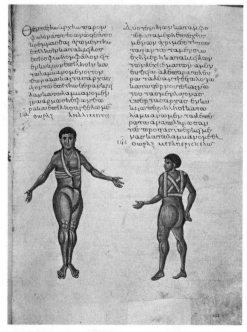

Fig. 11.6 Bandages elegantly modeled in an eleventh-century manuscript of Soranus.

on show in Elis (*Natural History* 28.34), whereas, in an ode written for a patron who claimed descent from Tantalus (*Olympians* 1), Pindar denies the whole story. Poets were free to take such licence. In another ode, honoring a patron who claimed descent from Heracles but was short in stature, Pindar asserts that Heracles himself, the archetype for physical power, was not very tall.

>———

Little or nothing is said about prosthetics in the surviving medical literature. A single example of a prosthetic limb survived from antiquity, an artificial right leg, knee to ankle, buried with its owner, probably an adult male, in his tomb discovered in Capua in the late nineteenth century. It was made of wood in a covering of bronze, and dated to about 300 B.C. The Royal College of Surgeons Hunterian Museum in London acquired it by uncertain means, but it was destroyed during the Blitz in 1941. A copy and some photographs are all that survive.

>———

The prophet Hegesistratus of Elis had once escaped from Sparta by sawing through his foot at the instep with an iron tool that had been smuggled into the prison. When the wound healed, he had a wooden foot made and, because of his hatred of Sparta, he helped the Persians conduct sacrifices in the Greek manner before the Battle of Plataea in 479 B.C. (Herodotus *Histories* 9.37).

The great-grandfather of Lucius Sergius Catilina, who attempted to subvert the Roman state in 63 B.C., was a hero in the Second Punic War. He was twice captured by Hannibal and kept in chains for twenty months, but twice he escaped. He had a prosthetic right arm made of iron so that he could continue fighting, and on two occasions his horse was killed under him (Pliny *Natural History* 7.104).

>———

Not long ago, there was a rich man in Asia Minor who had both his feet amputated as the result of an accident; they had, I believe, turned gangrenous because of frostbite when he was on a journey. After suffering this wretched misfortune, he dealt with it by having wooden feet made.

He used to get about with them strapped on and with his slaves to help support him (Lucian *The Ignorant Book Collector* 6).

Laelia, you wear teeth that you bought and hair that you bought, and you're not embarrassed. But what will you do for an eye? That's not something you can buy (Martial *Epigrams* 12.23).

MEDICINE FROM ANIMALS

Nature, the parent of all things, did not intend any creature to be born simply to eat and be eaten. She inserted medicines in their entrails—just as she put them in inanimate things also—for she wanted these very effective means of ensuring life to be derived from other forms of life. This is a particularly awesome point to ponder (Pliny *Natural History* 27.146).

I often hear it said that eating a fledgling swallow ensures against angina for a whole year. It supposedly helps, at the onset of that disease, to burn such a bird, preserved in salt, then grind it to powder and give it as a drink with honey water. Since this cure has widespread popular authority and cannot do any harm, I thought it best to include it in my book, even though I have read nothing about it in the usual medical sources (Celsus *On Medicine* 4.7).

Deer do not suffer from any diseases that involve fever. In fact, they provide medicines to guard against such ailments. They say that in recent times some ladies of the imperial family made a practice of eating venison every morning and were free of fever all through their long lives. It is believed that this is an effective precaution only if the deer has been killed with a single wound (Pliny *Natural History* 8.119).

The plant-based cures in Dioscorides's *Medical Material* are largely untainted by superstition, magic, and unfounded lore, but his remedies derived from animals are sometimes rather less persuasive. In Book Two, as a cure for toothache, he recommends rinsing the teeth with sloughed snakeskin boiled in wine, or frogs boiled in water and vinegar, or earthworms boiled in oil and poured into the ear on the side of the head opposite to the aching tooth. The uses he finds for dung (2.80) are many and various (see also p. 219 for another such Dioscoridean catalogue of medical applications of animal products). For example:

Type of Dung	Afflictions Relieved
cow	wounds, sciatica, tumors, bone inflammation, prolapsed uterus, and the smoke repels mosquitoes
goat	jaundice, difficulties with menstrual flow, baldness, gout, snakebite, skin infections, swollen glands, sciatica, and it also acts as an abortifacient
sheep	pimples, corns, warts, burns
wild pig	vomiting blood, pains in the side, hernias, convulsions, dislocations
donkey and horse	bleeding, scorpion stings
dove	tumors, carbuncles, burns
chicken	as with dove droppings, and also mushroom poisoning and colic
stork	seizures
vulture	acts as an abortifacient
mouse	baldness, bladder stones, children's constipation
dog	tonsillitis, and it also cleanses the stomach
human	tonsillitis, wound inflammation, and it also closes wounds
crocodile	is used in cosmetics for women's faces

Strains and bruises are treated with wild boar's dung gathered in spring and dried. This treatment is used for those who have been dragged by a chariot or mangled by its wheels or bruised in any way. Fresh dung also may be smeared on (Pliny *Natural History* 28.237).

>⎯

An ointment for bald patches. Take four drachmas of pepper, dried sheep dung, hedge mustard, and arugula seed, three drachmas of white hellebore and mouse droppings, and mix these ingredients up with the gall of a bull or a goat or a pig (Oribasius *Select Prescriptions* 4.1).

▬▬◀

I cured a peasant with growths on his knee and other parts of his body by applying goat-dung plasters, but that medication is too sharp for city ladies, little children, or anyone at all with soft flesh. . . . Some country folk are very hard-fleshed, like donkeys, and capable of swallowing goat-dung pills (Galen *The Mixtures and Properties of Simple Medicines* 12.298K).

Eating boiled viper meat makes the eyesight keener, tones up the nervous system, and checks scrofulous swellings. When you skin the snake, you should throw away the head and the tail, for they have no flesh on them. . . . Take out the entrails, wash what remains and chop it in pieces, and then boil it with olive oil, wine, a little salt, and dill. Some people say those who eat viper meat become a breeding-ground for lice, but that is not true. Others say that such food promotes longevity. Salts are also made from viper meat to counter the same complaints, but they are not so effective. A living viper is put into a new pot, along with a pint of salt, a pint of ground figs, and half a pint of honey. The pot is smeared all round the lid with mud, and baked in an oven until the salts turn to coals. The contents are then ground to a powder and stored. Spices are sometimes added to make the salts more palatable (Dioscorides *Medical Material* 2.16).

>⎯

In a broth with salt and olive oil, frogs are an antidote for the venom of any type of snake. This mixture is also effective against stubborn suppurating inflammations of the tendons. Frogs burnt to ashes and smeared on wounds in an ointment staunch blood flow. They cure baldness if rubbed in with liquid pitch. Dripping the blood of green frogs onto the eyelids prevents the eyelashes from growing again after they have been plucked. Boiling them in water and vinegar and then swirling the mixture round in the mouth is a good remedy for toothache (Dioscorides *Medical Material* 2.26).

At *Medical Material* 2.24, Dioscorides catalogues many medicinal properties of beaver testicles. For example, they stimulate menstrual flow, they are abortifacient, and they expel the placenta; they are effective against flatulence, colic, hiccups, deadly poisons, varicoceles, lethargy, trembling, convulsions, any sort of depression, and all nervous disorders.

Dioscorides goes on to comment: *the belief that the beaver, when pursued by hunters, rips off its testicles and throws them away is utterly unfounded.* That widespread notion appears, for example, at Aelian *History of Animals* 6.34: *A beaver understands why hunters pursue it so eagerly. It puts its head down and bites off its own testicles, which it then throws in the path of the hunters, just as a sensible person saves his life when caught by thieves by giving them all his possessions.* Some Roman authors imagined a link between *castor* (Latin for "beaver") and *castro* ("I castrate"). Dioscorides's reason for resisting this rural legend is very practical: *it is impossible for a beaver to take hold of its testicles, since they lie tight up against its body, as do those of pigs.*

The seal is like the beaver in its amphibious way of life and in its nature. It vomits up its gall, which is useful in many medicines, and likewise its rennet, which is a cure for seizures. It behaves this way because it realizes that hunters pursue it to obtain these substances. Theophrastus records that, when geckoes slough off their old skin the way snakes do, they swallow it immediately. If it can be snatched away from them before they swallow it, it is used to cure seizures. They say that gecko bites are harmless in Greece, but harmful in Sicily (Pliny *Natural History* 8.111).

One further non herbal Dioscoridean medication calls for particular mention:

> Gloios, *the grime collected from the baths, is able to heat, soften, and disperse various substances, and is good for anal fissures and lumps, if applied in ointment. A compress of grime and dust from the wrestling ground helps with tumors on the knuckles, and such a compress, if applied warm and used instead of an emollient or a heated pad, also gives relief to sufferers from sciatica. Grime scraped from gymnasium walls and from statues warms and dissolves inflamed growths and is suitable for treating abrasions and old sores* (*Medical Material* 1.30).

The head of a shrew, burnt to ashes and ground to a powder with antimony, is an excellent remedy for watery eyes (Pliny *Natural History* 29.118).

They say that the fat of dormice and shrews that have been boiled is very useful in preventing paralysis (Pliny *Natural History* 30.86).

Snails are especially good for stomach complaints. They should be blanched whole, then roasted over coals just as they are, and consumed with fish sauce and wine. It has recently been ascertained that African snails are particularly beneficial. [Pliny has just recommended eating African mice as a remedy for lung disease.] *People take care to eat an odd number of snails. Their juice does, however, cause bad breath* (Pliny *Natural History* 30.44).

Apollonius recommends the following cure for dandruff: Rub the patient's head with bull's urine, and then repeat the process in the same way with camel's urine. This procedure should be carried out for several days. But I would inform the patient that no one with any sense of personal hygiene would tolerate having the urine of any such animal poured over his head on even one occasion, much less daily for many days, especially since the complaint is so trivial and can easily be cured by other means (Galen *The*

Composition of Drugs According to Places 12.476K). For somewhat less drastic ways to cure dandruff, see pp. 219 and 221.

> ⟩———•

As a cure for a sore throat, Apollonius recommends drinking donkey's urine, as much as possible and as hot as possible. He says this is just as good for angina as well. But I am amazed at those who write about such remedies, for I know that, with hardly any exceptions, just about everyone would prefer to die sooner than drink donkey's urine (Galen *The Composition of Drugs According to Places* 12.982K).

> ▬▬►

Country folk have found out through experience that a person suffering severely from a tumor gains relief if he eats a snake (Celsus *On Medicine* 5.28).

Galen records, and apparently accepts as genuine, two cases in which patients suffering from leprosy were dramatically cured when they drank wine in which, unbeknown to them, a viper had drowned (*The Mixtures and Properties of Simple Medicines* 12.312K).

PERSONAL ATTENTION

Earwax is a fatal sign if it is sweet, but not if it is bitter (Hippocrates *Epidemics* 6.5). Who conducted such tests?

> ⟩———•

Many doctors believe that they should personally taste a patient's sweat or his earwax, for they suppose that they can draw deductions even from this (Galen *Distinctions in Symptoms* 7.76K).

> ▬▬►

Someone in Rome recently devised an oral technique for curing . . . sessile warts. . . . The person performing the procedure starts by placing his lips on them and sucking on them as if he were drinking milk from a teat, so as to draw them out and pry them free from the root; then he takes hold of them with his front teeth and quickly pulls them out (Galen *The Therapeutic Method* 10.1011K). Galen goes on to say that a doctor with sufficient skill and the best tools for the job—including a sharp quill made from an eagle's feather—does not have to resort to this rather extreme procedure.

MEDICAL ERRORS

Even doctors often make mistakes (Cicero *On the Nature of the Gods* 3.15).

I would strongly commend the doctor who makes only slight mistakes. One rarely meets with absolute accuracy, since most doctors seem to me to be like inexpert navigators. As long as the weather is calm, their mistakes are not evident. But, when they are in the grip of a severe storm or violent winds, everyone can readily see that it is their ignorance and errors that destroy the ship. So it is with bad doctors, who comprise the majority. So long as they are treating only minor ailments—and most common illnesses are of this sort, even the grossest errors would do patients no serious harm, and are rarely evident to the layman. But, when they encounter a serious, life-threatening illness, their mistakes and lack of skill are obvious to all (Hippocrates *Ancient Medicine* 9).

Hippocrates recorded that he had once been misled by the sutures on a person's skull. Such an admission with regard to matters of great importance is typical of great men (Celsus *On Medicine* 8.4). Celsus is referring to *Epidemics* 5.27: *A man called Autonomus died sixteen days after suffering a head injury. It was midsummer, and he had been struck by a stone on the sutures at the front and center of his skull. I did not notice that surgery was required. I was misled because the damage caused by the missile was directly on the sutures, as later became obvious.*

I have recorded the details of my unsuccessful attempt to cure a patient's spinal deformity, for good lessons can be learned even from experiments that turn out to be failures, provided it is made clear why it was that they failed (Hippocrates *Joints* 47).

I think the famous doctor Hippocrates behaved very commendably when he acknowledged some mistakes he had made, so as to prevent other people from repeating them later on (Quintilian *Education of the Orator* 3.6.64).

I have continued practicing as a doctor right into my old age, but to this day I have never committed a blunder, either in prognosis or in treatment, though I have seen many other doctors with the highest reputations doing so (Galen *The Affected Places* 8.146K).

◆━━━━━━◆

Galen seems no more of an idealist than his rivals when he describes as extremely funny the very public failure of a rival doctor to cure a liver patient. After a very long account of the case, we hear how the rival brought a group of the patient's friends to see him cured, only to find that, as Galen had predicted, he had died (*The Therapeutic Method* 10.909K). And he positively gloats at the ludicrous failure of a demonstration of the power of a much praised medication to cure gout; the cure is tried on a patient whose condition is only moderately severe, but overnight he is left almost paralyzed (*The Mixtures and Properties of Simple Medicines* 11.432K). Schadenfreude may have no place in the medical profession nowadays, but it was endemic and virulent in the cutthroat doc-eat-doc world of medicine in antiquity.

· XII ·

TREATMENT AND CURES II

DRUGS

A sick person who is sensible will turn to medicines only as a last resort, for diseases are like living creatures, and should not be provoked by drugs unless they have actually become life-threatening (Plato *Timaeus* 89a).

In its early days, the human race was reluctant to undergo surgery or cautery. This is still the case with very many people, indeed with almost everyone, and, unless they are compelled by necessity and it is their only hope for regaining their health, they refuse to submit to these procedures, which are barely endurable. I can therefore find no reason why anyone would keep the medical profession from using drugs, unless it is to expose his own ignorance. Doctors who have no experience of this type of treatment deserve condemnation for neglecting such an essential branch of the medical art, whereas those who do have experience of how useful drugs are, but still refuse to use them, are even more at fault, for they are consumed by prejudice, an evil to be abhorred in every living creature, but especially in doctors (Scribonius Largus *Prescriptions* Preface).

We are told that Herophilus, who was considered one of the greatest doctors, said that medicines are the hands of the gods. In my opinion, he was quite right, since drugs that have been tried and tested can indeed achieve the same result as divine intervention (Scribonius Largus *Prescriptions* Preface).

If you say that drugs in themselves are nothing, you will be correct, for they are nothing unless they are administered by someone who knows how to use them properly. Conversely, if you say that "drugs are like the hands of the gods," you will be equally correct, for they are a great help to someone who has been trained in the logical method and is naturally intelligent (Galen *The Composition of Drugs According to Places* 12.966K).

There is considerable discrepancy in the way doctors use medicines, whether in simple form or in compounds. Hence it is clear that each doctor is following his own opinion rather than relying on firmly established facts (Celsus *On Medicine* 2.33).

If I may be forgiven for saying so, doctors are entirely ignorant about drugs. . . . Preparing medications used to be an essential part of a doctor's work. But nowadays, if ever a doctor wants to make up a prescription that he happens to come across in some book, that means testing the ingredients at his wretched patients' expense, for he has to rely on pharmacists, and they spoil everything with their fraudulent adulterations. Doctors are now even buying ready-made plasters and eye ointments, and that only encourages the pharmacists to corrupt their wares (Pliny *Natural History* 34.108).

Sellers of medicines aim to win people's good opinion and are always trying to ingratiate themselves by saying whatever is most popular. That is how they earn their livelihood (Polybius *Histories* 12.25e).

It is important to devote time to personal examination of each medicine, so as to distinguish those that are effective from those that are useless.

For drug sellers are so crafty at tampering with medicines that they can fool even people with great experience in such matters (Galen *Antidotes* 14.7K).

━━━━➤

As I have said many times, recipes for medicines are better in verse than in prose, for not only are they easier to memorize, but they also guarantee the accuracy of the amounts of the various ingredients (Galen *The Composition of Drugs According to Kind* 13.820K).

Since Greek and Latin verse had strict rules for scansion, errors and deliberate changes could be detected very readily. For example, in preparing a concoction to relieve earache, Serenus Sammonicus says, "Then you will put garlic cloves, seven in number, and seven lupins in an earthenware pot." In Latin, this is one and a half hexameter lines: *allia tum septem numero, septemque lupinos/ cretaceam dabis in testam*. The nearest numbers all scan differently from seven (five, *quinque*; six, *sex*; eight, *octo*; nine, *novem*), so none of them could go undetected if it displaced seven in this line.

━━━━➤

Even without such a practical reason for preventing error and deliberate tampering, doctors might wish to show off their skill in versifying: *Marcellus of Side, a doctor who lived during the reign of Marcus Antoninus, wrote forty-two medical books in epic verse. His subject matter included werewolves* (Suda s.v. *Marcellus*).

━━━━➤

Galen lists the ingredients and the requisite quantities needed in a drug to prevent and reverse hair loss, but warns that the circumstances in which he came by it make the recipe only provisional. A medical friend of his found it in a leather notebook that had belonged to a deceased doctor. Unfortunately, the recipe was safeguarded with secret symbols, and Galen and other doctors were still working through the ingredients to determine the proper amount of each (*The Composition of Drugs According to Places* 12.423K).

Pharmacists sometimes listed the ingredients of a drug and their quantities wrongly, to mislead trade rivals. Confusion could arise without any such subterfuge, for it was not always clear which measurement system was in use. Galen, for example, complained when it was not specified whether the system was Roman or Greek, Athenian, Alexandrian, Ephesian, or some other one (*On the Composition of Medicines by Type* 13.893K).

In my father's time and my grandfather's, no doctor prescribed hellebore. The preparation and the dosage were not understood. If anyone actually did prescribe it, he would order his patient to make his will first, given that the risk he was about to undergo was so high. Most patients choked to death on hellebore, and only a few survived. But nowadays it seems to be quite safe (Ctesias *Indica frg.* 68).

There are many different pills with a wide range of purposes. Those that relieve pain through sleep are called anodyne. They should not be used except in dire necessity, for their ingredients are very active and harm the stomach (Celsus *On Medicine* 5.25).

A doctor who distributes exactly the same quantity and weight of a medicine to every patient is utterly ridiculous (Plutarch *Table Talk* 643c).

HERBAL REMEDIES

In the time of Hippocrates, and for many generations thereafter, simple and natural treatments predominated, but gradually experience, the most effective teacher of all things, and especially of medicine, degenerated into mere words and endless talk. For it was more congenial to sit in the schools listening to lectures than to go out into remote areas looking for the various herbs each in its proper season (Pliny *Natural History* 26.11). But the rejection of simple and cheap medicines may have started long before, if for a different reason. The ingredient most frequently included in medicines prescribed in the Hippocratic corpus is myrrh, an exceedingly expensive commodity imported from the East. Myrrh has antiseptic qualities, but it has been speculated that the primary motive for including it was to enhance the prestige of the doctors who prescribed such costly medicines.

The reason why there is so little research into the medicinal properties of various herbs is that only illiterate country folk who live surrounded by them make use of them; faced with hordes of doctors, the rest of us do not trouble to look for herbal remedies (Pliny *Natural History* 25.16).

Poisonous mushrooms can only be detected by country folk, especially those who actually gather them. But even such people can be fooled. For example, if there is a snake's hole nearby, and the snake breathes on a mushroom as it is developing, the mushroom's affinity with toxic substances ensures that it absorbs poison from the snake (Pliny *Natural History* 22.95).

Nature intended that our only medicines should be those that are widely available, easy to find, cost nothing, and are derived from the same sources as the food on which we live. But later on human deceit and lucrative swindling devised those dreadful workshops that promise each of us a way to prolong our lives, provided we are willing to pay for it. All at once people are singing the praises of highly elaborate compounds and mixtures, cures from Arabia and India are at a premium, a medication for some slight sore is imported from the Red Sea—even though the very poorest among us dines every day on foods that really should be the source of our medications. But if remedies were sought from the herbs and shrubs that grow in our own gardens, no art would be less highly regarded than medicine (Pliny *Natural History* 24.4).

Arcadia and Laconia produce medicinal herbs. That accounts for the Arcadian custom of drinking milk instead of taking medicines in the springtime, the season when the juices of such plants are at their peak. Milk is particularly rich in medicines in the spring. They drink cows' milk, for the cow eats more than any other animal and grazes on the greatest number of plant species (Theophrastus *History of Plants* 9.15).

Fig. 12.1 Medea, herbalist extraordinaire but a very bad advertisement for foreign medicine. Having demonstrated her powers of rejuvenation by transforming an old ram into a young lamb by chopping it up and boiling it in a cauldron of water mixed with her secret herbs, she persuaded the daughters of King Pelias to submit him to the same treatment. This time, however, she did not add the herbs, and thus her husband, Jason, was freed from his great enemy.

Some roots keep for a longer time, some for a shorter. Hellebore remains useful for thirty years, birthwort for five or six. . . . Of all drugs the one that lasts the longest time is the "driver," and the older it is the better it is. A doctor who is neither a charlatan nor a liar told me that he had some of it that was two hundred years old and still marvelously potent. He had been given it as a gift. The reason it stayed good so long was that it was kept moist (Theophrastus *History of Plants* 9.14).

When Chiron the Centaur was handling the weapons of Hercules, who was visiting him, an arrow fell on his hoof, and he was cured with centaury. (The plant has the alternative name "chironion.") . . .

Centaury is so effective in healing wounds that they say that pieces of meat join up again if they are boiled with it (Pliny *Natural History* 25.66).

The giant cedar produces a resin that is extremely effective against tooth-ache. It breaks the teeth and extracts them, thus soothing the pain. . . . I would be very hesitant about using it as a mouthwash in a vinegar solution to combat toothache, nor would I be keen to inject it into the ears as a remedy for deafness or earworms. But it does have one amazing quality: washing a man's genitals with it before sexual intercourse ensures against pregnancy (Pliny *Natural History* 24.11).

Xenocrates reports an amazing fact, if indeed it really is true. He claims that a woman's menstruation is delayed by a day if she swallows a cori-ander seed, by two days if she swallows two, and so on, according to the number of seeds (Pliny *Natural History* 20.218).

African fennel became famous thanks to the emperor Nero. At the start of his reign, while prowling the streets on his nighttime adventures, he had his face battered with punches. But he applied an ointment made from fennel juice, frankincense, and wax, and the next day he countered the gossip about the brawl by going about with his skin free from bruises (Pliny *Natural History* 13.126). Tacitus may be referring to this very incident at *Annals* 13.25: *A young man of senatorial rank fought back when set upon by Nero, but apologized when he recognized his assailant; this was a fatal mistake, for he was then forced to commit suicide. From that time on, Nero was careful to take a bodyguard of soldiers and gladi-ators with him when he went on such escapades.*

They say that mint will cure diseases affecting the spleen, provided that the patient tastes it in the garden, straight from the plant without plucking it, on nine consecutive days. As he chews it, he should declare that he is treating his spleen (Pliny *Natural History* 20.53).

Both varieties of the plant known as "thlaspi" [shepherd's purse] are effective against inguinal complaints. The experts recommend that anyone gathering it should say that he is picking it to treat ailments of the groin, any type of abscess, and wounds. They also recommend plucking it with one hand only (Pliny *Natural History* 27.139).

Near the end of his treatise *On Agriculture*, the elder Cato devotes two quite untypically effusive chapters (156–7) to recording the health benefits to be derived from cabbage, whether one eats it, drinks its juice, or applies it externally as a bandage or poultice. It stimulates good appetite, good digestion, and bowel movements. Bathing children in the urine of someone who has eaten cabbage ensures that they will be sturdy; such baths also promote clear vision, freedom from pains in the head and neck, and immunity to gynecological problems. Not the least of its great qualities is that it costs so little, though Cato, who was notoriously parsimonious, is enthusiastic enough to add, "even if it were expensive, you should still use it for the sake of your health."

Cato epitomizes the old Roman way of life, stridently resistant to the new practices being imported from Greece. (For his opinion of Greek doctors, see p. 37.) It is frequently assumed that his championing of the humble cabbage is part of this traditional attitude, but cabbage was in fact well established in the Greek world as a wonder vegetable. Pliny lists several Greeks who sang its praises (*Natural History* 20.78). Brief excerpts of a monograph on the cabbage in medicine, written about the time of Cato by Mnesitheus of Cyzicus are preserved by Oribasius (*Corpus Medicorum Graecorum* 6.1.1 p. 100). Cabbage is, moreover, one of the ingredients in pills found in the *Relitto del Pozzino*, the wreck of a ship that had sailed from Greece and went down off the coast of Tuscany in the period soon after Cato's death in 149 B.C.

MUSIC THERAPY

As I read very recently in a book by Theophrastus, many people have put on record their belief that, when pain in the hips is particularly severe, it can be relieved by soothing melodies played on the flute. There is also a book by Democritus that claims viper bites are cured by skilfully played flute music. That book informs us that flute music helps cure very many diseases. The human mind and the human body are so very intimately interconnected, and therefore there is a close link between physical and mental illnesses and their remedies (Aulus Gellius *Attic Nights* 4.13).

According to Theophrastus in his On Inspirations, *music is useful in the treatment of many ailments, both mental and physical, such as fainting, panic attacks, and long-term mental disturbance. He claims that pipe music cures sciatica and seizures* (Theophrastus *frg.* 88).

Asclepiades the doctor often employed music to restore the minds of the mentally unstable to their proper state. Herophilus, who was also a doctor, claimed that the pulses in the veins move with musical rhythms (Censorinus *The Birthday Book* 12).

The Pythagoreans used incantations to counter some illnesses, and they believed that music contributes greatly to health, provided that it is used appropriately. They also used phrases chosen from Homer and Hesiod to correct faults in the soul (Iamblichus *Life of Pythagoras* 29.164).

To prevent the womb from wandering, Mantias [a second-century B.C. pharmacologist] *used the music of flutes and drums when an attack was imminent* (Soranus *Gynecology* 3.29). For the wandering womb, see p. 95.

Some doctors approve of the use of music in healing, as Philistion's brother reports in On Remedies 22; *he records that when a musician played his pipe over them, the parts of the body that were in pain started to throb and quiver and the pain grew less acute. Some people say that Pythagoras invented music therapy, but in Soranus's opinion those who believe that a serious disease can be removed through tunes and singing seem to be laboring under an empty delusion* (Caelius Aurelianus *Chronic Diseases* 5.23).

BATHING

The Greeks call baths βαλανεῖον (balaneion) *because they throw* (βάλλω, ballo) *worries out of our mind* (St. Augustine *Confessions* 9.12).

Wine drunk in moderation gives relief to the soul and banishes pain from it. Other things have much the same effect, such as moderately hot baths. This is what inspires people to sing when they are in the bath (Rufus of Ephesus *On Melancholy frg.* 61).

I understand that it is customary among the barbarians for infants to be given frequent cold baths, whereas we Greeks cook our children with frequent warm baths. It is the children's nurses who have convinced us that this is a good thing. They appreciate the drowsiness that hot baths induce, for it means they are less troubled during the night, but they claim that children have difficulty sleeping if they have not been more or less soft boiled in the bath (Oribasius *Medical Compilations* 10.7).

Fig. 12.2 A horn and a water organ. What did they sound like together?

In the absence of chemical cleaning agents, *going to the baths is one of the worst things to do if one has a wound that is not yet free of morbid matter, for bathing makes it moist and dirty, and that often leads to infection* (Celsus *On Medicine* 5.28).

When people have been bitten by a mad dog, some doctors send them straightaway to the baths, and have them sweat for as long as they can tolerate it. They leave the wound undressed, so that the poison can drip out of it (Celsus *On Medicine* 5.27).

Fig. 12.3 Maybe some people found bathing to be soothing and relaxing, but by and large public baths seem to have been rather less salubrious than they are in the modern imagination of them. The deities most frequently honored in bath complexes were Asclepius and his daughter, Hygieia, so we may surmise that the sick constituted a large part of the clientele. In fact, the emperor Hadrian allowed only the sick to go to the baths before the eighth hour (2 p.m.) (Historia Augusta *Life of Hadrian* 22.7).

Scribonius Largus commends a particular type of plaster as being very serviceable for wounds and bites, for inhibiting tumors and pus, and for not falling off if worn at the baths (*Prescriptions* 214).

What do you suppose a visit to the baths entails? Olive oil, sweat, filth, water full of gloios [see p. 193], *an entirely disgusting affair* (Marcus Aurelius *Meditations* 8.24).

Some people do not even bother with a massage. They just anoint themselves with olive oil and get straight into the bath; sometimes they even take a strigil and scrape the sweat off themselves right there in the bath (Galen *Matters of Health* 6.406K).

When speculation about the number of people in Rome suffering from hernias happened to come up in conversation, the emperor Elagabalus ordered a list of all such people to be made, and then he had them brought to his baths, where he bathed with them. The group included even some high-ranking individuals (Historia Augusta *Life of Elagabalus* 25). The *Historia Augusta* is not altogether reliable; in the same passage, we are informed that Elagabalus had ten thousand pounds of cobwebs collected.

The baths, wine, and sex destroy our bodies, but the baths, wine, and sex are what make life worth living. This couplet is found several times in Latin graffiti (*Corpus of Latin Inscriptions* 3.12274c, 6.15258, 6.19007, 14.914), and is much like the anonymous Greek epigram "Wine and the baths and the urge for sex send us by a quicker path to Hades" (*Greek Anthology* 10.112). A slightly modernized version of the couplet survives in Italian: *Bacco, tabacco e Venere/reducono l'uomo in cenere* ("Bacchus, tobacco, and Venus reduce a man to ashes"). Aristotle puts the same idea more pedantically: *There are many people in good health whom no one would congratulate for their good health, because*

Fig. 12.4 Asclepius and his daughter, Hygieia, who is feeding the sacred snake.

they achieve it by abstaining from all or most human pleasures (Rhetoric 1361b).

SLEEP

Some doctors say that sleep comes upon us when exhalations from our food seep gently round our digestive tract and cause a sort of tickling (Plutarch On Isis and Osiris 384a).

What are the causes of sleep and death? According to Alcmaeon, we fall asleep when our blood retreats in our veins, we wake up when it comes flowing back, and we die when it retreats altogether (Pseudo-Plutarch On the Opinions of Philosophers 909d).

A cure for severe insomnia: you should tie the patient's arms and legs at the time when he usually goes to bed, and order him to stay awake. If he closes his eyes, force him to open them. Do this till he is sufficiently exhausted, then suddenly untie him, remove the lamp, and ensure that he is left undisturbed (Oribasius *Synopsis to Eustathius, His Son* 6.31, drawing on a lost work by Galen).

Sleep can be induced by:

> *wool-grease either diluted in a quarter of a pint of wine with a pinch of myrrh or mixed with goose-fat and myrtle wine;*

> *a cuckoo in a hare-skin pouch worn as an amulet;*

> *the beak of a young heron in a donkey-skin pouch attached to the forehead; the beak has the same effect by itself, if soaked in wine.*

Sleep can be prevented by:

> *The dried head of a bat worn as an amulet.*

(Pliny *Natural History* 30.140)

Fig. 12.5 Sleep and Death (helpfully labeled by the painter) removing Zeus's mortal son Sarpedon from the battlefield at Troy.

Doctors often make a lot of fuss and prepare countless medications without being able to free the patient from his disease. But sleep comes along unsummoned and cures every disease, freeing sufferers from countless pains. Night is a medicine not just for physical sufferings but also for mental illnesses, relieving our minds when they are afflicted with pain (John Chrysostom *Homilies* 49 p. 98).

Refusing to enter the bedroom of a patient who was sleeping, Erasistratus declared "I can hear a better doctor in there already" (Pseudo-Caecilius Balbus *Sententiae* 43).

ANIMAL DOCTORS

The hippopotamus has actually been our teacher in one particular medical procedure. When it becomes fat through its non-stop grazing, it comes out onto the riverbank and looks for a spot where the reeds have recently been cut. When it sees a very sharp stump, it presses its body against it to open a vein in its leg, and by this outpouring of blood it relieves its body, which would otherwise have become diseased. After the bleeding, the hippopotamus covers the wound with mud (Pliny *Natural History* 8.96).

Pliny goes on to note other remedies learned from the animal world. For example:

> *Deer have shown that the herb dittany is good for extracting arrows, because they eat that plant when they are shot, and the arrow is ejected*
>
> *Deer also eat crabs as a cure for spider bites*
>
> *A really good antidote for snakebite is the plant* [unnamed] *with which lizards treat their wounds whenever they join battle with snakes*
>
> *Swallows have shown that greater celandine is very good for the eyesight, because they use it to treat their fledglings if their vision is impaired.*

To say nothing about spiders, deer, and crabs, why does Pliny specify swallows? How might one come to notice if fledgling swallows were blind? Aristotle makes an equally surprising observation at *Generation of Animals 775a: If swallows have their eyes stabbed while they are still young, they recover their sight, for the blinding happens when they are hatched but not yet fully developed, and that is why their eyes take form and grow again.*

In the only surviving fragment of a work entitled *On Antipathy and Sympathy*, the otherwise unknown Greek writer Nepualius lists various types of self-medication practiced by animals:

> *If a lion is ill, it eats a monkey*
> *If a panther is ill, it drinks the blood of a dog*
> *If a tiger is ill, it eats human excrement*
> *If a monkey is ill, it drinks its own urine*
> *If a goat has been shot, it eats the herb dittany and this ejects the arrow*
> *If an eagle is ill, it eats a tortoise*
> *If a swan is ill, it eats frogs*
> *If a leopard is ill, it drinks the blood of a wild goat*

Since a hibernating bear spends forty days without food or any kind of nourishment, the excessive colliquescence causes its intestines to fold up and become compressed. The bear realizes this, and so, when it emerges from its den, it eats some of the plant called wild arum. This induces flatulence, which opens and widens the bear's intestinal tract, making it capable of admitting food. Once the bear's intestines fill out again, it eats some ants, and this allows for a very easy evacuation. That is all I need say, my fellow human beings, about the natural process by which bears empty and fill themselves—a process that has no need of any doctors or medications (Aelian *History of Animals* 6.3).

A dog that is troubled by overeating knows that, if it eats a particular herb that grows in dry stone walls, it vomits up everything that is upsetting it, along with phlegm and bile, and a great quantity of excrement is also evacuated. It thereby ensures health for itself, with no need of doctors to assist it. It also voids a substantial amount of black bile, which, should it remain in its body, causes madness, a dreadful disease among dogs. Dogs that are full of worms eat chaff, as Aristotle says [History of Animals 612a]. *Dogs that have been injured have their tongue to treat them; with it they lick the wounded part and restore it to health, dismissing the need for bandages, plasters, and complex medicaments* (Aelian *History of Animals* 8.9).

Elephants help each other when they are being hunted, and defend any one of their number who is exhausted. If they can remove him from danger, they anoint his wounds with the tears of the aloe tree, standing round him like doctors (Philostratus *Life of Apollonius* 2.16).

ACCIDENTAL CURES

It is worth learning from any and every source about medicines that are for drinking or for applying to wounds. These facts were not discovered by deduction, but rather by mere chance, and not by experts so much as by ordinary people (Hippocrates *Affections* 45).

Some medical discoveries were made accidentally. For example, the couching of cataracts was devised when a goat with a cataract recovered its sight after being stabbed in the eye by a sharp reed. Drenching with clysters was devised thanks to the ibis's habit of filling up the skin round its neck like a douche bag with water from the sea or the Nile and injecting it into itself through its beak from behind (Pseudo-Galen *Introduction or The Doctor* 14.675K). Severus Iatrosophista says of the latter treatment: *when the ibis, a gluttonous bird that gorges on shellfish, becomes constipated, it applies its rather eccentric cure, thus obtaining relief and enabling itself to fill up again with food* (*On Clysters* 1).

A would-be assassin inflicted a divinely providential wound on Jason, the cruel tyrant of Pherae. He ambushed him and struck him with a sword. In so doing, he burst a tumor that none of the doctors had been able to cure, thereby freeing him from a deadly affliction (Valerius Maximus *Memorable Deeds and Sayings* 1.8 ext. 6).

Fig. 12.6 The African ibis is no longer found in Egypt, where its self-medication was no doubt first observed.

Experience has taught us that a person who has been bitten by an asp should drink vinegar. They say that this was discovered when a boy was bitten by one and then suffered dreadfully from thirst, partly because of the bite and partly because of the excessive heat. He was in a dry region and could find no other liquid, so he drank some vinegar that he happened to have with him, and that saved his life (Celsus *On Medicine* 5.27).

The governor of Egypt sentenced some convicted criminals to be thrown to ravening wild beasts. As they were going into the theater designated for the punishment of thieves, a woman selling things by the roadside took pity on them and gave them some of the citron she was eating. They took it and ate it, and very soon after were exposed to the asps, dreadful savage creatures. The asps bit them, but they were not harmed at all. The governor was baffled. Eventually he asked the soldier who was guarding the criminals whether they had eaten or drunk anything. When he learned that they had been given pieces of citron, the next day he ordered one criminal to be given a piece of citron, but not the other. The one who ate it suffered no harm when he was bitten, but the other died as soon as he was bitten. Since many further experiments produced the same result, citron was proved to be an antidote for all deadly drugs (Athenaeus *Wise Men at Dinner* 3.28).

FOREIGN MEDICINE

Just as agriculture promises food to the healthy, so medicine promises health to the sick. There is no part of the world where medicine is not found, for even the most backward peoples have discovered the use of herbs and other easily available remedies to help against wounds and diseases (Celsus *On Medicine* Preface 1).

There are considerable differences between races. For example, we are told that the inhabitants of Egypt, Arabia, Syria, and Cilicia are subject to various types of intestinal worm not found at all in Thrace and Phrygia. This is far less remarkable than that these parasites are found among the Thebans in Boeotia, but not among the Athenians, in the neighboring region of Attica (Pliny *Natural History* 27.145).

Fig. 12.7 Gladiators fighting one another or wild animals probably ranked higher as a spectator sport than leopards (or lions or tigers or bears) mauling victims who were securely tied to stakes or delivered as meals on wheels.

Plants and other remedies were in use among the Egyptians, as Homer testifies when he says, "The land of Egypt is very fertile, bearing many drugs that are beneficial when mixed, and many that are deadly." It is likely that much information about surgery was discovered by the first doctors when they cut corpses open for mummification (Pseudo-Galen *Introduction or The Doctor* 14.675K).

Helen threw a drug into the wine, a drug that dispels sorrow and anger, and brings forgetfulness of all evils. Anyone who drinks it when it is mixed in the wine-bowl, does not let fall a tear from his cheeks all day long—not even were his mother and father to die, nor even were his brother or his dear son to be butchered with a bronze sword before his very eyes. Such were the drugs that the daughter of Zeus possessed, excellent drugs, given to her by Polydamna, the wife of Thoth, from Egypt, where the wheat-bearing fields produce abundant drugs, some excellent, some deadly, and every man is a skillful doctor, for they are of the race of Apollo Paean [the god of healing] (Homer *Odyssey* 4.220–32).

In Egypt, medicine is organized as follows: each doctor devotes himself to one single disease, never more, and the whole country is full of doctors, with some specializing in the eyes, others the head, others the teeth, others the stomach, and others the more obscure forms of sickness (Herodotus *Histories* 2.84). Herodotus's report is confirmed by the Stele of Iri-ka-Ra, erected in Luxor about five centuries earlier. But there were, or had been, exceptions. The Stele of Irenakhty, from the late third millennium, proclaims him as *Eye-Doctor at the Palace, Doctor of the Stomach at the Palace, Shepherd of the Rectum, Interpreter of Liquids, Physician at the Palace, Inspector of Physicians at the Palace, Chief of Physicians at the Palace, and Scorpion Charmer.*

In Egypt, doctors are allowed to change to a different treatment after four days, but if they make any modifications sooner than that, they do so at their own risk (Aristotle *Politics* 1286a).

Leprosy used to be found only in Egypt. When the pharaohs contracted it, it was fatal for their subjects, because part of the treatment was to bathe in tubs of warm human blood (Pliny *Natural History* 26.8).

The Egyptians are, apart from the Libyans, the healthiest people in the world. In my opinion, the reason for this is that they live in an unchanging climate. For it is change, especially from one season to another, that causes most diseases (Herodotus *Histories* 2.77).

The following custom is practiced by some, perhaps all (I can't say for sure), of the Libyan nomads. When their children are four years old, they burn the veins at the top of their head, or in some cases the veins at the temples, with greasy sheep's wool. They do this to ensure that phlegm flowing down from the head does not harm them at any time in their life, and they attribute their remarkably good health to this. The Libyans are certainly the healthiest of all known peoples, but I can't confirm that this is definitely the reason. If a child has convulsions during the procedure, they counter the attack by pouring goat's urine over him. I am reporting what the Libyans themselves say (Herodotus *Histories* 4.187).

The traditional Babylonian way of treating the sick is very wise. They do not have any doctors. Instead, the sick are brought to the marketplace, where people come up to them and give them advice about their ailment, if anyone has either personally suffered from such a complaint or knows someone else who has done so. When they come up and give advice, they recommend the procedures by which they themselves or some person they know escaped from a similar illness. It is not permissible to pass a sick person in silence without asking what is wrong with him (Herodotus *Histories* 1.197).

I am not going to discuss medicines made with ingredients brought here for sale from India or Arabia or any other foreign part of the world. Substances produced so far away do not suit our remedies; they do not grow for us, in fact they do not even grow for the native population there either, for otherwise they would not be selling them on to people elsewhere.

It is reasonable that anyone who wishes to should buy them for making perfumes, or unguents, or any such luxury items, or as a contribution to religious ceremonials, since we pray to the gods with incense. I intend to demonstrate that it is possible to maintain good health without such stuff, and I shall do so even if it is only to put those people to shame who indulge in the modern decadent way of life (Pliny *Natural History* 22.118).

In India, there is a law that anyone who discovers a deadly substance is put to death, unless he also finds an antidote for it. In that case he receives a reward from the king (Strabo *Geography* 15.1.22).

The Padaeans are a nomadic Indian tribe who eat raw meat. They are said to practice the following custom when any man or woman in the tribe falls ill. If it is a man, the men who are his closest friends kill him, declaring that, because he is wasting away with disease, he is spoiling the meat for them. He denies being ill, but they disagree and kill him and have a feast. Likewise, if a woman falls ill, her closest female friends do just what the men do (Herodotus *Histories* 3.99).

Raw bacon is regarded as a panacea by the Franks [the German tribe who gave their name to France], *making all other medicines unnecessary. It can be chewed or applied to wounds* (Anthimus *On the Observance of Foods* 14). Bacon poultices may seem outlandish, but note Dioscorides's recommendation: *Cutting up chickens and applying the segments to the wound gives relief from snakebites; but the chicken has to be changed regularly* (*Medical Material* 2.49). Would such remedies be any less efficacious than steak on a black eye?

LISTS OF REMEDIES

Some suggestions for the treatment of a patient with digestive problems:

After exercising, he should take a walk, but not a very long walk

After dinner, he should take a short walk, little more than a stretch after leaving the table

In the early morning, he should take a longer walk

He should take a warm bath and be rubbed down with unguents

Let him have plenty of sleep in a soft bed

He should have a certain amount of sexual intercourse

Reduce his food intake by a quarter over a ten-day period

(Hippocrates *Diet* 3.80)

Lion fat is said to counteract treachery

Elephant fat and deer fat, applied as an ointment, drive away snakes

He-goat fat gives relief from gout, if mixed with saffron and the droppings of she-goats (Sheep fat has the same effect)

Pig fat is good for disorders of the womb and buttocks, and for burns

Donkey fat turns scars all the same color

Goose fat, like that of poultry in general, is good for women's ailments, cracked lips, facial blemishes, and earache

Bear fat is good for chilblains, and supposedly reverses hair loss

Viper fat is good for dull vision and cataracts, when mixed with equal parts of cedar oil, Attic honey, and aged olive oil. Smeared fresh by itself in depilated armpits, it ensures that the hair does not grow again.

(Dioscorides *Medical Material* 2.76)

A solution of vinegar and salt water is good for gangrenous and septic ulcers, dog bites, and the bites of venomous creatures. When patients are operated on for stone, it stops bleeding if the wound is bathed in it immediately after surgery. It also gives relief to sufferers from rectal prolapse. It is used as a suppository in cases of dysentery complicated by septic ulcers, though this must be followed up with an enema made with milk. If swallowed or used as a gargle, it rids the body of leeches, and cures dandruff and other such skin complaints (Dioscorides *Medical Material* 5.15).

*The human bite is one of the most dangerous. It can be cured with earwax.
This need cause no surprise, given that earwax, especially that obtained
from an executed person and applied while still fresh, cures even scorpion
stings and snakebites. Earwax is also effective against hangnails, as is a
human tooth against snakebites, if ground to a powder* (Pliny *Natural
History* 28.40).

At *Natural History* 20.23, Pliny lists many medicinal qualities of rad-
ishes. For example, whether in a drink or worn as an amulet, they
help in the treatment of asthma, depression, edema, seizures, lethargy,
intestinal worms, liver complaints, back pains, deafness, poor vision,
hair loss (in women), and pubic lice. They also check excess phlegm
and bile, and reduce an enlarged spleen. They are effective in purges,
diuretics, and emetics (for those who have eaten too much). In an
ointment, they cure snakebites, and a piece of radish placed on a scorpion's back will kill it. They are aphrodisiac (though some link this
benefit with damage to the voice).

In praise of spitting (Pliny *Natural History* 28.35):

> *Spitting while fasting drives away snakes*
> *Spitting wards off seizures*
> *Spitting protects us against magic spells and the bad consequences of
>   meeting a person who is lame in the right foot*
> *Spitting in one's lap wins pardon from the gods for presumptuous aspirations*
> *It is customary to spit three times to ensure the efficacy of any medicine
>   when it is being administered*
> *It is customary to mark fresh boils with spittle while fasting*

Pliny has still more good things to say about saliva (*Natural History*
28.37):

> *Smearing them with saliva while fasting cures papules and leprous spots,
>   bleary eyes, and cancerous growths*
> *Neck pains are relieved if saliva is applied to the back of the right knee
>   by the right hand, to the back of the left knee by the left hand*
> *Spitting on a creature that gets into a person's ear makes it come out*

*Spitting on one's urine during micturation acts as a protective charm, as
does spitting into one's right shoe before putting it on, and likewise
spitting when going past any place where one has ever been in danger*

>——•

The virtues of cress (Anonymous Byzantine *Farm Work* 12.26):

*Mixed with bean flour and a small amount of myrrh oil, cress seeds cure
pustules and scrofulous swellings of the glands in the neck (cabbage
leaves should be used instead of linen bandages)*
Drunk with wine and mint, they expel roundworms and tapeworms
Boiled with goat's milk, they cure chest problems
Used as a fumigant, they drive away snakes
They say that those who eat cress have a sharper intelligence
Cress seeds inhibit the sex drive
Drunk with honey, they cure coughing
They are also applied to spreading ulcers
Cress juice checks hair loss
Mixed with goose fat, cress cures dandruff and little sores on the head
Mixed with yeast, it brings boils to a head
They say that cress juice, poured in through the ears, cures toothache

Treatments for Ears, Eyes, and Teeth

EARACHE

*For bruised ears: Hippocrates advises leaving them to heal themselves,
but our patients often pressure us to treat them somehow, so here are some
methods you might try. . .* (Paul of Aegina *Medical Compendium* 3.23).

◣━━━━━◗

Dioscorides's *Medical Material* is predominantly concerned with
herbal remedies, but the small section at the start of Book Two on
cures to be derived from animals contains many remedies for ear troubles. The following are to be smeared on or instilled into the affected
ear. They are not to be taken orally:

Chicken fat
Fox fat
Goose fat
Goose fat with earthworms

Goose fat with lanolin (also good for genital sores)
Cockroaches' entrails, boiled, or ground to a powder with oil
Millipedes, ground up, and warmed with oil of roses in a pomegranate rind
Spiders, boiled in oil of roses
Pig's gall
Bull's gall, mixed with the milk of a goat or a woman
Bull's urine, mixed with myrrh
Dog's urine, boiled in a pomegranate rind
Goat's urine
Wild boar's urine
Snake's skin, boiled in wine

Small creatures and little stones have a tendency to fall into people's ears. If a flea gets in, a little bit of wool should be inserted; the flea clings to it and can be extracted. . . . A vigorous sneeze also dislodges foreign bodies, as does a powerful jet of water through an ear syringe. Another method is to balance a plank of wood in such a way that neither end touches the ground, and then tie the patient to it, lying on his side so that the affected ear is turned towards the ground and projects out beyond the end of the plank. The other end of the plank at the patient's feet is then struck with a mallet; this shakes the ear and whatever is in it falls out (Celsus *On Medicine* 6.7).

For earache. Wrap some wool round your finger and pour some oil on it. Then put the ball of wool in the palm of your hand and place it under the patient's ear so that he thinks that something has come out of his ear. Then throw the wool on the fire. This is a trick (Hippocrates *Epidemics* 6.5.7). When Galen discusses this passage, he refuses to believe that Hippocrates would advocate any sort of trickery and declares, "it is better to suppose that Hippocrates simply didn't write this passage" (*Commentary on Hippocrates's* Epidemics VI 17*b*.269K).

DEAFNESS

Fever sometimes causes hearing loss, but the trouble can be completely dealt with if the patient has a nose bleed or a bowel movement. Nothing acts as effectively against deafness as a bilious bowel movement (Celsus *On Medicine* 2.8).

Fig. 12.8 *Long ago, Cutius Gallus had vowed these ears to you, son of Apollo, and he placed them here when his ears were cured* (*Corpus of Latin Inscriptions* 3.7266). A typical offering in the temple of Asclepius at Epidaurus, except that the inscription is in Latin, not Greek, and the dedicatee has a Roman name. The worship of Asclepius at Epidaurus was not interrupted by the Roman conquest of Greece in the second century B.C., even though that conquest culminated in the destruction in 146 of Corinth, the most prosperous city in mainland Greece, only thirty-five miles away to the north.

Asclepiades used to cure the profoundly deaf by means of trumpet-blasts (Martianus Capella *The Marriage of Philosophy and Mercury* 9.926).

People become deaf and dumb at the same time, and ear complaints transform into lung diseases. Some people cough when they scratch their ear (Pseudo-Aristotle *Problems* 961b).

Congenitally blind people are more intelligent than deaf and dumb people (Aristotle *On the Senses* 437a).

EYE TROUBLES

An infant with congenital strabismus is treated by attaching a mask to his face, so that he looks straight ahead. A lamp should be placed directly in front, not shining on him from the side. If the child still looks off towards his nose, little balls of purple wool should be attached to the outer corners of his eyes, out towards his temples, so that, by looking steadily at them, he will correct his eyes (Oribasius *Synopsis to Eustathius His Son* 8.51).

An attack of dull vision may be preceded by:

> *chronic indigestion*
>
> *bouts of drinking undiluted wine*
>
> *sunstroke*
>
> *a burning sensation in the head*
>
> *a chill*
>
> *reading or bathing immediately after a meal*
>
> *vomiting at unsuitable times*
>
> *immoderate sexual intercourse at unsuitable times*
>
> *the violent retention of one's breath, as happens with trumpeters*
>
> (Aëtius On Medicine 7.50)

There is a weakness of the eyes that allows people to see adequately by day, but not at all during the night. Women with a regular menstrual cycle are immune to it. The eyes of those who suffer from it should be smeared with the bloody juice that drips from a roasting liver; a goat's liver is best, and the liver of a he-goat is preferable to that of a she-goat. The patient should also eat the liver itself (Celsus *On Medicine* 6.6).

The sharp-tasting juice of the turnip, extracted at harvest time and mixed with woman's milk, is used as an eyewash and to treat impaired vision (Pliny *Natural History* 18.130).

Aconite has a root that glistens like alabaster and is shaped like a scorpion's tail. They say that touching a scorpion with aconite root paralyses it, whereas it is revived by white hellebore. It is used in medicines to relieve pains in the eyes. If you throw down aconite root wrapped in pieces of meat for them to find, it kills leopards, wild boar, wolves, and all kinds of wild animal (Dioscorides *Medical Material* 4.76).

If a sty develops in your right eye, grip it with three fingers of the left hand, while facing east under the open sky, and say:

> A she-mule does not give birth, and a stone does not produce wool. May no head grow for this disease, and if it does grow, may it wither away.

When you have said this, touch the earth with the same three fingers and spit. Do this three times.

(Marcellus On Medicines 8.190)

When troublesome eyelashes are plucked, they can be prevented from growing back by the application of:

> hedgehog's bile
>
> the white of a gecko's eggs
>
> the ashes of a salamander
>
> the bile of a green lizard in white wine, left in the sun in a copper jar till it thickens to the consistency of honey
>
> the ashes of baby swallows mixed with the milky sap of the spurge plant
>
> snail slime

(Pliny Natural History 29.116)

An ophthalmologist called Justus cured many patients suffering from purulent flux of the eyes by making them sit up straight in a chair, then taking hold of both sides of their head and shaking it so vigorously that we *could clearly see the pus being moved downwards* (Galen *The Therapeutic Method* 10.1019K).

The left eye should be operated on with the right hand, the right eye with the left hand (Celsus *On Medicine* 7.7).

TOOTHACHE

Toothache ranks among the greatest of all torments. . . . If the pain is such as to necessitate extraction, a peppercorn without its outer husk or a peeled ivy berry inserted into the cavity splits the tooth, which will then fall out in pieces. Or the spiny tail of a stingray is roasted, then ground to a powder and added to resin, and this mixture is smeared round the tooth, making it loose. . . . These are among the remedies recognized by doctors (Celsus *On Medicine* 6.9).

At *Natural History* 32.80, Pliny recommends scraping the gums with fish-bones or the sting of a stingray as a cure for toothache, or washing the mouth out with the brains of a dogfish boiled down in olive oil. He then goes into detail on the important contribution that frogs make to dentistry:

> *Frogs are boiled down in vinegar, one at a time, and used as a mouthwash. If a patient objected to the unpleasant taste, Sallustius Dionysius used to suspend several frogs by their back legs so that the fluid in their mouths could drip into the boiling vinegar. Patients with stronger stomachs were made to chew frogs boiled in their own juice.*
>
> *Some doctors tie a whole frog to the patient's jaw* [to ward off or relieve toothache]. *Others reduce ten frogs in three pints of vinegar to a third of the volume to secure loose teeth.*
>
> *Others boil down the hearts of forty-six frogs in one pint of old olive oil in a copper pot, and pour the liquid into the ear on the same side of the face as the aching jaw.*
>
> *Others apply to the sore teeth a mixture of boiled frog's liver beaten up with honey.*

Fig. 12.9 A votive set of terracotta teeth.

Drip the fat of a headless cockroach heated up in rose water into the appro-
priate ear [on the same side of the face as the aching tooth] (Galen *The*
Composition of Drugs According to Places 12.861K). This recommendation, which Galen quotes from the first/second-century A.D. physician Archigenes, is wonderfully gross, but it is perhaps even more
gross in the textually corrupt version given by Aëtius three centuries
after Galen, where "headless" has been transformed into "the one that
farts" (*tes bdeouses* instead of *tes kephales deouses*) (*On Medicine* 8.35).

· XIII ·

GENERAL MEDICINE

The passages cited in this section are particularly miscellaneous. But since, to use Hippocrates's phrase, at least they do no harm, it seemed better to isolate them together here rather than to insert them ectopically somewhere else or excise them entirely.

><

The elements from which the world is made are air, fire, water, and earth; the seasons from which the year is made up are spring, summer, winter, and fall; the humors from which animals and humans are composed are yellow bile, blood, phlegm, and black bile. The humors are all combined with moisture and heat, dryness and cold. Blood, air, and spring are moist and hot (though there is some dispute whether this applies to air), and yellow bile, summer, and fire are hot and dry, whereas black bile, earth, and fall are cold and dry and phlegm, water, and winter are cold and moist (Pseudo-Galen *On Humors* 19.485K). The term *humor* is derived from the Greek word *chymos*, meaning "sap" or "juice," the sense "wit" being a much later development. The idea that the human body is composed of four humors probably had its origin either in Egypt or in Mesoptamia, but it was the Greeks, about 400 B.C., who first formulated the principle that health depends on their being in proper balance with each other, and also in harmony with the elements and the seasons. Humoral theory was strongly attacked by Paracelsus in the sixteenth century, but survived till the middle of the nineteenth century, when it was finally swept aside for good and all by the new and true discoveries in cellular pathology. Few people nowadays are aware of the origins of such terms as "melancholy," "phlegmatic," and "sanguine." Not many other beliefs so wholly lacking in any proper scientific foundation have impeded progress for so long.

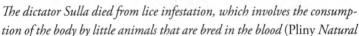

Here is a simple example of the sort of confident nonsense that the humoral theory engendered. To quote a Greek proverb, a single drop tells you everything about the whole jarful:

> *Why is it that phlegm often moves up from the feet to the head and eyes, even though it is heavy and cold, and therefore has a natural tendency to move downwards? The phlegm does not move upwards of its own accord. Each individual part of the body has the power to reject it, and chases it off upwards, until it reaches the weakest part of the body, and that part, since it is so weak, is unable to shake itself free of it, so it is weighed down by the phlegm and suffers fluxes because of it. It is just as when a large group of people throw a burning coal from one to the next; each person exerts himself to throw it to someone else, until it reaches the weakest person and stays with him* (Pseudo-Alexander of Aphrodisias *Problems* 3.15).

Lice tend to infest children's heads, men's heads less so, and women's more than men's. People with lice on their head suffer less from headaches (Aristotle *History of Animals* 557a).

The dictator Sulla died from lice infestation, which involves the consumption of the body by little animals that are bred in the blood (Pliny *Natural History* 26.138).

Bald people tend not to suffer from varicose veins. If a bald person does get varicose veins, his hair grows again (Hippocrates *Aphorisms* 6.34).

People who lisp are particularly vulnerable to long bouts of diarrhea (Hippocrates *Aphorisms* 6.32).

When his liver expands in the direction of his diaphragm, the patient becomes delirious. He thinks that snakes and all kinds of other such animals appear before his eyes, and armed soldiers in combat, and he himself seems to be fighting with them. . . . This disease mostly afflicts people when they are traveling abroad, going along a lonely road; but it does strike at other times also (Hippocrates *Critical Days* 3).

If you were to mix blue or red dye with water and give it to a very thirsty animal to drink (especially a pig, since it is not a beast that cares much for appearances), and if you were then to cut its throat while it was still drinking, you would find that its trachea is dyed by the drink (Hippocrates *The Heart* 2).

There are circumstances in which even healthy people can find themselves unable to pass urine. For example, at meetings of the assembly or the senate, or at the law court or a banquet. When someone retains their urine for an unusually long time, the bladder distends and consequently they cannot pass urine (Galen *The Affected Places* 8.407K). The emperor Claudius would have understood this difficulty: *It is said that, after hearing about someone who almost died because of his modest restraint, Claudius even considered publishing an edict excusing the passing of gas during dinner* (Suetonius *Life of Claudius* 32). However logical it might seem, we need not draw the inference that there actually was a law against farting.

Sneezing occurs when the brain is heated or the cranial cavity fills with moisture. The air inside overflows, and makes a noise because it has to escape through a narrow passage (Hippocrates *Aphorisms* 7.51).

Fear is accompanied by a loosening of the bowels, because the muscles that normally keep the passage for waste products closed are left without

the soul's strength as it withdraws farther into our body, and they there-
fore relax the bonds by which they were holding back the waste products
until they had an opportunity to dispose of them (Macrobius *Saturnalia*
7.11.9).

Some Stoic philosophers think that anger is aroused in the chest when
the blood boils around the heart. The reason why this particular loca-
tion is assigned to anger is simply that the chest is the warmest part of
the whole body. Anger builds up only gradually in people with excess
moisture [in their combination of humors], *because they do not have*
a store of heat, but acquire it through movement; this is why the angry
outbursts of children and women are fierce, but not very consequential,
and can be sparked by trivial causes. During those periods of life when
dryness predominates among the humors in the body, anger is vehement
and strong, but stable, without growing worse, because cold is then tak-
ing over from heat, which is waning. Old people are tetchy and queru-
lous, as are sick people and those whose heat has been used up either
through exhaustion or through loss of blood. The same applies to those
who have wasted away through thirst or hunger, and to the anemic, the
badly nourished, and the weak. Wine inflames angry passions, because it
increases heat. Some people boil over when they are drunk, others when
they are just slightly tipsy: it depends on the individual. This is also why
red-haired people and those with ruddy complexions are particularly
susceptible to anger: their blood is in a constant state of restless motion
(Seneca *On Anger* 2.19).

Everything on the right side of the body is stronger, and everything
on the left correspondingly weaker, the reason being that the right
side is regulated by the body's heat, whereas the left is dulled by
contact with the cold that controls that side (Macrobius *Saturnalia*
7.4.21).

Doctors do not worry as much about fevers that have some clear and sub-
stantial cause as they do about those that arise mysteriously and gradually.

Likewise, the unrelenting petty bickering between husband and wife day after day goes unnoticed by most people, but that is what creates a rift between them and spoils their life together (Plutarch *Marital Advice* 141*b*).

Fig. 13.1 A drunken old woman clutching a rather large wine jar.

What sort of doctor would fail to give any advice to a patient when he was ill, but would then turn up at his funeral and explain to the mourning family the treatment that would have cured him? (Aeschines *Against Ctesiphon* 225).

What sort of doctor invites people to be his patients? I hear that doctors in Rome nowadays actually do advertise their services. But when I lived there, it was the patient who called in the doctor (Epictetus *Discourses* 3.23).

Theophrastus tells a story about flames shooting out from a person's eyes, and Megethius, the doctor at Alexandria, told me that he had seen a flame emanating from the hip of someone with sciatica and burning the bed sheets (Simplicius *Commentary on Aristotle's* About the Heavens 7 p. 602).

A woman was suffering from the delusion that she had swallowed a snake. Her doctor cured her by giving her an emetic, and then surreptitiously inserting a snake into the bowl into which she vomited. A man was in great distress because he imagined that a dead man had called to him by name. His doctor cured him by masquerading as the ghost of the dead man, killed by robbers in the cemetery at the city gates (Galen *Commentary on Hippocrates's* Epidemics II 2.208W-P).

≻══

If a patient is afflicted by headaches, it helps to bathe his head in very hot water, and to expel phlegm and mucus by making him sneeze (Hippocrates *Affections* 2). This might be more effective than Pliny's suggestion that headaches can be relieved *by smearing one's forehead with the grime produced by pouring vinegar on door hinges, or by wrapping round one's temples the rope with which someone has been hanged, . . . or by tying a woman's brassiere round one's head* (Pliny *Natural History* 28.49, 76).

▬▬►

This use for nooses and brassieres may seem bizarre, but it fits a pattern: *it is said that, in order to counter the headaches caused by drinking too much wine, Dionysus, the god of wine, tied a band round his head. . . . This is allegedly the origin of the custom whereby kings wear a crown* [διάδημα (*diadema*, literally "a thing tied round")] (Diodorus Siculus *The Library* 4.4).

⚱

Some doctors order their patients who are suffering from jaundice to keep their eyes fixed on something either made of gold or gold in color, and they recommend having blankets of that color on the bed (Caelius Aurelianus *Chronic Diseases* 3.78). The theory is that the similarity in color will draw the unhealthy color out of the patients into the golden object, but Aurelianus comments that the process is just as likely to work in reverse, and that in any case gold-colored objects might depress the patient by reminding him of his illness.

≻══

Love, like epilepsy and other such seizures (see p. 155), was thought by many to be an affliction sent by the gods, a notion that the great Galen felt moved to oppose: *the pangs of love are not a divine disease, but rather a purely human condition, unless of course one gives such credence to mythological stories as to accept that there are people driven to*

Fig. 13.2 Dionysus and two maenads. The hare is a traditional gift between lovers. The inscription names Dionysus and the artist who painted the jar (DIONYSOS AMASIS ME POIESEN, "Dionysus Amasis made me.")

this suffering by some tiny, newborn deity armed with burning torches (*Commentary on Hippocrates's* Prognostics 18*b*.19K).

Just as plants are rooted in the earth, so we ourselves are rooted to the air by our nostrils and our whole body (*Anonymous London Medical Papyrus* 3.21).

"Their helplessness makes sick people hard to please" [Euripides *Orestes* 232]. *They find their wives irritating, they criticize the doctor, they grumble about their bed, and, as Ion says* [*frg.* 56] *"friends annoy them when they come, and offend them when they leave." But then their illness is cured and they are restored to sound health, and that makes everything fine and pleasant. The man who yesterday was revolted at the thought of eating eggs and dainty cakes and bread made with the best flour today tucks in eagerly to a hearty meal of coarse bread with olives and water-cress* (Plutarch *On Tranquility of Mind* 466c).

Nature is its own physician. It devises its own methods for itself without recourse to reasoning. For example, blinking, and the functions of

Fig. 13.3 and 13.4 Eros was originally envisioned as a vigorous adolescent. His portrayal as a chubby and cherubic little chap was a later development.

the tongue, and all other such things. Nature produces what is needed without education, without having to learn anything—tears, nasal secretions, sneezes, ear wax, saliva, expectoration, inhaling, exhaling, yawning, coughing, hiccups, and so on, the excretion of urine, and the evacuation of both kinds of wind, that from food and that from breathing, and things specific to women, and things that affect the rest of the body, sweating, itching, stretching, and all suchlike things (Hippocrates *Epidemics* 6.5).

The followers of Erasistratus maintain that food is ground up in the stomach; those of Plistonicus, that it putrefies; the Hippocratics, that it is cooked by the body's heat. Then there are the supporters of Asclepiades, who consider all such speculations worthless and irrelevant; they believe that there is no such thing as digestion, and that food is distributed round the body in the same crude state as it is swallowed (Celsus *On Medicine* Preface 20).

Medicine is one of the creative arts, but not in the uncomplex way that architecture or carpentry or weaving is an art; a better comparison would

be with the repairing of a house that has been damaged or the mend-
ing of clothing that has been torn (Galen *The Composition of the Art of*
Medicine 1.303K).

MEDICINE AND COOKERY

Doctors should have at least a basic knowledge of cookery since, when two
foods are equally healthy, the one with the more pleasant taste is easier to
digest (Galen *Capacities of Foodstuffs* 6.609K).

Cookery has insinuated itself into medicine, and claims to know which
foods are good for the body. If a cook and a doctor had a competition
to decide who knows better which foods are good and which are bad,
and if the competition were judged by children or by adults as lack-
ing in sense as children are, the doctor would starve to death (Plato
Gorgias 464d).

Dreaming about boxing is altogether bad. It foretells not only dis-
grace, but also actual loss, since the face becomes disfigured, and there
is loss of blood, which symbolizes money. Such dreams are lucky only
for those who earn their living from blood, by which I mean doc-
tors, animal sacrificers, and cooks (Artemidorus *The Interpretation*
of Dreams 1.61).

Even if a man is not a good person, he can still be a doctor or a ship's pilot
or a teacher or indeed a chef (Seneca *Letters* 87.17).

The doctors who were with the army during the German war had the
opportunity to dissect the bodies of the barbarians, but they did not learn
any more than cooks learn when they cut up meat in the kitchen (Galen
The Composition of Drugs According to Kind 13.604K).

Medicine has an understanding of all human sciences and is superior to
the art of cookery. It is, however, insignificant in contrast to the divinely

inspired cures for all illnesses and suffering, such as have been revealed by the oracle at Delphi, both to individuals and to mankind in general (Aelius Aristides *To Plato on Rhetoric* 35).

MEDICAL ARSON

There was a hostile tradition that Hippocrates cut out potential competition by burning the medical records stored either on Cos or in Cnidus, a nearby city on the mainland with a great reputation in medicine (Soranus *Life of Hippocrates* 4).

Galen suspected that the Alexandrian physician Heracleianus burned his father Numesianus's works on anatomy to deprive others of the benefit of them.

Galen himself lost many of his writings and important medical stores in the great Roman warehouse fire of A.D. 192. The tract in which he discusses his reaction to this loss, *Avoiding Distress*, was discovered as recently as 2005.

It is said that Paracelsus began his lectures on medicine at Basel in the sixteenth century by burning works by Galen and Avicenna as a gesture against the deadening influence of tradition.

MEDICAL WISDOM

It is no good waiting till after you have cured him before saying to a sick person "Pay up!" (Medieval Latin proverb).

Giving advice to an old man is the same as giving medical treatment to a corpse (Democritus *frg.* 302).

A doctor is merely a consolation for the mind (Petronius *Satyricon* 42).

Philosophy is medicine for the mind (Cicero *Tusculan Disputations* 3.6).

When the usual remedies do not have any effect, doctors try the opposite ones (Seneca *On Mercy* 9.6).

If your stomach and your lungs and your feet are fine, there's nothing more that all the wealth of kings could give you (Horace *Epistles* 1.12.5–6).

There are some people who seem to be excellent doctors for themselves, but could not do anything to help anyone else (Aristotle *Nicomachean Ethics* 1180b).

It is better to be sick than to tend the sick. Being sick is a simple thing, but tending the sick is a combination of mental anguish and physical work (Euripides *Hippolytus* 186–8).

The good thing about pain is that, if it lasts for a long time, it can't be severe, and if it is severe, it can't last long (Seneca *Letters* 94).

Time, the universal doctor, will cure you (Philippides *frg.* 32).

MEDICAL PROBLEMS

Why do people shiver after sneezing or urinating? Is it because both actions cause the veins to empty, and cold air coming in then causes shivering? (Pseudo-Aristotle *Problems* 887b).

Why is it that urine smells worse the more time it spends in the body, whereas it is the opposite with feces? Is it because feces becomes drier the longer it stays long in the body (and what is dry is less susceptible to decay), whereas urine becomes thicker as it loses its freshness, and not so much like the liquid originally drunk? (Pseudo-Aristotle *Problems* 907b).

Why do we pass gas when we urinate? Because the bladder, when it is full, presses down on the rectum, but, when the bladder is then relaxed, the air trapped in the rectum slips out (Pseudo-Alexander of Aphrodisias *Problems* 4.16).

Why is it that the armpits smell worse than any other part of the body? Is it because there is very little ventilation there? Moisture does not circulate there, and hence there is an unpleasant smell, brought on by putrefaction. Or it may be because the armpits are never moved or exercised (Pseudo-Aristotle *Problems* 908*b*).

Why do those who come in contact with some diseases fall sick, but no one becomes healthy through contact with healthy people? Is it because disease is movement, but health is rest, and disease moves things, but health does not? (Pseudo-Aristotle *Problems* 886*b*).

Why is it that everyone who is outstanding in philosophy, politics, literature, or any of the other arts obviously suffers from melancholy, in some cases so acutely as to be afflicted by the illnesses that arise from black bile [μελαίνη χολή, *melaine chole*]*?* (Pseudo-Aristotle *Problems* 953*a*). The discussion that follows is one of the longest in the *Problems*, and no clear and succinct answer is given.

Why is it that, whereas all the other parts of the body relax after death, the testicles alone are drawn upwards? Because men ejaculate sperm when they die. Sperm tends to be emitted when the testicles are retracted, and so they stay up after death (Cassius Iatrosophista *Problems* 47).

Why do drunkards like to drink cheap wine? Because those who drink a lot have dilated pores. High quality wine is fine and hurries through large pores without being stopped, whereas cheap wine, not being fine, is stopped and lingers, and that is when it seems to provide pleasure (Cassius Iatrosophista *Problems* 48).

Why is it that, when they are asleep, people pass gas more often than they sneeze or belch? The reason is that, as the stomach region heats up during sleep, the liquids in the stomach are turned to vapor, and this vapor makes its way to the nearest exit (Pseudo-Aristotle *Problems* 963*a*).

Why does fat waste away when people take exercise? Is it because fat melts when it is warmed up, and movement heats it, whereas actual flesh does not melt? (Pseudo-Aristotle *Problems* 880*b*).

Why does the region round the stomach run most to fat? Is it because the stomach is near to the food supply? Whereas the other parts of the body draw their nourishment from the stomach, the stomach constantly draws nourishment for itself. Or might it be because the stomach takes the least amount of strenuous exercise, given that it has no joints? (Pseudo-Aristotle *Problems* 881*a*).

Why does a wound heal more readily if inflicted by a bronze instrument rather than by an iron one? Is it because bronze is smoother, and so rips the flesh less and inflicts a smaller wound? Or is it because, even though iron has a sharper blade, bronze cuts more easily and less painfully? One thing is sure: bronze has healing qualities, and this gives the recovery process a strong beginning. Since the medicine is applied at the very moment the wound is inflicted, healing starts that much more quickly (Pseudo-Aristotle *Problems* 863*a*).

Why is it that, although both eyes and both ears are so similar, one eye shares the suffering of the other eye, but ears do not do this? It is because the eyes are not just so similar, they are also very close together, whereas the ears are widely separated (Cassius Iatrosophista *Problems* 17).

Michael Psellus, writing in eleventh-century Constantinople, copied the following and many other such observations in an often highly abbreviated form from Pseudo-Alexander's *Problems*, collected perhaps eight hundred years earlier:

> *People often shiver when they pass urine, because a sharp bile flows out with it and bites the urine-holding bladder, and this rouses the whole body to act in sympathy with that part. This happens particularly to children, since their greed for food makes them produce rather a lot of waste matter*

Fig. 13.5 According to one version of the myth, the Greeks were initially unable to find Troy and had to return to Greece. During that first expedition, Achilles wounded Telephus with his spear. The wound would not heal, but Telephus received an oracle that "the one who caused the wound will also heal it." By promising to show the Greeks the way to Troy, he persuaded Achilles to heal him by scraping the rust from his spearpoint into the wound.

When infants fall to the ground, they do not suffer fractures, since they yield to the ground. Likewise, a sponge does not break, whereas an earthenware pot does

People's hair and nails do not, as some assert, continue to grow when they are dead; they merely give the impression of doing so as the flesh around them wastes away

(*Opusculum* 55.642, 655, 770)

MEDICAL LANGUAGE

Doctors in antiquity generally expressed themselves in a rather less technical manner than they do nowadays, but what their language lacked in precision it perhaps gained in vigor. Consider these vivid Hippocratic similes, a figure of speech rarely to be found in modern medical literature:

If you put an olive into a narrow-mouthed cruet and it turns sideways, it is hard to get it out again. Likewise, a woman's labor is made difficult if the child turns sideways in her womb (Diseases of Women 8.78).

A person afflicted with typhus takes on a pale, washed out, and sallow complexion, like a bag full of urine (Internal Affections 43).

In the acute and rapidly fatal form of jaundice, the patient's whole skin is very like pomegranate peel in color, or greener than green lizards (Diseases 3.11).

Hippocrates was not alone in drawing such comparisons. Here are a couple of examples from the fragments of Herophilus:

Because hellebore is so powerful, doctors were initially reluctant to use it in doses large enough to have the required effect, either as a purge or as an emetic. But in fact it has the excellent quality of going through the system too quickly to do harm. Herophilus boosted hellebore's popularity when he compared it to a very brave general, one who stirs up everyone in a town under siege, and then personally leads them out to fight (Pliny Natural History 25.58).

In its original state, in women who are still virgins, the opening of the uterus is soft and fleshy, spongy like the lungs and soft like the tongue. But in women who have borne children it becomes more callous, like the head of an octopus or the larynx, as Herophilus says, for it is made callous by the passage of secretions and of babies being born (Soranus *Gynecology* 1.10).

Obscurity is not commendable: *What would be the point in a doctor prescribing that a patient should eat "earth-born, grass-treading, house-carrying, blood-lacking creatures" instead of saying "snails" like everybody else?* (Cicero *On Divination* 2.133).

Nowadays we don't need medical help just for wounds and seasonal ailments. No, because of our laziness and unsuitable way of life, people fill themselves up with fluxes and flatus, as if their bodies were a marsh. But isn't it disgusting, the way we thereby force the clever followers of Asclepius to find more and more names for ailments—terms like flatulence and catarrh? (Plato *Republic* 405d).

The Roman name *Caesar* was thought to be derived from the Latin verb *caedere* "to cut," an early member of the family having been cut from his mother's womb. Caesarean sections are not, however, discussed by medical writers and were probably not a normal procedure in antiquity.

In his veneration for the Good Old Days, Galen rants about how the old simplicity and clarity has gone out of language, to be replaced with tortuous arguments over every syllable. He conveniently forgets about the difficulties Herophilus faced five hundred years earlier in getting his descriptions of types of pulse accepted (see p. 78):

Nowadays, if a doctor calls a strong pulse "vehement," a second doctor says that a "vehement" pulse is "big," "full," and "rapid." ... And so on, till even a seventh and an eighth doctor turn up to give their interpretation of such terms. What sort of battle do you think there will be then? The sort of battle we often see at the temple of Peace and in the sickroom, where some people can't hold their fists in check (The Different Kinds of Pulse 8.494K).

Galen himself is not averse to making fine distinctions of his own, subtle enough that other doctors might find them hard to follow. For example:

There is a total of fifteen types of exhaustion: four are simple, from wounds (A), from tension (B), from inflammation (C), from dieting (D), and eleven are combinations (AB, AC, AD, BC, BD, CD, ABC, ABD, ACD, BCD, ABCD) (Matters of Health 6.217K).

"Clitoris" is a Greek word, but was not much used in antiquity. The lexicographer Pollux rather curiously defines it as "the little piece of flesh dancing in the middle" (*Onomasticon* 2.174), the remarkable thing about this definition being that "dancing" (*skairon*) is an anagram of "little piece of flesh" (*sarkion*).

Archigenes's greatest mistake was in using terms that are appropriate for a sensation other than the one he was writing about. For example, describing a pain in the kidneys as harsh, or a pain in the bladder as astringent. Those are terms for humors that are recognized by the tongue and our sense of taste. . . . So we can have no more understanding of what Archigenes means by calling a pain harsh or astringent than we would have if he called it blue or red or gray or some other color (Galen *The Affected Places* 8.113K).

There was no term, in either Greek or Latin, to denote what we call the common cold.

Galen records that, "one of the currently fashionable professors almost choked me" during an argument about terminology held in public (*The Different Kinds of Pulse* 8.571K).

The caudal vertebrae are still known as the *coccyx*, which is Greek for "cuckoo." Presumably the name is derived from its shape. It is hard to see why it was imagined that the tailbone looks like the beak of a cuckoo in particular, for many other birds seem just as eligible. (Most bones have Latin names, given to them by the Romans long ago. The Latin for "cuckoo" is *cucŭlus*; perhaps the Romans hesitated to use their own word because of its similarity to *cŭlus*, a not altogether polite term for the not very distant anus?) A rather different explanation is given by a late medical writer:

> *According to Galen, the coccyx bone is so called because the winds that come out from there through the fundament make a sound like "cuckoo" when they strike against it. It is a metaphor derived from the bird that goes "cuckoo"* (Meletius *On the Nature of Man* III).

Empedocles, comparing *puos*, colostrum, and *puon*, pus, declared that milk is corrupted blood (*frg.* 59), but Aristotle denies this, arguing that milk is digested blood (*Generation of Animals* 777*a*).

Alopecia ["baldness," literally "foxiness"] *is a disease that affects the head, a metaphor from the animal, for it is said that any place where a fox urinates becomes infertile for that year* (Ancient commentator on Callimachus *Hymn* 3.79).

Galen, though he spent so many years at the imperial court in Rome, apparently felt no need to learn Latin, or any other language but Greek: *Everyone can learn Greek, which is a mellifluous language. Should you wish, however, to learn any of the languages spoken by barbarians, you should be aware that some of them sound like the noises made by pigs or frogs or crows, for they are without charm, and some people speak them as if they were snoring, hissing, or squeaking* (*The Different Kinds of Pulse* 8.586K).

Medical writings in any language other than Greek lack prestige even among the uneducated who do not know Greek. When it comes to health matters, people have less confidence if they know what is going on (Pliny *Natural History* 29.17).

Celsus, an elder contemporary of Pliny, takes a different view of the use of Greek as the language of medicine:

> *The Greek terms for the private parts are more admissible than the Latin ones. They are in common use, for they are now standard in just about all medical books and discussions. Not even the widespread use of the coarser Latin terms has made them acceptable in decorous discourse* (*On Medicine* 6.18).

· XIV ·

RESPICE FINEM

DR. DEATH

Anyone who claims to be a doctor is trusted straightaway. Medicine is the only profession in which this happens, even though there is no other profession in which falsehood is more dangerous. But we pay no heed to that danger, for everyone finds the sweetness of wishful thinking so seductive. Moreover, there is no law to punish ignorance that costs lives, and no precedent for redress. Doctors learn through endangering our lives, conducting experiments that lead to people's death. Only doctors have total immunity if they kill people. In fact, the criticism is transferred to the patient, who is faulted for self-indulgence: those who die are actually considered to have brought their death upon themselves (Pliny *Natural History* 29.17).

Sudden death snatched the flourishing years away from his so innocent soul, for the doctors operated on him and killed him (*L'Année épigraphique* [1911] 191, from an epitaph).

A sick person who makes his doctor his heir is treating himself badly (Publilius Syrus *Sententiae* M 24).

Crateas the doctor and Damon the mortician had an arrangement. Damon would steal the shrouds from the corpses and send them to his friend Crateas to use as bandages. Crateas responded by sending Damon all his patients for burial (Anonymous *Greek Anthology* 11.125).

We are all worried about my dear daughter Severiana, for she is unwell. She is longing for healthy country air, ... and we believe that, if we refuse our patient's wish, her illness will get worse. So we have decided to get away with our whole household from the stifling heat in the city and thereby to escape the advice given by the doctors, who sit round the sickbed arguing. With their limited expertise and unlimited visits, they are so very conscientiously killing off countless sick people (Sidonius *Letters* 2.12).

There is no doubt that all those doctors strive for publicity through some novel treatment, buying their fame at the expense of our lives. This is the cause of those awful diagnosis-competitions at the patient's bedside, with no doctor agreeing with any other, for fear of seeming subordinate; it is also the cause of that miserable epitaph "I died of a surfeit of doctors" (Pliny *Natural History* 29.11). Pliny himself escaped this wretched end, famously dying of asphyxiation in the eruption of Vesuvius on August 24/25 A.D. 79.

When someone asked the Spartan king how they could conquer the Thracians, he replied, "By appointing our doctor as general, and our general as doctor" (Plutarch *Sayings of the Spartans* 231a). The point is that doctors are more successful than generals at killing people.

Yesterday, Marcus the doctor took the pulse of the stone statue of Zeus; today, even though it is Zeus the immortal and is made of stone, the statue is being carried out for burial (Lucillius *Greek Anthology* 11.113).

Andragoras bathed with us, and dined cheerfully, and yet he was found dead in the morning. Do you wonder what might have caused such a sudden death, Faustinus? He saw the doctor Hermocrates in a dream (Martial *Epigrams* 6.53).

Alexis the doctor gave purges to five patients, and emetics to five; he visited five, and he put ointment on five. Now, for all of them, there is one night, one medicine, one coffin maker, one grave, one Underworld, and one lamentation (Callicter *Greek Anthology* 11.122).

When Marcus fell ill, the soothsayer Diodorus told him he had only six days to live. But Alcon the doctor is more powerful than the gods and the fates, for he proved the prediction to be false: he felt the hand of the patient, who would have lived if he had not touched him, and Marcus immediately lost his six days (Ausonius *Epigrams* 77).

To those suffering from intestinal obstruction, death is happiness. It is not right for a responsible doctor to bring this about. But it is right for him to give the patient rest with narcotics if he sees that his symptoms are inescapable (Aretaeus *On the Treatment of Chronic Diseases* 2.5).

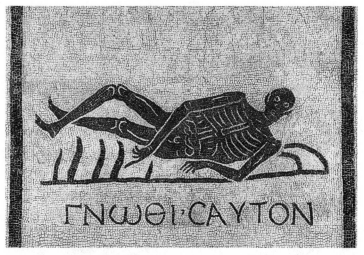

Fig. 14.1 GNOTHI SAUTON "know yourself." The rather weird figure, well on its way to being no more than a skeleton, is reclining as if at a banquet. The sentiment, rather like *memento mori* "remember (that you are going) to die" and *carpe diem* "enjoy the day," is a solemn reminder of human mortality.

Twin brothers, whose mother and father were still living, fell sick. The doctors who were consulted said that they were both suffering from the same illness. The other doctors despaired of saving them, but one said that he could save one twin if he were allowed to examine the other twin's internal organs while he was still alive. With their father's permission, he cut one of the boys open and carried out the examination. The other twin was cured, but their father was accused by their mother of maltreatment (Quintilian *Major Declamations* Preface 8).

A justification for vivisection: *It is not cruel, as most people maintain, that remedies should be sought for innocent people's ailments in all future ages through the sufferings of just a few criminals* (Celsus *On Medicine* Preface 26).

Oh, healing Death, do not disdain to come to me. You are the only physician for incurable ills, and no pain afflicts a corpse (Aeschylus *frg.* 399*b*).

Death is the doctor that finally cures our diseases (Sophocles *frg.* 698).

Death is the universal antidote (Artemidorus *The Interpretation of Dreams* 4.71).

GLOSSARY

I N LIEU of explanatory footnotes accompanying the text, this glossary defines briefly some of the people, places, events, and institutions referred to most often and most prominently in the book. It is not comprehensive; further information is readily available in reference sources such as the *Oxford Classical Dictionary* (Oxford University Press, 4th ed., 2012).

Adamantius: fifth-century A.D. doctor and philosopher.

Aegina: island fifteen miles off the Athenian coast.

Aelian (Claudius Aelianus, c. A.D. 165–c. 235): author of *On Animals* and *Miscellaneous History*, rich sources of curious lore.

Aelius Aristides (A.D. 117–c. 185): sophist, hypochondriac, and man of letters, author of a wide range of prose works, much admired in antiquity, but often rather boring.

Aeneas: prince of Troy and son of the goddess Venus; the legendary founder of the Roman people.

Aeschines: fourth-century B.C. Athenian orator.

Aeschylus: with Sophocles and Euripides, the greatest of the fifth-century B.C. Athenian tragedians.

Aesop: semilegendary composer of fables.

Aëtius of Amida: sixth-century A.D. doctor.

Africa: Roman province, mostly in modern Libya and Tunisia.

Agamemnon: king of Mycenae, leader of the Greeks at Troy.

Agrippa (Marcus Vipsanius Agrippa, c. 63–12 B.C.): a close personal friend of Augustus and leader of the victorious forces at Actium.

Alexander of Tralles: sixth-century A.D. doctor.

Alexander the Great (356–323 B.C.): king of Macedon and conqueror of the Persian empire.

Alexandria: founded by Alexander at the western edge of the Nile delta in 331 B.C., a great cosmopolitan center of learning and culture.

Ali ibn Ridwan: eleventh-century Arab scientist.

Ammianus Marcellinus (c. A.D. 325–after 391): the last great Roman historian.

Anonymous Byzantine *Farm Work*: tenth-century compilation on agriculture.

Anthimus: sixth-century A.D. doctor, author of a Latin treatise on dietetics.

Antony (Marcus Antonius, 83–30 B.C.): Julius Caesar's lieutenant, lover of Cleopatra, and Octavian's rival for power.

Apuleius: second-century A.D. Roman writer.

Arcadia: region in the central Peloponnese.

Archigenes of Apamea: second-century A.D. Greek doctor.

Aretaeus of Cappadocia: first-century A.D. Greek doctor.

Aristophanes (c. 455–c. 388 B.C.): Athenian writer of comedies.

Aristotle of Stagira (384–322 B.C.): incalculably influential scientist and philosopher.

Artaxerxes II: King of Persia (ruled 405/4–359/8 B.C.).

Artemidorus of Daldis: second-century A.D. author of *The Interpretation of Dreams*.

Asclepiades of Bithynia: second/first-century B.C. Greek doctor.

Asclepius (Latin **Aesculapius**): god of medicine.

Athenaeus of Naucratis: late second-century A.D. author of *Wise Men at Dinner*, a ragbag of discussions on literature, philosophy, law, medicine, and other topics.

Attica: the hinterland of Athens.

Augustus (63 B.C.–A.D. 14; before 27 B.C., referred to as Octavian): the first and most influential Roman emperor (ruled 31 B.C.–A.D. 14).

Aulus Gellius (c. A.D. 125–after 180): author of the *Attic Nights*, a collection of quotations and discussions on wide-ranging and miscellaneous topics.

Ausonius (Decimus Ausonius Magnus, of Bordeaux, c. A.D. 310–394): teacher and writer.

Avicenna (c. 980–1037): Persian polymath, a latter-day Aristotle.

Bithynia: region in northwest Asia Minor (Turkey).

Boeotia: region in central Greece, north of Attica.

Caelius Aurelianus: fourth/fifth-century A.D. Latin medical writer.

Caesar (Gaius Julius Caesar, 102 or 100–44 B.C.): the greatest Roman of them all.

Caligula (Gaius Julius Caesar Augustus Germanicus, A.D. 12–41, more formally known as Gaius): Roman emperor (ruled 37–41).

Callimachus of Cyrene: third-century B.C. scholar and poet in the Alexandrian Library and at the Ptolemaic court.

Cassius Iatrosophista: author of a collection of medical *Problems*, of unknown date.

Catiline (Lucius Sergius Catilina, 108–62 B.C.): leader of a conspiracy in 63 B.C. to overthrow the Roman government.

Cato (Marcus Porcius Cato, 234–149 B.C.): an iconic advocate of the traditionally simple Roman way of life, the *mos maiorum* ("the custom of the ancestors"); his like-named great-grandson (95–46 B.C.) had a similarly conservative attitude to politics and life in general.

Celsus (Aulus Cornelius Celsus, 25 B.C.– A.D. 50): the author of an encyclopedia, of which only the books on medicine survive.

Censorinus: third-century A.D. scholar and writer.

Centaurs: half-man horses and half-horse men, associated esp. with Thessaly.

Chrysippus of Soli (c. 280–207 B.C.): head of the Stoic school at Athens.

Cicero (Marcus Tullius Cicero, 106–43 B.C.): the greatest of all Roman orators, and a leading politician in the late Republic.

Cilicia: region in southeast Asia Minor (Turkey).

Claudius (Tiberius Claudius Nero Drusus Germanicus, 10 B.C.–A.D. 54): the fourth Roman emperor (ruled 41–54).

Cleopatra: Cleopatra VII, the last Greek ruler of Egypt, the lover of Julius Caesar and of Mark Antony, with whom she was defeated by Octavian at Actium.

Cnidus: Greek city in southwest Asia Minor (Turkey).

Columella (Lucius Junius Moderatus Columella): first-century A.D. writer on agriculture and trees.

Commodus (Lucius Aurelius Commodus Antoninus, 161–192 A.D.): son of Marcus Aurelius and mad emperor par excellence (ruled 180–192).

Constantine the Great (Flavius Valerius Aurelius Constantinus Augustus, c. A.D. 272–337): Roman emperor (ruled 306–337).

Cos: island in the Aegean Sea.

Ctesias of Cnidus: physician to Artaxerxes II of Persia (ruled 405/4–359/8 B.C.), author of historical and geographical accounts of the Persian empire, rather unreliable and now mostly lost.

Cyranides: a treatise on medical magic lore, probably first collected in the fourth century A.D.

Delphi: sanctuary and oracle of Apollo in central Greece.

Democritus of Abdera (c. 460–? B.C.): atomist philosopher.

Demosthenes (384–322 B.C.): the greatest Athenian orator.

Dieuches: fourth/third-century B.C. medical writer.

Dio Chrysostom (c. A.D. 45–after 110): orator and popular philosopher.

Diodorus Siculus (c. 90–c. 27 B.C.): author of a universal history in Greek.

Dionysius I (c. 430–367 B.C.): tyrant of Syracuse.

Dionysius of Halicarnassus (c. 60–after 7 B.C.): Greek author of a history of Rome down to the First Punic War and of various treatises on rhetoric.

Dioscorides of Anazarbus: first-century A.D. author of *Medical Material*, a very influential five-book study of the plants used in medicine.

Domitian (Titus Flavius Domitianus, A.D. 51–96): Roman emperor (ruled 81–96).

Dorotheus of Sidon: first-century A.D. astrologer.

Drachma: basic unit of Greek coinage, of varying value in different poleis.

Elagabalus (Marcus Aurelius Antoninus Augustus, c. A.D. 203–222): Roman emperor (ruled 218–222).

Empedocles of Acragas (c. 492–432 B.C.): natural philosopher.

Ephesus: Greek city on the west coast of Asia Minor (Turkey).

Epictetus: first/second-century A.D. Stoic philosopher, a slave in his early life.

Epidaurus: city in northeast Peloponnese, esp. famous as a cult center of Asclepius.

Erasistratus of Ceos: fourth/third-century B.C. physician at Alexandria.

Eunapius of Sardis (c. A.D. 347–414): Greek intellectual and historian.

Euripides: with Aeschylus and Sophocles, the greatest of the fifth-century B.C. Athenian tragedians.

Firmicus Maternus: fourth-century A.D. astrologer.

Galen of Pergamum (Claudius Galenus, c. A.D. 129–c. 217): the most influential of ancient doctors, magnificently opinionated.

Gargilius Martialis: third-century A.D. writer on gardens and medicine.

Gauls: the people of modern France and surrounding regions.

***Gnomologium Vaticanum*:** fourteenth-century compilation of wise sayings, drawn mostly from classical sources.

Gorgias of Leontini (c. 480–c. 380 B.C.): Greek philosopher, orator, and politician.

***Greek Anthology*:** a collection of about 3,700 epigrams by hundreds of poets on a vast range of subjects, written over a period of about 1,600 years.

Hadrian (Publius Aelius Traianus Hadrianus, A.D. 76–138): Roman emperor (ruled 117–138).

Halicarnassus: Greek city in southwest Asia Minor (Turkey).

Helen: daughter of Zeus and Leda, wife of Menelaus.

Heraclitus: sixth/fifth-century B.C. philosopher.

Herodian (c. A.D. 170–c. 240): author of a Greek history of Rome from A.D. 180 till 238.

Herodotus of Halicarnassus (?–c. 425 B.C.): author of the *Histories*, an account of the Persian Wars and the peoples involved.

Herophilus of Chalcedon (c. 330–260 B.C.): physician at Alexandria. As with Erasistratus, his importance would be better appreciated if more of his writings had survived.

Hesiod: eighth/seventh-century B.C. author of the *Works and Days* and the *Theogony*, and much other poetry, now mostly lost.

Hippocrates of Cos (c. 470–c. 400 B.C.): father of Western medicine.

***Historia Augusta*:** the *Augustan History* is a thoroughly unreliable collection of biographies of second- and third-century emperors and usurpers, of uncertain date and authorship. The citations from it should be regarded with particular skepticism.

Homer: the greatest of all poets; if he ever existed, he probably lived in the eighth century B.C.

Horace (Quintus Horatius Flaccus, 65–8 B.C.): a leading poet of the Augustan age.

Iamblichus of Chalcis (c. A.D. 245–c. 325): Neoplatonist philosopher.

John Chrysostom (c. A.D. 350–407): Christian theologian.

Josephus (Titus Flavius Josephus, A.D. 37–after 100): author of the *Jewish Wars* and *Jewish Antiquities*.

Julian (Claudius Julianus Apostata, c. A.D. 331–363): Roman emperor (ruled 360–363).

Julius Africanus: second-century A.D. author of a chronicle of world history and of the *Kestoi*, a wide-ranging collection of miscellaneous information.

Justinian I (Flavius Petrus Sabbatius Justinianus, A.D. 482/483–565): ruler of the eastern empire (ruled 527–565), who commissioned the compilation of the *corpus iuris civilis*, the most significant and influential Roman legal texts.

Laconia: region in the southern Peloponnese, home of the Spartans.

Latium: region in central Italy, around Rome.

Libanius of Antioch (A.D. 314–393): Greek teacher and orator.

Lucian of Samosata: second-century A.D. author of essays, dialogues, and narratives commenting wittily and satirically on literature and contemporary culture.

Lycurgus: semilegendary Spartan legislator.

Macrobius (Ambrosius Theodosius Macrobius, late fourth/early fifth centuries A.D.): a grammarian and philosopher, author of, most notably, the *Saturnalia*, a dialogue on many subjects, esp. literary criticism of Vergil.

Marcellinus: second-century? A.D. author of a monograph on pulses.

Marcellus Empiricus: fourth/fifth-century A.D. medical writer.

Marcus Aurelius (Marcus Aurelius Antoninus Augustus, A.D. 121–180): Stoic philosopher and emperor (ruled 161–180).

Marius (Gaius Marius, c. 157–86 B.C.): leading military and political figure in the late second and early first centuries B.C.

Martial (Gaius Valerius Martialis, c. A.D. 40–c. 101): prolific writer of epigrams, a few of which are better than the others.

Martianus Capella: fifth-century A.D. author of a Latin encyclopedia of the liberal arts.

Menander (c. 344–292/1 B.C.): Athenian writer of comedies.

Michael Psellus (A.D. 1018–after 1081): prolific author of works on history, philosophy, rhetoric, science, and literature.

Mimnermus: seventh-century B.C. Greek poet.

Mithridates (132–63 B.C.): Mithridates VI (ruled 120–63) of Pontus in modern Turkey, Rome's most dangerous foreign enemy in the first century B.C.

Mnesitheus: fourth-century B.C. Athenian medical writer.

Nero (Nero Claudius Caesar Augustus Germanicus, A.D. 37–68): Roman emperor (ruled 54–68).

Octavian: see **Augustus**.

Oribasius: fourth-century A.D. Greek doctor.

Paracelsus: sixteenth-century Swiss scientist, who preferred to be known as "Second to Celsus" rather than by his actual name, Philippus Aureolus Theophrastus Bombastus von Hohenheim. Although he had a reputation for arrogance, the term "bombastic" owes nothing to him.

Parthia: the Parthian empire, which extended over much of the area from the Mediterranean to India and was a serious threat to Rome's eastern possessions.

Paul of Aegina: seventh-century A.D. Greek doctor.

Pausanias of Magnesia: second-century A.D. author of *A Description of Greece*, a detailed account of most of the regions in the Roman province of Achaea.

Peloponnesian War: fought in 431–404 B.C. by Sparta and its allies against Athens and its allies.

Pergamum: Greek city near the west coast of Asia Minor (Turkey).

Pericles (c. 495–429 B.C.)**:** Athenian political and military leader.

Petronius (? Petronius Arbiter, probably Neronian)**:** author of the *Satyricon*, a satirical novel.

Philemon: fourth/third-century B.C. writer of comedies.

Philippides: fourth/third-century B.C. writer of comedies.

Philo of Alexandria: first-century A.D. Jewish scholar and philosopher.

Philogelos: late antique collection of jokes mocking characters and professions, rather than individuals.

Philostratus (c. A.D. 170–c. 250)**:** Greek sophist, to whom a wide range of works are attributed.

Phlegon of Tralles: second-century A.D. writer of miscellanies.

Photius (c. A.D. 810–c. 893)**:** Patriarch of Constantinople and author of *The Library*, 280 chapters providing accounts of books he had read.

Phrygia: region in west-central Asia Minor (Turkey).

Pindar (c. 518–c. 438 B.C.)**:** Boeotian lyric poet.

Piraeus: port of Athens.

Plato (c. 429–347 B.C.)**:** the philosopher to whom the European philosophical tradition is a series of footnotes.

Pliny the elder (Gaius Plinius Secundus A.D. 23–79)**:** author of the *Natural History,* an endlessly fascinating encyclopedia, conveying (by Pliny's computation) twenty thousand facts. Modern scholars would boost that total to approximately thirty-seven thousand.

Pliny the younger (Gaius Plinius Caecilius Secundus, A.D. ?62–?113): nephew and adopted son of Pliny the elder.

Plutarch (c. A.D. 45–127): as well as biographies of prominent Greeks and Romans, he also wrote the *Moralia*, essays on a broad spectrum of philosophical, religious, and literary topics.

Pollux: second-century A.D. lexicographer.

Polybius (c. 203–120 B.C.): author of the *Histories,* an account in Greek of Rome's expansion in 220–146 B.C.

Pompey (Gnaeus Pompeius Magnus, 106–48 B.C.): leading military and political figure at the end of the Roman Republic.

Porphyry of Tyre: third-century A.D. Neoplatonist philosopher.

Posidonius of Apamea (c. 135–c. 50 B.C.): Stoic philosopher, scientist, and historian.

Priam: the last king of Troy.

Procopius of Caesarea: sixth-century A.D. historian.

Pseudo-Alexander of Aphrodisias: author of a collection of medical *Problems*, of unknown date.

Pseudo-Caecilius Balbus: second?-century A.D. compiler of an anthology of quotations from philosophers.

Pseudo-Demades: unknown author of the speech *On the Twelve Years,* falsely attributed to the fourth-century B.C. orator Demades.

Pseudo-Melampus: unknown author of a short Greek treatise on the lost art of divination by moles (the worrying epidermal features, not the burrowing subterranean creatures).

Ptolemy (Claudius Ptolemaeus): second-century A.D. Greek astronomer.

Publilius Syrus: first-century B.C. writer of Latin mimes, plays on everyday themes, known mostly from a collection of aphorisms said to be drawn from them.

Punic Wars (264–241, 218–201, 149–146 B.C.): the three wars fought by Rome against the Carthaginians (whose origin in Phoenicia in the Eastern Mediterranean is reflected in the term "Punic").

Pyrrhus (319/8–272 B.C.): king of Epirus in western Greece, who invaded Italy in 280 to fight the Romans.

Pythagoras of Samos: sixth-century B.C. philosopher.

Quintilian (Marcus Fabius Quintilianus, c. A.D. 35–c. 100): author of *The Education of the Orator*, a highly influential treatise on rhetoric.

Rhegium: city on the Straits of Messina (modern Reggio di Calabria).

Rhodes: island off southwest Turkey.

Rufus of Ephesus: first/second-century A.D. Greek doctor.

Scribonius Largus: first-century A.D. author of a book of drug recipes.

Scythians: barbarians living north and east of the Danube.

Seneca the younger (Lucius Annaeus Seneca, ?4 B.C.– A.D. 65): politician, philosopher, dramatist, and advisor to Nero.

Serenus Sammonicus: second?/fourth?-century A.D. author of a book of drug recipes, written in verse.

Sextus Empiricus: Skeptic philosopher, probably second-century A.D.

Sidonius Apollinaris: fifth-century A.D. Christian writer.

Simplicius: sixth-century A.D. Neoplatonic philosopher.

Socrates (469–399 B.C.): the Greek philosopher par excellence.

Sophocles: with Aeschylus and Euripides, the greatest of the fifth-century B.C. Athenian tragedians.

Soranus of Ephesus: first/second-century A.D. Greek doctor who practiced in Rome, and deserves to be more widely known.

St. Augustine (Aurelius Augustinus, A.D. 354–430): author of *The City of God, Confessions*, and more than a hundred further works.

St. Basil (c. A.D. 329–381): bishop and theologian.

St. Clement of Alexandria (c. A.D. 150–c. 212): Christian apologist and philosopher.

St. Isidore (c. A.D. 560–636): theologian, scholar, and patron saint of the Internet.

Stobaeus (Iohannes Stobaeus [John of Stobi (in Macedonia)]): probably fifth-century A.D. author of an anthology of extracts from prose and poetry on many topics.

Strabo (?64 B.C.–A.D. ?24): author of a voluminous treatise in Greek, the *Geography*.

Suda: tenth-century Byzantine historical encyclopedia.

Suetonius (Gaius Suetonius Tranquillus, c. A.D. 70–after 130): author of biographies of Julius Caesar and the first eleven emperors, as well as of poets, rhetoricians, and teachers.

Sulla (Lucius Cornelius Sulla Felix, c. 138–78 B.C.): ruled Rome in the early years of the first century B.C.

Syracuse: Greek city on the east coast of Sicily.

Tacitus (?Publius Cornelius Tacitus, c. A.D. 56–c. 117)**:** the greatest Roman historian.

Teles: third-century B.C. Cynic philosopher.

Tertullian: second/third-century A.D. theologian.

Thebes: city in Boeotia.

Theodore Priscian: fourth/fifth-century A.D. author of *Easily Obtainable Recipes*.

***Theodosian Code*:** Roman law code commissioned by Theodosius II (ruled 408–450).

Theognis of Megara: sixth-century B.C. Greek poet.

Theophrastus (c. 370–c. 287 B.C.)**:** successor to Aristotle as head of the Lyceum.

Thessalus of Tralles: first-century A.D. doctor.

Thessaly: region of central Greece, associated esp. with magic.

Thrace: region in modern Greece, Bulgaria, and European Turkey.

Thucydides (c. 455–c. 400 B.C.)**:** Athenian admiral and author of an account of the Peloponnesian War.

Tiber: the river that flows through Rome.

Tiberius (Tiberius Claudius Nero, 42 B.C.–A.D. 37)**:** Roman emperor (ruled 14–37).

Tiresias: legendary Theban prophet.

Trajan (Marcus Ulpius Nerva Traianus, A.D. 53–117)**:** Roman emperor (ruled 98–117).

Tralles: city in western Asia Minor (Turkey).

Trojan War: setting for the Homeric epics, probably in the thirteenth century B.C.

Valerius Maximus (flourished in the Tiberian period)**:** author of a moralizing collection of *Famous Deeds and Sayings*.

Varro (Marcus Terentius Varro, 116–27 B.C.)**:** a voluminous author on many topics, whose only works to survive complete or in substantial part are his *On Farming* and *On the Latin Language*.

Vegetius (Publius Flavius Vegetius Renatus, of unknown date in the Late Empire)**:** author of *On Military Affairs* and *On Veterinary Medicine*.

Verus (Lucius Aurelius Verus Augustus, A.D. 130–169)**:** Roman emperor (ruled jointly with Marcus Aurelius 161–169).

Vespasian (Titus Flavius Vespasianus, A.D. 9–79): Roman emperor (ruled 69–79).

Vettius Valens of Antioch (8 February A.D. 120–?): author of a treatise on astrology.

Vitruvius (?Marcus Vitruvius ?Pollio, before 70–c. 25 B.C.): author of a highly influential treatise on architecture.

Xenocrates of Chalcedon (c. 396–c. 314 B.C.): head of the Academic school of philosophy at Athens.

Xenophon (c. 430–354 B.C.): Athenian soldier and writer on philosophy, politics, history, hunting, and horses.

Xerxes I: King of Persia (ruled 486–465 B.C.).

Zeno of Citium (335–263 B.C.): founder of Stoicism.

Zenobius: second-century A.D. collector of Greek proverbs.

COIN IMAGES

ALL IMAGES of coins, at the chapter heads and throughout the interior, are reproduced courtesy of Classical Numismatic Group, Inc., www.cngcoins.com.

CHAPTER I: A rather tough looking Asclepius on a coin minted c. A.D. 236 by Maximinus the Thracian, at 8' 6" reputedly the tallest of the Roman emperors.

CHAPTER II: Asclepius with his daughter Hygieia on a coin minted in Pergamum, the home-city of the great Galen.

CHAPTER III: Asclepius on a coin from Epidaurus, his greatest cult-center.

CHAPTER IV: Asclepius examining a bull's hoof (with its leg bent rather unrealistically).

CHAPTER V: Asclepius borne aloft on an eagle's wings.

CHAPTER VI: Asclepius, holding his staff, the caduceus, with his sacred snake coiled round it, being carried along by a winged serpent on a coin minted in Pergamum to commemorate a visit to the god's temple there by the Roman emperor Caracalla in A.D. 214.

CHAPTER VII: Asclepius with his sacred snake.

CHAPTER VIII: Asclepius's snake wrapped round his caduceus.

CHAPTER IX: The Roman goddess Salus (Health) on a gold coin of c. A.D. 65.

CHAPTER X: Asclepius being conveyed in a chariot drawn by Centaurs.

CHAPTER XI: The Roman emperor Caracalla visiting the Pergamene shrine of Asclepius, whose rather squat statue stands on a pillar.

CHAPTER XII: A small statue of Asclepius and his snake atop a rather intriguing foot.

CHAPTER XIII: A woman pouring a libation into a dish held by Asclepius.

CHAPTER XIV: The goddess Salus (Health) feeding Asclepius's sacred snake on a coin issued in thanksgiving for the safe birth of a child or children to Faustina, wife of the Roman emperor Marcus Aurelius. Faustina (whose name means "Lucky Woman") had at least thirteen children, including two sets of twins, but only two girls and one boy survived to adulthood. The boy, Commodus, ruled as one of Rome's most unsavory emperors.

ILLUSTRATION CREDITS

Fig. 1.1	Public domain.
Fig. 1.2	Public domain.
Fig. 1.3	© Vanni Archive/Art Resource, NY.
Fig. 1.4	© Erich Lessing/Art Resource, NY.
Fig. 1.5	Public domain.
Fig. 1.6	Courtesy of the Classical Numismatic Group.
Fig. 1.7	Public domain.
Fig. 1.8	Public domain.
Fig. 2.1	Photographed by Carole Raddato.
Fig. 2.2	© DeA Picture Library/Art Resource, NY.
Fig. 2.3	Science Museum, London, Wellcome Images.
Fig. 2.4	© Erich Lessing/Art Resource, NY.
Fig. 3.1	©Kathleen Cohen.
Fig. 3.2	Berlin/Antikensammlung, Staatliche Museen/Juergen Liepe/ Art Resource, NY.
Fig. 3.3	Sites & Photos/Art Resource, NY.
Fig. 4.1 and 4.2	Images courtesy of Shutterstock, Inc.
Fig. 4.3	Wellcome Library, London.
Fig. 4.4	Public domain.
Fig. 4.5	Public domain.
Fig. 4.6	Photographed by Carole Raddato.
Fig. 4.7	Image courtesy of Shutterstock, Inc.
Fig. 4.8	Photographed by Nina Aldin Thune.
Fig. 6.1	© Erich Lessing/Art Resource, NY.
Fig. 6.2	Mongol01984, Creative Commons License.
Fig. 6.3	Science Museum, London, Wellcome Images.
Fig. 7.1	Public domain.
Fig. 7.2	Public domain.
Fig. 7.3	Science Museum, London, Wellcome Images.
Fig. 7.4	HIP/Art Resource, NY.
Fig. 7.5	Dave & Margie Hill/Kleerup from Centennial, CO, USA.
Fig. 7.6	Public domain.
Fig. 7.7	Photographed by Marie-Lan Nguyen.
Fig. 7.8	Art Resource, NY.

Fig. 8.1	Public domain.
Fig. 8.2	Photographed by Calidius.
Fig. 8.3	Photographed by Stefano Bolognini.
Fig. 8.4	Public domain.
Fig. 8.5	Image courtesy of Shutterstock, Inc.
Fig. 9.1	Public domain.
Fig. 9.2	Fletcher Fund, 1956.
Fig. 10.1	Photographed by Sailko.
Fig. 10.2	Wellcome Library, London.
Fig. 10.3 and 10.4	Courtesy of the Classical Numismatic Group.
Fig. 10.5	Photographed by Shakko.
Fig. 10.6 and 10.7	Photographed by Carole Raddato.
Fig. 10.8	Public domain.
Fig. 11.1	Wellcome Library, London.
Fig. 11.2	Sheila Terry/Science Photo Library.
Fig. 11.3	Public domain.
Fig. 11.4	Wellcome Library, London.
Fig. 11.5	Science Photo Library.
Fig. 11.6	Album/Art Resource, NY.
Fig. 12.1	Photographed by Anagoria.
Fig. 12.2	Photographed by Carole Raddato.
Fig. 12.3	Public domain.
Fig. 12.4	Erich Lessing/Art Resource, NY.
Fig. 12.5	Public domain.
Fig. 12.6	Photographed by Bernard Gagnon.
Fig. 12.7	Public domain.
Fig. 12.8	© Kathleen Cohen.
Fig. 12.9	Wellcome Library, London.
Fig. 13.1	Photographed by Marcus Cyron.
Fig. 13.2	Photographed by Marie-Lan Nguyen.
Fig. 13.3 and 13.4	Photographed by Yair Haklai (13.3) and Marie-Lan Nguyen (13.4).
Fig. 13.5	© DeA Picture Library/Art Resource, NY.
Fig. 14.1	Public domain.